BOTHY TO BIG BEN
...and Beyond

The Queen Mother chats to the author at the Royal Smithfield Show in 1984. On the right with the catalogue is Denis Emus, Chairman that year, and next to him is Earl Ferrers, the Show President

BOTHY TO BIG BEN
...and Beyond
An Autobiography

BEN COUTTS

THE MERCAT PRESS
EDINBURGH

First published in 1988 by Aberdeen University Press
This revised edition published in 2001 by Mercat Press
James Thin, 53 South Bridge, Edinburgh EH1 1YS
www.mercatpress.com

ISBN: 184183 0275

Ben Coutts' previous books include:

Auld Acquaintance
A Scotsman's War
Bred in the Highlands
A Stick, Hill Boots and a Good Collie Dog

All are available from Mercat Press

Typeset in Bembo at Mercat Press
Printed and bound in Great Britain by
Bell & Bain Ltd., Glasgow

Contents

Illustrations

Acknowledgements

I can't believe it is 13 years since I wrote the first edition of *Bothy to Big Ben*, but a lot of water has flowed under the bridge since then. I am 13 years older and could not write another whole book, but Tom and Seán, who work for Mercat Press and have now published four books of mine since taking over from Aberdeen University Press, have been most helpful with this revision. Sally as always supports any mad idea I come up with and I could not live without her. My two added chapters have been typed by Isobel Johnston, just as competently as she has done so many chapters of my recent books.

Max Hastings, my old pal, now moved on from being the Editor of the *Daily Telegraph* to be Editor of the *Evening Standard*, has allowed me to use an article he wrote for the *Field* as the Foreword, thanks Max. Judith Stowell, who painted my portrait, warts and all, for my 85th birthday, has allowed the use of it on the cover. To all, many thanks.

Max Hastings on the left with the author on the right, dwarfing Sally in the middle, on a visit to Woodburn in the year 2000, forty-plus years since he was in Scotland as the author's student

Foreword

Although almost all my happiest days are spent in the countryside, I cannot claim to be a countryman. I earn my living in the city. My standing as a naturalist is shaky, to put it politely. But I am lucky enough to know some great countrymen. From these, over the years, I have learnt just enough to be able to bluff my way across the plough on a sunny day.

I was drinking with one of them in his bungalow in Perthshire a few weeks ago, and thinking what a vast pity it is that so few politicians of any party know anyone like him. Ben Coutts is 84 now, and long retired from farming, which has been his life. But he and his wife Sally still cram more into their days than most of us manage at half their age.

'Sal and I get by on fifteen thousand a year' Ben says cheerfully. He has never had any money, but he has travelled most of the world thanks to two Nuffield scholarships and ten years as chief executive of the Aberdeen-Angus Society, parties with the best and every winter gets up to Smithfield where he judged for so many years. Sally, who is English and heavenly, picks-up at the local shoots and has shown herself a maestro at schooling driving ponies for 20 years.

I admire Ben boundlessly for two reasons. First, he is a walking encyclopaedia of everything to do with the Highlands, hill farming and stock. Second, he is a peerless enthusiast. He can and does talk forever about the things he loves. He is a big, formidably tough, even fierce man. I remember an otherwise intractable German pointer none of us could manage on the hill, until Ben had a quiet word with it. The dog never ran in again.

Ben is also one of the warmest and most exuberant characters I know. He started life as a son of the manse. His parents wanted him to be a vet. But as a teenager in the barren Thirties, he came south and became a farm labourer and groom in Sussex. He joined the Sussex Yeomanry in 1936 (to get an annual holiday at their camp, otherwise he wouldn't have got any time off). He rose through the ranks to be a Sergeant Major at the outbreak of the war. After the Eritreian and Abyssynian campaigns he was commissioned back into his own regiment, something that is most unusual and of which he is justly proud, and he finished the war as a Captain. After the early part of the war he was posted to the famous garrison of Tobruk, where while he was inspecting his gun positions, a passing shrapnel fragment blew off his nose.

In 1942, he was sent home on the liner *Laconia*, which met a German torpedo off the West Coast of Africa. Most of the 2600 people on board died swiftly. The survivors, including Ben, spent two days on a raft and five in a lifeboat before being rescued. He came home to pass most of the next two years having his face rebuilt by the legendary Archie McIndoe.

Captain Coutts returned to hill farming in Scotland after the war and spent most of the next 30 years with his own sheep and cattle on the hills of Inverness-shire and Argyll, then factoring Highland estates (he likes to tell of the keeper who, asked if there was vermin on his hill, answered 'only a puckle hoodies and a factor'), and finally served 10 years running the Aberdeen Angus Cattle Society.

He still laments the passing of the good old days when a shepherd castrated lambs with his teeth, and works himself into a fever of rage about the modern mania for crossbreds. 'It costs no more to feed good cattle than bad cattle, Max!' he exploded one day, in the midst of a sorry pack of Holstein crosses.

My father met Ben in the Fifties while making a television film about red deer damage to Highland farming. When father despaired of my 15-year-old delinquency at home, he dispatched me to spend a summer holiday on the Coutts farm near Laggan. It was a revelation. I felt the rough edge of the Coutts tongue almost daily, whether for oversleeping when I was supposed to bring in the cows for hand-milking, or pointing a 20-bore the wrong way walking-up a grouse. But I fell in love with the Highlands and I was captivated by farm life, even if my fitness for it seemed doubtful.

In the years since, I have met Coutts dancing like a dervish in a London restaurant in his kilt, campaigning as liberal candidate for Perth and Kinross against Nicky Fairbairn, broadcasting his farming diary for so many years on BBC Scotland and venting his rage against Scottish Nationalism at every turn. If he has a vice, it is in believing that the old ways were always the best, yet his matching virtue is a love for the land and the beasts that graze it, which marks every good countryman.

He was always a quick man with a gun. I remember him sitting on a Sutherland hillside gossiping while others looked for a fallen grouse. Suddenly two more birds burst out of the heather. Ben, aged 50-something, was up and had shot them before I reached my feet. He is an untruthful man in some respects, for instance in suggesting a wee dram when that adjective has been conspicuous for its absence from everything in his life.

His invective is fierce, deployed in those braw, gravely northern cadences against political correctness, modern politicians, the decline of small farming, the damage done by breath-testing to Scottish social life. His friendships are legion, many with stockmen as devoted as he is. I have learnt from him all manner of improbable things, such as that you will never make a decent stick handle from the horn of a hand-fed ram, which bears a tell-tale soft white streak at its heart.

I still fear his rages. Some years ago, I was proud of myself for retracing Montrose's 1644 winter march through to snows from Blair Atholl to Inverary. Ben was factoring Blackmount in Argyll when I rang to announce my triumphant arrival, after a hard passage across the frozen hillsides. 'You bloody fool!' he roared, 'You're the sort of idiot our stalkers have to be dragged out of bed every few days to pick off the hill with a busted leg!' I was crestfallen.

Today he has reluctantly given up shooting, and knows he won't go to the hill again. But he has published half-a-dozen slim volumes of autobiography, written with the verve and passion of a man who can talk all night about shepherding, dogs, grouse, sheep sales, whisky, forestry or any of the things that matter most above the Highland line. I love him dearly. I owe him more than I can say for what he has taught me and for the way of life that he so nobly represents.

MAX HASTINGS
Author, broadcaster and Editor
of the *Evening Standard*

1
The Family

I suppose it must have been father's forebears, who belonged to Strathdon in Aberdeenshire and who were crofters, who instilled the love of farming in my veins, for all my life I have never wanted to be anything else. My grandfather had left Strathdon to become a chemist, and his vocation, if one calls being a chemist a vocation, took him to Manchester. It was there that my father was educated and brought up. Breeding again told in Dad's blood, as he was determined to be a Church of Scotland minister. His Mater, as he called his mother, always backed him in his determination to cross the Border again, even though she herself was English.

Time and again the readers of this yarn will get fed up with my references to breeding. If you've bred as many sheep, cattle and horses as I have, either for myself or other people, you will realise what a haphazard job we humans make of the whole business. We males go to a dance, like the look of the lass, take her out a few times, decide we're 'madly in love', marry her and then wonder why our offspring don't come up to the standard which we expected. In stock breeding we take fantastic care with pedigrees, as did and do many of our aristocratic families. When careful breeding comes off in stock breeding we call it 'line breeding': when it doesn't we call it 'in breeding'; but every now and then you need a complete out cross, and I think that Dad and Mother must have been that super out cross that came off.

Mother died in August 1987 just five days short of her 101st birthday. She had only three weeks in hospital and but five days discomfort and no pain. As the minister said in his appreciation, 'She was indeed a remarkable woman'; and as her lawyer and friend Dick Barclay confided in me, 'Heaven will never be the same, now Rose is there they'll wonder what's hit them!' She had, until her last five days, what an old shepherd of mine called 'all her facilities'. Also from crofting stock, she was a Fleming related to the famous writing brothers Peter and Ian, and I advisedly put Peter first when I talk of writers. Dad must have been brilliant, as he was an MA at eighteen. He had to spend some years tutoring before he could enter the Church of Scotland. This was to prove invaluable to him and to us, his family, as he learnt a lot of taste, and I always wish he had earned more money to enjoy some of the taste that he had.

Part of his time during the early days of his ministerial life, before the First World War, was spent in Rangoon among a lot of hard-drinking Scottish tea planters, and it was among them that he got a taste for the 'cratur'. But I never even knew he drank until I came back wounded from the Second World War. It was then that he told me about his Rangoon days, and how shiploads of girls came out looking for wealthy tea-planting husbands. They were known as 'the Fishing Fleet'—but fortunately for the six children in our family, thank goodness he didn't get hooked!

He was immensely humble as befits a minister, but was very proud of his family, and I only wish he had lived to see some of the success that the six achieved. He had a most glorious fund of clean stories: I wish I had written more down in the few years that we really got to know each other, because if you read on you will see that we had a turbulent period. Being a minister and a brilliant (and, more important, short) speaker, he was often asked to say grace. If there was only one water glass on the table it was 'Oh Lord, for all the least of all thy mercies', but if there were sherry, wine and port glasses, his hands would be held aloft and he would almost sing—and he had a superb baritone voice—'Oh, Bountiful Jehovah...'

Mother's family had had a bit of money and her father, an MP for Aberdeen and then Lord Provost, was not amused when she married an impecunious Church of Scotland minister. She used to tell the story of the Church Treasurer in Dad's Aberdeen charge coming to the Manse when summoned by Mother—and believe me she had that ability to the end—to paint the Manse. Screwing his bonnet in his hands in nervousness, he announced that the Kirk Session (the ruling body in the Church of Scotland) had given him 10 shillings to spend on redecorating the Manse. History doesn't relate what Mum's reply was but I'm glad I wasn't there!

When Lord Provost, Grandfather had an official chauffeur called Gray. After Grandfather demitted office Gray got a job in the Aberdeen Fish Market and used to send a wooden box (originally constructed to hold 144 eggs) full of discarded but beautifully fresh fish to mother by train each week. From memory the cost in old pence—not shillings—was 10d.! What I do remember clearly is how much we, as schoolboys, hated collecting the box at the station, as all our school chums baited us with calls of 'Smelly Fish Coutts'. Believe it or not, when one sees the price and scarcity of fish today, in the twenties it was considered the poor man's meat. Sadly, as in so many other aspects of life in Britain today, it is greed that has devastated our once thriving fish stocks.

Before he married, Dad had a ferocious bull terrier called Beeloo who

Father and Mother, Melrose 1939

used to pick fights with the guard dogs that were used to look after the fish yards in Aberdeen. During their engagement Mum used to exercise him, and the dog used to swim the Dee to pick a fight, but after the marriage Mum got her way, as she was to get it during many, many years of married life, by getting rid of Dad's beloved Beeloo. Mum was greatly encouraged by Dad's Beadle (the Church of Scotland's Church Officer) who said 'Yon's no a meenester's dug, yon's a miner's dug'.

Father's ministry in Aberdeen was long enough for Mother to produce two boys: Robin who was born deaf and whom Father with infinite patience taught to lip-read brilliantly; and Fleming (later Sir Walter) who, I am told, as Chief Secretary in Kenya during the troubles, had probably more to do with Kenya's stability than anyone else. My authority is no less than the late Sir Martin Gilliatt, the Queen Mother's Secretary, who worked with him. After Kenya, brother Wally become Governor and then the only Governor General of Uganda.

Dad's next move was to St George's and St Peter's in Glasgow, one of the churches that has been phased out in the churches' amalgamation programme.

I think this must have been a very hard charge, as I know what a magnificent visitor Dad was and he would have had well over 1,000 in the congregation. It was during Dad's ministry in Glasgow that he suffered a nasty growth in his throat. He always maintained it was due to the fact that, although he had a strong voice, in front of the pulpit there was a huge gap and above it the steeple, which is where his voice went if he didn't bellow. Anyway, he had to have an operation carried out by the leading Ear, Nose and Throat surgeon in Glasgow—whom Dad called, ignominiously, 'the top snout-howker in the business'! The said gentleman went on to be knighted for his work, but not only did he cut a nasty sac out of Dad's throat, but he never charged him a penny. That's how highly the ministry was regarded in the twenties.

The twenties were hard times in Glasgow, as the shipyards that had produced the vessels that helped win the First World War, and had made 'Clyde-built' a name to be respected world wide, were laid bare and thousands of first-class tradesmen were thrown out of work. I well remember as a boy accompanying Father to see an ex-Clyde riveter from one of the well-known shipyards. He lived in one of the notorious Glasgow slums, where you went in through a 'close' (an alleyway) that was dark both night and day with a feeble wee gas light flickering at the end of it. After climbing endless stone stairs we arrived at the one-roomed flat. There was a tiny coal fire in a huge old-fashioned metal range, so polished one could see one's face in it. The man and his wife were both 'perjink' (Scots for clean and fastidious). When Dad asked his church member why didn't he and his wife come to the soup kitchen that the church was operating for the unemployed, to this day I can still feel a tear come to my eye at his reply. Showing us both hands, he said 'there's the best ten riveting fingers on the Clyde, and nobody will employ them.' A proud man. How sad that successive governments, and workers striking, have ruined one of Scotland's great industries. Who, in the thirties, would ever have dreamt of a ship like the *Queen Mary* being built anywhere else but the Clyde—they certainly wouldn't have imagined it being built in France!

Talking of slums and the closes that led into them, Dad told me a lovely story after we'd had a few drams and not long before he died (aged 84). I hope he'll forgive me putting it in print, but it's a classic. During the Depression years Dad was holding a Bible class cum tea-and-scones evening in one of the deprived areas near the Clyde. On the evening in question he was particularly pleased with the number of lads present, because usually the female sex, as in church, predominated. After clearing up and congratulating himself on the turn-out, he was walking up the neighbouring street on his way home, when out of a nearby close he heard a female voice saying: 'Hold my Bible, Jock, and I'll tak them doon mysel'! Nuff said.

But the war came along and soon Dad was off. During that time I was born in 1916 and brother Frank in 1918. Brother Frank, after starting as a bobby on the beat outside Buckingham Palace, became a regular soldier, rose through the ranks to Brigadier, played rugby for Scotland, became that most cherished person in a regiment, their Hon. Colonel, got his CBE and was President of the Scottish Rugby Union.

After the war Father was called to Milngavie outside Glasgow, where Maisie, the only girl, was born. She was the only one that had Dad's love of art, both painting and music. Philip was the youngest; he had fantastic musical ability, served in the Colonial Service with distinction and was awarded his MBE. Latterly he controlled the Scottish Wool Board, but is sadly no longer with us. So, all in all, my parents produced six of us, four of whom have been decorated. Probably Robin, the eldest but deaf, could be the brightest, and Maisie, in this male-chauvinist dominated world, has not had the same chance to make her mark in public life.

Milngavie was the charge Mother enjoyed most. The manse was not as draughty as most. Father was on the magnificent salary of £600 pa, she was surrounded by people whom she liked, and she took part in Gilbert and Sullivan operas etc. Father's Session Clerk, Hugh Buchanan, was especially kind to us all. He in turn was a great friend of Neil Munro (or Hugh Foulis, which was his *nom de plume*). I remember Neil reading some of his writings and poetry with that lovely Highland lilt of which I became so fond. One of his great characters was John Splendid, of whom he said, 'He was better in the promise than the performance.' How many John Splendids I've met in life!

Then there was the time when Neil told us that he was running out of inspiration but seemed to get it in the middle of the night, so he put a pencil and pad under his pillow. At lunchtime the next day he suddenly remembered that he had written something and dashed upstairs, only to find that what was on the pad was, 'Paraffin oil is good for the boil.' Neil's Para Handy stories are West Highland classics, but they were even better when he read them.

Glasgow Academy had a wonderful scheme that gave minister's children a cheap and first-class education, and they also gave reductions for numbers. When Philip went, Dad said they were almost owing him money!

2
Schooldays

Why do people continue to call schooldays 'the happiest days of your life'? For me I thank God that Dad was such a stickler for education. 'You can carry it round the world like a belt', he used to say, and how right I proved him to be. But at the time I loathed school from the first day to the last.

There was no doubt at all that Glasgow Academy had the ability to turn out good citizens—and, in my day, good rugby players, though sadly I was not one of them. It also made good politicians, judging by the high esteem in which the late Donald Dewar was held. I had one teacher, a certain Baggy Aston, who taught English and for whom I would work like a slave, but apart from that one subject my exam marks and reports were abysmal. Baggy got his nickname because he wore flannel trousers, at least 22 inches at the turn-up, that were the fashion at Oxford where he had been educated and where the trousers were known as Oxford bags. Baggy hated the slovenly Glaswegian speech, in which butter becomes 'burrer'. He always loved Father's story of the Glaswegian mother who rewarded her daughter, a recent recipient of an English prize, with a long tram ride from one end of Glasgow to the other. In these days the tram-cars had wooden seats: after three hours sitting on them the mother and child got off, and the girl, very sore, said 'I wish I hadnae goed', whereupon mother said, 'An you just won an English Prize—what you mean is I wish to Goed I hadnae went.'

Baggy had leadership, and any small success I have had in broadcasting, TV and public speaking must stem from Mum and Dad's rearing and Baggy's tuition. My broadcasting career now spans fifty years. I think there are few left now to have broadcast on farming matters with A.G. Street, Ralph Wightman and John Charrington. I also appeared on Cliff Michelmore's 'Tonight' programme along with Wilfred Pickles and Esther Rantzen; contributed regularly to 'Matter of Opinion', the Scottish equivalent of 'Any Questions', and for several years during the eighties had my own farming programme called 'Ben Coutts' Diary'.

Glasgow Academy had a marvellous old headmaster called Ted Temple who, like many of his era, thought no one had a future unless they were classical scholars. The best example of this way of thinking was John Baird's father who was a fellow Church of Scotland minister with Father. When Father congratulated the old man on his son's success in inventing TV, he responded, 'He'll never get anywhere: he couldn't pass his Latin exams.' I don't know how many countless hours I spent staring out of the vast panes of those windows and dreaming of the weekend when I'd either be at Balmore or Killearn helping on a farm.

Father really did work hard, and I sometimes wonder what modern ministers/parsons/priests would think of his workload. We hardly saw him, as he was out every night at prayer meetings, religious instruction, women's meetings and constant visiting. He visited every single member at least once a year, plus all the calls on the sick. He would put many modern ministers to shame with the standard of his preaching. His sermons were never more than 10 to 15 minutes, which I have found is the hardest type of sermon or public speech to do. His great saying about this was: 'If you don't strike gold in ten minutes, stop boring'!

Although he was seldom seen by us, he kept an eagle eye on us all. I well remember being told by him to be home on the family bicycle, his, by a certain time from the Gilchrists' farm at Balmore. We were at the hay with the Clydesdale horses and the 'tumblin' Tams', that huge horse-drawn fork, that once it was full coming up a row of hay was tumbled over, leaving a heap of hay to be forked into the cole or small stack. It was one of my favourite jobs and I lost track of time, getting home in the dark at least two hours late. I suddenly panicked, as I knew Father would be upset, so I thought I would be clever and let down a tyre. I told Father I'd had a puncture. My face, as always, must have given me away, as Father went out to the bike, came back in and said, 'Burnaby, the bathroom and the slipper for you.' He was a dab hand with a slipper with one's head over the bath, and as he finished he said, 'That's not because you were late but because you lied to me.' What a super lesson, and one I've never forgotten.

Things have changed today. Now we hear of a headmistress controlling an unruly boy only to be given the sack. It seems to me that there is now no discipline instilled into the youth of the country. This used to be started in the home, then was continued in schools and in my case carried on in the Army. I was sad when this country gave up National Service, as I know many who went to it very reluctantly but came back saying how much good it had done them in terms of discipline.

Mr Gilchrist from Balmore was one of Father's members, and he and his family were more than kind to me. They worked hard in those days. The boys were no sooner home from school than they were yoked to some job or other. All the cows were hand-milked and the milk driven by pony and cart in big cans to Glasgow or the local railway station.

Another family who were very kind to me were the Browns at Westerton, Killearn. Old man Brown had a delivery service for taking beef from the Glasgow slaughterhouse to butchers' shops. He had invented a long narrow cart that one could push into a butcher's shop door, containing a side or two of beef which could be pushed right up to the chains which pulled them up to the hanging hooks. These 'meat barrows' were pulled by fast trotting Irish ponies, and the service was called 'Brown's Express Delivery'.

The 'do-gooders' of today would throw their hands in the air if nowadays they saw a half side of beef exposed to the air! To my way of thinking we have taken hygiene too far, and have no antibodies left to defend us from all those mysterious ailments which were never known, or publicised, in my young day. An example of this is the experience of my daughter Pippa. She had worked for the Save the Children Fund for two years in Sudan, two in Eritreia and two in Ethiopia, where she was part of a team of aid workers. When everyone in the team, with the exception of Pippa, were stricken with severe stomach problems, the Medical Officer asked her, 'Where were you reared?' Answer: 'On a Scottish farm.' 'What milk did you drink?' Answer: 'From the farm, hand-milked by Dad.' Whereupon the Doc said, 'That's the explanation—you're the only one with antibodies!' Nuff said.

Old John Brown, like many butchers of his era, was no mean judge of a horse: many of those ponies were sold on at a profit and some came to Westerton for his family to ride. As I was friendly with his son 'Coupie', I learnt to ride with them. Coupie was an accomplished whip and won the National Single Horse Driving Championship. The Browns also had Aberdeen-Angus cattle and Border Leicester sheep, a very usual combination of stock for pedigree breeders until very recently. Bob Adam of Newhouse, Allan Grant of the Thorn, the Templetons of Sandyknowe, the Stewarts of Kinimouth, and Struthers were just a few of the leading Scottish stockmen who had these breeds of cattle and sheep.

I owe a great debt to the Brown family for those happy, carefree, hardworking weekends, and Mrs Brown's cooking was superb (especially after Mother's). One was never short of lemonade in that household, something we never saw in the Manse. I often wonder what would have happened had I taken 'Pa Broon's' (he was always nicknamed that after a cartoon) advice when he said, 'You ought to become a sporting parson, Burnaby.' What a lovely thought!

To return to Father—another member of the family and I once spilt a lot of split barley on the kitchen floor on which someone had come a cropper, and we boys had fled and hid in the rhubarb patch. Father appeared at the back door and said, 'I'll see you after six in my study', and from then on not one game we started was any good because of the dreaded six o'clock. I used this technique to good advantage in the war, when as a Sergeant Major I used to march the 'prisoner and escort' as far as possible before confronting the officer/judge: it's amazing how the time-lag saps one's confidence, and many a cocky offender crumpled when he eventually faced his judge.

We didn't see much of Dad, but how much we as a family owed him. I thought he never drank, little realising what he had to give up to educate us. The big snag as far as I was concerned was that he wanted all of his family to go to university or college, and I, a slow maturer who hated learning and loved the outdoors, was set on a collision course with him. He had a great friend, whom he had met when he was minister at Coldstream, and this person was highly respected in farming circles—in fact, he was knighted for his administrative work for farming—one Sir Joshua Ross-Taylor. (Some local farmers naughtily called him the Knight of the Thistle because they didn't think much of his practical farming.) It was to Sir Joshua Dad went for advice about my future. Sir Joshua was adamant that without capital there was no future for me in farming, and without a farming background there was no chance of a manager's job, as in the late Twenties and Thirties there were scores of farmers' sons looking for work. 'Make him a vet,' said Sir Joe, 'and if he is successful he'll be able to buy his own farm.' So my school teachers were told to try to prepare me for my leaving certificate. However, Dad was told that he would be better to take me away and get some private tuition for the EIS certificate, which at that time was the sort of back entrance into the Vet College and not as high a standard as the Higher Leaving Certificate. I scraped in, and will never forget a wee French tutor, sorely tried because I had difficulty in memorising slices of Molineux's *Poudre aux Yeux*. To this day I have problems in memorising.

I realise now that I was slow to mature and the fact that I was flat-footed as well ruled me out of being good at sport, but I did manage to win the 'best drilled and dressed recruit' in the Officers Training Corps, and thoroughly enjoyed their summer camps.

In 1932 I managed to get into the rifle shooting team and represented the school at Bisley. My flat feet were so bad that I had to go to hospital and have the bones manipulated into place, and have huge plaster cast boots put on them, but to this day one foot still gives me a lot of trouble. Looking back I wonder how our parents managed to afford to give us all they did: not only a first-class education but allowing us to pursue some sort of sport and giving us holidays. There was no National Health Service then, but I suspect the local doctor, who was a great friend, may not have sent in a bill.

In Scotland the minister, the doctor and the schoolmaster were held in very high esteem in the Twenties and Thirties, but I don't think the same can be said today. One of the reasons our educational system is having problems in recruiting teachers is, I have no doubt, because socially the profession has been degraded. The same goes for ministers: this country is no longer interested in the Church as money has become God. The Church is used by all too many as a place to marry in, to christen children in and when the time comes to have a memorial service in. The story is told of the Church of Scotland minister whose church was invaded by mice. He went to speak to the local R.C. priest, as he had heard that the priest had got rid of a similar invasion of mice. When asked how he had done it the priest, an Irishman, said, 'Sure and bejasus, I christened them, and so I never saw them again until till they died!' As for doctors, after the lengthy period of study and work they need in order to qualify, they make one human mistake and then face litigation! How values have changed.

One lived very frugally then and, as our staple breakfast was porridge and one morning roll, by eleven o'clock we were starving and more than ready for that mug of soup and another roll that was our lunch. Mother would have been the first to admit that she was not interested in food but, as all five boys grew to be over six feet tall, whatever she gave us must have been wholesome. One of Father's best friends, a highly successful Glasgow lawyer, once said, 'There is nothing to beat a Manse upbringing because of the Christian background and the fact that there is no spare cash with which to spoil the children.' I couldn't agree with him more.

3

School Holidays

Mother had been given a cottage in St Fillans, Perthshire, as a wedding present from her father and we either went there or Mother let it and spent the money on taking us somewhere else. The island of Arran and the Lake District were two of these holidays, and whenever we arrived anywhere I made straight for the nearest farm and was never seen again for the rest of the holidays. One of Mother's sisters had married a Border farmer who had moved down to Norfolk. I loved working with his men, but I was so terrified of my Aunt that I developed a nervous complaint of wetting the bed, which I'm glad to say I've never had since, but it didn't exactly endear me to Aunt Elizabeth.

One of the finest sights I have ever seen in farming used to occur every morning at Uncle Willie's farm, when ten pairs of highly polished chestnut Suffolk Punch horses emerged from the horse barn. They were so quiet they weren't stabled, as most farm horses in Scotland were, with partitions between them: the twenty were tied up in one long line in the barn.

It was usually harvest time when I was staying in Norfolk and I was given the job of 'Hodye' boy. His job was to ride the horse that was in the shafts of the huge old harvest waggons that were pulled by two horses, one in the shafts and one in front in the traces. I had to pilot the waggon from stook to stook, and when I was about to start the horse I had to shout to the two men building the cart load 'Hold ye', which in broad Norfolk had become 'Hodye'. The pay was 2s. 6d. per week, which was wealth indeed in those far-off days. Another job that I got after harvest was finished was 'turkey boy'. Thousands of turkey were fattened in Norfolk for the London Christmas market. Immediately the stooks were cleared from the fields, temporary perches were erected and flocks of turkeys were set free, to be controlled during the day by two boys with long ash poles and guarded against foxes at night by a watchman. It was a much more monotonous job and not half so much fun as harvest, in which one was part of a gang and I was with my beloved horses.

I'm afraid I got on better with the farm staff than I did with my relations, much to my Aunt's annoyance. On Saturday mornings, when the huge staff of horsemen, cattlemen, shepherd, gardener and the harvest casual labour, of which I was one, lined up to touch their forelocks and get their pay, my

Aunt was not amused to see me join them. Norfolk was very feudal in those days, and coming from Scotland where we were 'a' Jock Tamson's bairns', I couldn't understand this attitude at all and was always missing when the family were going to 'take tea' with their neighbours. When it was found that I had been bathing in the canal with the other 'Hodye' boy I was really in trouble, and even more so that I hadn't worn a bathing suit. I did however condescend to sing in the village choir, as all my pals were in it, but I wasn't too keen about being dressed up in the gown etc. because of course in Scotland most choirs are not gowned. My lasting impressions of those Norfolk holidays were of constant sunshine, the smell of peaches ripening on the wall outside my bedroom, and the appalling condition of the workers' cottages compared with their counterparts in Scotland. No wonder the farm workers' union started in East Anglia.

I went back to Narborough this year, 2000, and found fantastic changes, but of course it is seventy years since I worked there. The horse barn where those lovely Suffolk Punches were stabled is now a row of flats. The farm is completely split up and the part I saw was, like so many farms today, grazed by horses. I was able to show the present owner of Church Farm, Uncle Willie's old home, the window where we lined up for our pay and touched our forelocks! Also the spot where the pump used to stand, that had to be manually pumped for two hours each morning to provide enough water for the cistern in the loft to keep the house supplied with water. I'll bet the modern mains water is not half as good as that which came up from that old well.

Arran holidays couldn't have been more different, because we stayed in a farmhouse while the farmer and his family moved into a shack behind. I was accepted as an unpaid casual labourer, doing whatever chores were necessary, and I don't know why, but the small potatoes that were kept back and boiled up for the hens were the best I have ever tasted in my life. Was it because I was virtually stealing them? Or because Arran potatoes were then world-famous, thanks to Donald McKelvie and his Arran Banner, Arran Pilot etc.? Much more likely because they were just partially washed, and boiled up in an old cast-iron three-legged pot. How I wish the average housewife would think about flavour in a potato instead of wanting potatoes that have no eyes (almost an impossibility), that must be washed, round in circumference etc. This has filled supermarkets with potatoes that are bland and flavourless because of too much nitrogen. But thank goodness there are still some growers around who have kept the likes of Sharpe's Express, Duke of York, Kerr's Pink and the Daddy of them all, Golden

Wonder, where the likes of wee gardeners like me can procure seed.

I made great friends with the shepherd on the neighbouring 'big' farm and was allowed to help him drove the blackfaced wether lambs over the 'string road' from Machrie Bay to Brodick, where they were put on the boat en route for the Ayr or Lanark market. To this day I always marvel at how the shepherds kept their lots separate as they got closer to the boat.

This shepherd, Archie McDiarmid, is still alive and did a first-class broadcast about the old days at the bicentenary Arran Show in 1986, which was graced by Her Royal Highness Princess Anne. He it was who tried to train me in running a sheep dog. Looking at the success of 'One Man and His Dog' I wish he had succeeded, but it's a gift you either have or haven't. He it was also who, when on his holidays in Glasgow, introduced me to the Arran Societies Ceilidhs, which were so well attended between the wars that they filled the St Andrews Hall. The Gaelic language was still much in use, especially among the old folk, and if you didn't know how to dance you soon had to learn all the reels and quadrille jig time. A quiet dance was a Boston or Military Two Step!

All my holidays were spent farming. The St Fillans ones were the tops for me, as I looked on Perthshire as home and I have always loved the hills. Murdo Nicholson was one of my early mentors. He was tenant of a north-facing small farm on Lochearnside called Ardtrostan. As the farm was a poor one he made his money out of summer visitors by selling milk to them. Murdo was a *Sgianach*, a Skye man. He went every year to Oban where he bought dairy-type heifers from his fellow Skye men or other islanders. These he took home to St Fillans, had them bulled by his neighbour's bull, calved them down and had keen laddies like myself milk them. Many a time I got landed in the 'grip' as we called the dung channel, but it was great experience. The heifers were dried off in the winter and when they calved down the second time they were often sold to shepherds, stalkers, or gamekeepers —for the 'hoose coo' was a really good perquisite in those days of poor wages. It was with Murdo that I ploughed my first furrow, and a pretty crooked one it was. Not helped by the fact that one horse was a Clydesdale and the other a Highland pony, which not only had to plough, harrow etc, but took the milk to the village each morning in a gig. Murdo had lost two sons in the First World War, and of his two remaining sons, the one who worked on the farm wanted to, and did, join the police, and the youngest was what was then called a 'mongol', i.e. had Down's Syndrome. We lads all accepted him and played football with him, and I'm sure he had a much happier upbringing on the farm than being shut away in a home. One of my

Keepers, ghillies and a young Ben Coutts, St Fillans, 1934

favourite memories of Murdo was of his taking me to my first Oban Cattle Sale. It was up that magical railway line, sadly to go with the Beeching axe, from St Fillans to Balquhidder and on up past Crianlarich and Tyndrum to Taynuilt and Oban. From that day to this Oban has held me in its spell. I well remember Murdo telling me as he went in to the pub for the umpteenth time that he had to go in with his Skye friends for another 'refresh'— 'but tell your father it's only lemonade I'm drinking.' Even in those boyhood days before I knew about alcohol, the old *Sgianach's* breath didn't seem to smell of lemonade!

Caravans were almost unheard of, and the old man was not at all amused when one had been parked in what he called his 'good Coo Pairk' without his consent. 'Come on, laddie, we'll just go away down and see what he's up to.' When we got there Murdo accosted the man by saying, 'You've been in my good Coo Pairk for two days without as much as by my leave.' The stranger in a very English voice, and obviously knowing something about farming because the 'Pairk' was a mass of tansy (ragwort), replied, 'Your good cow meadow? It's nothing but a lot of weeds.' Quick as a flash the old *Sgianach* replied, 'There was no weeds here till you cam.' Poor Murdo must turn in his grave, as the 'Coo Pairk' is now a caravan site and does nothing to enhance lovely Lochearnside.

In this day of modern farming, when cash flow is all-important and many farmers who have overstretched themselves are going to the wall, I look back wistfully and think of old Murdo and his way of life, because that's what it was. He was a first-class stockman who bought his heifers wisely and well, he used his neighbour's bull as I've said, and never spent money unless he had to. He got cash from the 'veesitors' in the summer for his milk and potatoes, he reared a super family, he was an Elder in the Kirk and thereby did his bit for the district, and he had a wonderfully dry sense of humour. What a different lifestyle from some modern farmers, so often chasing a will o' the wisp existence.

It was at St Fillans that I was to receive my first, if not my last, rebuff from the fair sex. Wally, Frank and I decided to attend the Lochearnhead dance that was held annually on Glasgow Fair Saturday, when the local 'talent' was augmented by many Glaswegians. We set off on our bicycles and pedalled the seven miles up the lochside. In those days the girls sat on one side and the lads on the other, and when the band struck up there was a dirty dive across the hall to grab the lady of one's choice. I picked out a 'smasher'. After arriving breathless in front of the person that I thought was to be my partner I said, 'Will you dance?' She looked me up and down once or twice and then said 'Na' in broad Glasgwegian and I, completely taken aback, and rather fancying myself as a dancer said, 'Why not?' Whereupon she replied, 'Your feet's ower big.' Exit Coutts to Lochearnhead Hotel, where Willie Cameron, the owner, said 'I know I shouldn't be serving you because I know your age and that you are the minister's son, but by the look of you you're needing a drink.' I became very friendly with the Cameron family, and had the honour to present their cattleman, Neil, with his Royal Highland Long Service Medal, and also to make the speech at his grand-daughter's wedding. And Ewan, Willie's son, became not only a fellow councillor but a good friend of mine.

Lochearnhead, like many villages I have known in the last fifty years, has completely changed, as there has been a rash of building. What saddens me is those people who emigrate from the towns, join the local community council, want to run the district their way, and completely disregard the views of the locals who have survived—and it was a case of survival for many years—and who, all too often, are not, shall we say, as vociferous as the incomers.

4

Glenartney

Glenartney is probably best known because of its mention in 'The Lady of the Lake' where Walter Scott talks about 'The stag at eve had drunk its fill'.

To me it is still one of my favourite glens in Scotland, as I have so many happy boyhood memories of it. The hills around Loch Earn were mostly owned by the Earl of Ancaster, the owner of Glenartney. John Ferguson, his estate manager, was in charge of the labour, both shepherds and keepers around St Fillans, and so it was inevitable that I should get to know the Glen. 'Shauchan' Ferguson was one of the best organisers of labour I've ever come across, and with a bothy full of young lads like myself, quite apart from stalkers, keepers, a cattleman, a lorry man and larderman, he would have us all doing some job or other within minutes of 'yoking' time, which in those days was seven o'clock. If it was wet I used to be forever cutting kindling wood or cleaning deer saddles, both jobs that were to stand me in good stead in years to come. I little realised in those far-off days how much I was absorbing that would be of use to me when I myself was in charge of a squad of men. I learned that men want direct orders as to what to do. They might not always be the right orders, but workers can't abide ditherers.

I spent many happy holidays in Glenartney both in the bothy and with the shepherd's family, the MacNabs, who were kindness itself. How the MacNab family existed on the pay they received, while feeding a ravenous Ben Coutts for £1 a week, I'll never know. But deer's liver and home-made scones have never tasted the same to me since those far distant days. In the summer there was an endless round of clippings, when we went as a squad in an ancient Model 'T' Ford lorry to clip the sheep on all the different sheep farms owned by the estate. With other boys I did the 'crogging', which means taking the sheep to the shearer, and old Shauchan used to stand at the gate and let the sheep go. Catching a blackfaced ewe in mid-air may be good practice for rugby, but it can also be dashed sore on the hands at the end of a long day; however woe betide any one of us who missed, for we didn't get a suck at the lemonade bottle the next time it was passed round.

Glenartney has always been famous for its deer forest and also for its ponies. It used to breed its own Highland ponies and get them broken, and then rent them out to grouse moors and deer forests. Peter McIntyre had been a rough-riding sergeant in the Scottish Horse, and he got lads like myself to help him break the ponies in the old but large stable at the Comrie railway station. Looking back, I suppose they broke them there rather than at the top of the Glen because (a) there was an abundance of keen, free labour, (b) the ponies saw a bit of traffic but nothing compared with today, and (c) the blacksmith was in Comrie—and a bad-tempered one he was.

I remember that John Ferguson had lent twelve ponies to Dunblane Show to be used for musical chairs. Dunblane Show was on Glasgow Fair Saturday then, and Peter McIntyre, myself and A. N. Other set off from Comrie with four ponies each, riding one, leading one and with two 'tailed' on behind, a very usual way of getting a lot of Highland ponies moved with a minimum of labour. We went as far as Braco on the Friday and set off early on Saturday for the Show. It was the days of charabancs, and on Glasgow Fair Saturday they were full of yelling Glaswegians. You never saw such a shambles, and I know at one point I had my led pony and its 'tailer' both on the other side of a low wall that verged on the main road. I still can't think how we got to the Show but get there we did, and my only consolation was that I got my first ever Show ticket for being third in the mounted musical chairs. I had bagged what I thought was the best pony, but I couldn't run as fast as the chap that won. Little did I think then that I would go on to serve on the Highland Pony Society Council, appear on their judges list, judge at the Highland Show, and to this day do the commentary at the Scottish and English Highland Pony shows with over a hundred ponies competing at each show.

August was of course the month for grouse shooting, and in the Twenties and Thirties many family incomes were greatly helped by the six shillings a day brought back by the schoolchildren for their day's grouse beating. In fact many children would be clothed for the winter with this money. Comrie was a great centre for the 'hunts', as the grouse shoots were called. Mr McPherson of the local ironmonger would supply beaters for Glenartney, Fordie, Invergeldie, Dunira, Lochside (St Fillans), Ardvorlich, Edinample and Glenbeich. Sadly there are now few grouse left and, although it is fashionable in some circles to decry what they call the 'grouse moor' image, I for one have a lot to thank it for. Discipline, a will to turn out looking smart, a respect for my elders and betters, the pleasure of physical fitness and the love of a good clean sport—all these things I learnt or partly learnt on the grouse moors.

There is a combination of reasons for the sad decline of grouse stocks in recent years. There are fewer keepers, so there is less heather burning which regenerates the young heather on which the grouse feed. Overstocking of sheep is another problem: there is a headage payment as an incentive to keep as many sheep as possible, but there are fewer shepherds and so ewes are often left on one piece of land, where they eat out the heather. But to my mind the most detrimental factor is the R.S.P.B., which won't allow any control of the raptors who live on grouse. I love all birds of prey, except for the hoodie crow, but raptors are multiplying at an alarming rate. Grouse, and with them keepers, are diminishing. Are we to put birds before people?

Christmas holidays in Glenartney were extra special for me as I went there on my own and stayed the whole time, usually with the MacNabs. I always hoped and prayed that the road would get blocked with snow and although the good Lord has answered many of my prayers since then he never answered that one. We only just got out one year, much to my annoyance. On deer forests the females (hinds) have to be culled, and December/January are the usual months for this. I always wonder why so much importance is put on stalking a stag, who at the end of the rut may well not be at his most alert, shall we say. Few people enjoy stalking hinds which are much more alert animals and therefore harder to stalk. It was on Christmas holiday in Glenartney that Fisher Ferguson, John's son, taught me to stalk and it's a sport I love to this day. We had a lot of hinds to cull then as numbers had been pushed off a neighbouring area because of afforestation. It was quite usual for me to come back with four ponies, all tailed, with two hinds on each. Thank goodness, so adept were the stalkers at securing the hinds that I never had a casualty. The stalkers would just leave me to come home on my own.

The late Fisher Ferguson retired to St Fillans and loved to talk of the 'good old days'. He was a first-class shot, not only with a rifle but also the shotgun. He was picked for the clay pigeon team for the Olympics but, because of pressure of work, his father wouldn't let him go. Can you imagine that happening today?

I remember him once running nigh on three miles to head off some hinds, three miles over rough hill and bog land. When he got in front of them he dropped fourteen with fourteen shots. Some shooting, some man. But they were tough in that Glen then, no Agocats, Weasels or Sno-tracks. Old 'Baldie' McNaughton, who also retired to St Fillans, told the story of walking from St Fillans to Glenartney, some five miles, doing a full day on the hill of 20 to 30 miles. When he got back to Auchinner at the head of Glen Artney, old 'Shauchan', instead of offering to have him driven home, looked up at the moon and said, 'It's a braw night for cycling back to St Fillans.' Seventeen miles!

What fun we used to have at New Year time! Mrs Ferguson, a Fisher from Balquhidder, a family who were famous for their hospitality, musical ability and sense of fun, was a wonderful hostess, and some forty of us would sit down to New Year's Day lunch after the annual clay pigeon shooting. There was great rivalry between Glenartney, Comrie, Crieff and Killin at the clay pigeons. One of the star turns of the Glenartney team was 'Uncle Bob', Mrs Ferguson's brother. He was rather fond of a dram, and to ensure that he was fit to shoot well we young lads were told to entice him into the cow byre with a bottle and then shut him in. Such was his strength that he charged the door with his shoulder, completely shattering it and came out unscathed to get 'gently fu'. But 'fu' or sober he could play a fiddle as well as or better than I've ever heard since, and with his sister playing the piano there was no way one couldn't learn to dance well. Learning to keep time to that super music was to stand me in good stead in the years to come, though I did not realise it at the time. Last year, at the Royal Smithfield show, a titled lady came up to me and said: 'I'll never forget the dance you gave me all those years ago. You Scots have a natural sense of time, thanks to dancing all your reels.' Conceit-making, but obviously I had progressed since I was so sharply rebuffed at Lochearnhead in the twenties!

'Uncle Bob' was a name to be conjured with when I was a boy. As a sergeant in the Scottish Horse had he not galloped into the square in Crieff and demanded to take over the Drummond Arms Hotel in the name of his Colonel, the Duke of Atholl? Had he not been reduced to the ranks by the same Duke for telling him to 'go to hell'? Also in his cups he decided he didn't like his Aberdeen-Angus bull, so he shot him and told his shepherds they could eat some decent beef instead of the interminable braxy mutton that one got then. Was it not he who, a great clay pigeon shot when sober, told his terrified housekeeper that he was fed up feeding her hens, which were her perquisite, so he sat outside the henhouse door, made her throw them out one by one when he shouted 'Pull' (the signal to release clay pigeons) and then shot them one by one? What a character, but oh! how kind to an impecunious laddie like me.

The New Year always finished with a singsong, and although to this day, after broadcasting regularly since 1947, I have butterflies in my tummy whenever I am on the air, they are as nothing compared to those I had when I rendered 'Bonnie Strathyre', my party piece. Every song or recitation— and everyone, but everyone, including the juniors, had to do something—was followed by John Ferguson leading 'Jolly good song, jolly well sung, jolly good fellows everyone, if you can beat it you're welcome to try, but please just remember the singer is dry', and around again came the bottle. Songs and recitations like 'McAlistar' were interspersed with dances. Old fashioned waltzes and the St Bernard's Waltz were looked on as respites and lassie's stuff compared with Broon's Reels (Duke of Perth) and eightsomes. Happy days and happy people. There is but one family at the head of the Glen now. What a lot TV and technology have to answer for!

5
Ponyman

As Lochside grouse moor was only two miles from the village of St Fillans, it was obvious that I should go there for the grouse beating and, thanks to my old Glenartney mate Pat McNab who was head ponyman, I was made one of his assistant ponymen. Loch Earn is seven miles long, with St Fillans at its east end and Lochearnhead at the west. On the north side of the loch there were three day's grouse beating: Lochside, the Derry and Ardveich, all owned by the Earl of Ancaster and keepered by a great character called Sandy Campbell. His nickname was the 'Rooster', because he looked for all the world like a bantam cock. His favourite saying was 'I'll bet ye', although he would never have seen a racecourse, or a racehorse for that matter. He was extremely good at showing sport and was a great vermin killer, so that in my day he always had good shooting for his tenants. On the south side of the loch there were two moors: one, Edinample, which was badly keepered and had waist-high heather so there weren't many grouse; and the second, Ardvorlich, owned by Major Stewart and keepered by Joe Bremner. Sandy and Joe were at daggers drawn.

As Lochside didn't have a shooting lodge the tenants stayed in Ardvorlich and came round the loch to the northern moors. In the Thirties a Mr Mordaunt took all five moors and the pattern was the same each week: Lochside Monday, Derry Tuesday, Wednesday Ardveich, Thursday Edinample and Friday Ardvorlich. The younger bloods shot ptarmigan on Ben Vorlich on the Saturday. To shoot ptarmigan one must be above 3,000 feet, as that's where they live. They are amazing survivors when you think how much of their feed is covered in snow each winter, and one sees them dive into snow to get to their food supply.

Gleneagles Hotel, I am told, was good value for money in the Thirties, so the young guns used to go there to the dinner dances on a Friday night, with the result that they weren't as fit as usual on the Saturday. There was the famous occasion when the person who was at the bottom of the firing line—one goes round and round the top of the mountain after ptarmigan and the going is tough—started slipping further and further down the hill. Sandy, who was directing operations, shouted down, 'Come up the hill, Mr X.' Poor Mr X was not feeling at all well and kept losing ground, where-upon Sandy bellowed at him again. After the third bellow Mr X said, rather pathetically, 'Have a heart, Campbell, I'm not feeling too well to-day', where-upon Sandy, pointing down to Loch Earn, said, 'If you don't like the performance there's the road.' It was the word performance that tickled me. Old Sandy was a hard but fair boss and he ran his 'performance' with the precision of a good Regimental Sergeant Major.

I had two years with the ponies at Lochside, one under Pat McNab and the second season, after I had brilliantly failed my veterinary exams, I went back as head ponyman. The head ponyman, who got £2 per week and the use of the bothy, was there each and every day, whereas the second ponyman got 7 shillings per day (1 shilling more than the beaters) but he was only there on a daily basis. I was friendly with Pat so I was as often in the bothy as I was in my own house. It was the head ponyman who had to catch the ponies (usually a wet job as the pony park was knee high in bracken), tie them up—there were four of them, two pannier ponies and two riding ponies—make breakfast and tidy up appearances. If it was Monday there wasn't so much of a rush, although Sandy always had us on parade long before we were needed, and he was right, for so many things could go wrong at the last minute. If it was Tuesday it was another matter, for the ponies had to go 'West the Loch' as Sandy called the Derry and Ardveich. The same system applied: riding one, leading one and two tailed, so it was necessary to be up betimes. The panniers and the other saddle came on in an ancient Morris Oxford driven by Sandy's son Tommy. And with all the gear dumped in the canvas hood, that canvas must have been tough! It was too bad if it was raining: the occupants of the car just got wet. The gear had to get there and there was no room in the car itself. One pannier pony had the lunch, the drinks, coats etc. and I, as a then teetotaller, was in charge of it. The slopes around the Loch are steep and one had to be sure that the girths, breeching etc. were secure before descending. Sandy always left me to the back of the cortège, and when I was checking the girths he would take a good long slug at the whisky bottle. When the guns were in their butts and waiting for the drive it was our job to 'flank' at one or other end of the line of butts. It sounds easy, but I've seen many a drive ruined by an over-enthusiastic flanker sending all the birds to the other end of the line. But they were halcyon days, lying in the sweet-smelling heather waiting for the drive to come in. And we were tremendously fit: Pat and I thought nothing of cycling to Glenartney on a Friday or Saturday night for the dances. The distance was 26 miles!

As you can guess, Sandy liked his dram, and the year that I was head ponyman he used to give me money to buy his whisky. Ma Campbell was

Head Ponyman, Lochside, St Fillans, 1934

very much against Sandy's love of the bottle or the 'weakness' as we call it in the Highlands. Because of this I had to bury the bottle in the 'kist' in which we kept the oats for the ponies. The kist had two sides, one with bruised oats and one with whole oats for Ma's hens. I was just preparing to hide the bottle when I heard the old targer coming, so I jammed the bottle into the hen's corn as it was nearer. It was, of course, found, and that was the end of the butter and scones that Ma used to leave at the bothy. No one would live in that bothy nowadays. The mattress was filled with oat chaff and was extremely lumpy, but we were physically tired and so we thought nothing of it. The fire always smoked and took ages to boil the heavy old kettle, and of course the water was outside and the loo was an old bucket privy.

But you only remember the good things, and one was the 'tips' received. With £2 per week for a wage, a tip of one of those lovely old white English fivers was riches indeed. I'll never forget the day I saw my first magical fiver. We had come off the hill when one of the guests realised he had left his spectacles in one of the butts. He was going south by train from Gleneagles that night and said to Sandy he would be lost without them. As one moves up two butts at each successive drive, I, who had been detailed to fetch them, found out from the 'Gent' which butt he started in at the first beat, and then I knew which ones he had occupied later. Luckily for me they were in the second line of butts, but by the time I got back the party was long gone. I got on my bike and cycled round to Ardvorlich, some seven miles round the loch. I told the butler why I'd come and he said he was sure the gentleman would want to see me. When he came down he was full of praise for my recovery job, and it was then I saw my very first fiver! I don't remember the bike ride back, I was in cloud-cuckoo land. Whenever possible I now try to tip as well as I can afford, as I well remember the pleasure that tip gave me.

As I said earlier, Sandy and Joe Bremner were at daggers drawn. At that time I couldn't see why, but in hindsight they were such entirely different characters. Joe was a tall, good-looking, kilt-wearing, easy-going Highlander, whereas Sandy was an aggressive, hardworking Scot, not too tall, and he couldn't see why the 'Toffs', as we called the tenants, took such a shine to Joe. One of Sandy's favourite occupations was to watch the Bremners' cottage, which was directly over the loch from his own, through his telescope—known in the keepering and stalking fraternity as your 'glass'. His comments to us assembled round him were as wonderful as they were assorted, and some are not printable. Usually they had something to do with Joe not being such an early riser as was he, for obvious reasons, as Sandy had to organise ponymen, ghillies and beaters, while Joe only had to wait for the 'Toffs' to pick him up and bring him round to our side of the loch. But the classic occasion was when we were all 'on parade', ponies saddled, boots polished, an hour before the off as was Sandy's wont, and he as usual was looking over the loch to see what was stirring. He suddenly shouted at me, 'Ben, you won't believe it—the bugger's looking at me through his glass!'.

6
The Ettrick Shepherd

Father had been called to a Border charge in Melrose, which delighted his rugby-daft family but annoyed Mother, because he had taken a drop in his salary to go there. He was dearly loved there by all, and to this day I meet boys who went to the local prep school St Mary's, and who remember, perhaps not the content of his sermons, but the fact that they enjoyed them. He was also loved by the old. He told a story against himself about two old ladies, one aged seventy-plus called Miss Jean and the other in her eighties, both single. For a joke one day he said to Miss Jean, 'Tell me, at what age do you give up thinking about getting a man?' and Miss Jean blushed and said, 'You'll have to ask my sister.'

They say there are three religions in the Borders: rugby, horses and the Church—in that order. Rugby was the only topic of conversation in Melrose, and with its famous seven-a-sides the subject didn't change much in half a century. Things are different now with the advent of professionalism. I'm the first to agree that international rugby was bound to go that way, and my goodness how it has quickened up the game. I can see the sense also in Edinburgh and Glasgow having a professional team each, but for Border and other small clubs to go professional I think is just plain daft. All the fun and loyalty to town and district have gone out of the window. Back in the thirties when I played for the (yellow and black) Melrose, there was a near-riot when it was suggested that, because the back row forwards (of which I was one) were all farm workers and too slow, the club might introduce someone from Musselburgh! With the players on the pitch nowadays, you wouldn't know who you were shouting for, Melrose, New Zealand or Fiji.

Much as I enjoyed my Saturday games, it was the nearby valley of Ettrick that drew me like a magnet. For I had met a sheep farmer called Robin Johnstone who tenanted the farm of Broadgairhill right up at the top of the valley and he agreed that when I had any spare days he would add to my scanty knowledge of sheep. To my mind the Border sheep men are the best in the world, and I say that having seen shepherding in the rest of Scotland, Sussex, USA, Mexico, Brazil, New Zealand, Australia and South Africa. I jumped at the idea, and instead of swotting for the vet exams I spent every available second at Broadgairhill. In Edinburgh too I was more game to train with the 4/7th Dragoon Guards who supplied horses for the Vet College

OTC than I was to swot. As for a chance of hearing that legendary trumpeter, Nat Gonella, Coutts was first in the queue for a seat in the 'Gods'. Money was scarce: one just ate less because one had to do a bit of what we called 'poodle faking', which was entertaining some of the fair sex. But it was in Ettrick that I really wasted most of my time. As things have turned out, the time was not wasted, but so far as exams were concerned it certainly was. Robin was a bachelor and had an old housekeeper who made the most wonderful scones and marmalade but would—apart from Mother, God bless her—be one of the worst cooks there ever was. The diet was staple and monotonous, braxy mutton, well hung, being the background, and poached salmon appearing on the menu at least twice a week. 'Burning the water' was our favourite pastime. This is shining torches on the pools where the salmon lay: the Ettrick river was full of them in autumn, being a tributary of the Tweed.

While one held the torch the other wielded a trident, called a Leester, such as you see Britannia holding on an old British coin. Robin was adept at the job: he would need to have been to live! But the water bailiffs were not amused and were always trying to catch us. Sadly, no longer are the upper tributaries of the Tweed full of salmon. This is due to many factors: radar tracing the fish before they get back to spawn, greed on the part of those who have the netting rights, and far too many seals and cormorants which the do-gooders won't allow to be controlled. The old Border poacher who took his 'one for the pot' would turn in his grave to see how few salmon there are today.

The river and most of the land belonged to the Duke of Buccleuch at that time. Walter, the last Duke, roared with laughter when I told him the following story. Robin, Jimmie Thomson, the single herd, and I were road-making in Rangecleuch, the next small valley or 'cleuch' past Broadgairhill, in the autumn and the salmon were 'running' up the burn to spawn. We had a 'cleek' with us, which is a type of fisherman's gaff, and had six lovely salmon on the bank when suddenly we saw the bailiff's motorbike at the bottom of our road, which was then in no condition for a motorbike. Quick as a flash Robin said, 'Ben, take the salmon and the cleek and go out over the hill to the farm and hide the salmon in the hay and we'll be back at tea time.' I could climb in those days and I was soon out of the bailiff's sight. Next day was Saturday: Robin, if we weren't busy, let me off to play rugby and used to lend me his motorbike to go home. He suggested I take a salmon with me for Dad, and I hid it in my rugger togs. Imagine my horror when I approached Ettrick Bridgend, now famous because David Steel lives there, to be stopped by the local policeman who had the two water bailiffs behind him. The conversation went something like this. 'Aye, aye, Ben, playing Hawick today?' 'Many fish up the Rangecleuch Burn?' 'Are you cleeking many?' Flat denial by Coutts whose face is all the time getting redder and redder and the sweat is beginning to ooze gently as he sees the headline in the local paper, *The Border Telegraph*, 'Son of well known minister had up for poaching salmon.' After about five minutes the policeman said, 'On your way and don't do it again.' And I never have poached another salmon. That policeman used a lot of psychology, so sadly lacking in many of the force today.

When I first went to Robin's I was meant to be working at the Vet College, but I promised him that after the OTC camp in Blair Atholl I would go back to him for that summer until I was wanted as ponyman at Lochside. As the spring and early summer wore on, I knew that I hadn't worked hard enough for my exams, and also that I simply hadn't my heart in the work. I've never been any good at Maths, and the first year subjects were in those days Physics and Chemistry (both depending on Maths) and Zoology and Botany, with one practical subject, Animal Husbandry, which I loved. As the day for the results grew nearer I got more and more morose, wondering how I was to face Father. The results were sent to us at Blair Atholl and I had failed ALL four of the written papers, but had come out first in Animal Husbandry. The rest of the camp was a disaster, which was annoying because I had a good cavalry charger and had been enjoying it all. John Ritchie, later to become Sir John Ritchie, head of the Government Veterinary Service, was our officer and he was great fun. But back home I had to go, tail between my legs, and tell Dad I'd failed. He couldn't have been nicer and just said quietly, 'Burnaby, I have three more to educate so you'll have to make your own way in the world.' Thirty years later, when I told him that I had been paid £20 for broadcasting on the BBC's *Matter of Opinion* programme he grunted, 'Ridiculous—and you couldn't even pass your Vet College exams.' Dear, dear Dad: education was the be-all and end-all to him. But I feel shame for the amount of money my education cost my parents.

But Robin's invitation still stood and I was off to learn to work his dog 'Joff' and to shear and all the hundreds of things shepherds have to learn. At the time it didn't seem to matter to me that I was only to get pocket money. Farming was going through tough times in the Thirties, and Robin was very hard up. In fact he told me that if he hadn't been managing three farms for his brother-in-law he wouldn't have been able to continue, and he lived sparsely.

The lamb sales were the highlight of a shepherd's year. In those days the lambs (five months old) were walked through the hills to Lockerbie and we lay out with them at night in a 'stell', a round stone-walled enclosure, and went on to the market in the morning. My memory may be playing me false but I think the lot that I accompanied, which were not the 'tops' but the seconds, made 6s. 6d. What I do remember is that Robin came round the circuitous road in what he called 'The Motor' which was an ancient Austin Seven. How Robin and I and Eck Storrie, the head shepherd on his brother-in-law's farm, plus four dogs, got into it, goodness only knows. I also remember that Robin and I, being both over six feet tall, towered over the windscreen, but after a beer or two it didn't seem to matter and we sang rugby songs the whole way home.

August came and I was back as head ponyman at Lochside, and Mr Mordaunt enquired how I had fared in my exams. I said I was going back to shepherd on the Borders after the grouse shooting was finished, and he said that if that didn't materialise he had a friend, a certain General Turner, who might help me.

Looking back over the years, that spell at Broadgairhill was to have a lasting effect on my future. There is something tremendously solid about the Border farmers and shepherds. Can it be the fact that they are descendants of the famous Border Reivers? Here we are in a new millennium, with farming in a crisis similar to those days of yore, seventy years ago. The huge difference nowadays is that people expect a standard of living we never dreamt of in the thirties. But of one thing I'm certain, and it is that the Border stocksmen who have not been stupid enough to get overdrawn with the bank will still be farming in the future, and producing the first-class stock that has made Scotland famous. As far as I was concerned, their love of their beloved stock and their lovely rolling countryside made an indelible impression on me.

7

Lavington Park

I loved my ponyman's job and wished it could have gone on for ever and ever. During that last year Mr Eustace Mordaunt, who was a very caring boss, introduced me to General John Turner, manager of the Lavington Stud, Petworth, Sussex, for the Hon Mrs MacDonald-Buchanan. General Turner said to me, 'I may have a job for you about Christmas time. It'll be £2 per week seven days a week, no holidays unless you join the Territorials.' He was one of the old school who called a spade a bloody shovel, and expected complete respect from all his staff. At the time of his offer I was hoping to continue to shepherd for Robin, but the lamb and wool sales were so bad in 1936 that, when I went back to him in September of that year, he told me that I should try and look for another job that would give me a living wage. Unfortunately we all have to live, and as Mother used to say, 'How are you going to get a wife silk stockings when you can't even make enough money to keep yourself?' So it was with a sense of reluctance that I wrote to General Turner saying I would accept his job.

I was to leave by the night train from Melrose (sadly Beechinged later on) and I had had my final game with Melrose at Hawick. As a farewell present the boys gave me a blown up 'FL' (nowadays known as a condom, but then called a 'French Letter') decorated with the yellow and black Melrose colours. Father had one of his dreary teetotal cousins staying at the Manse and such was the state of my inebriation that I forgot I still had the balloon-like object in my lapel. She probably wouldn't know what it was but Dad was *not* amused. So ended my old life and I started a new one.

I don't think I've ever felt so lonely as I did when I got off the night train in London. 'The drink was dying in me', like that lovely Snaffles picture of someone facing Beechers Brook in the Grand National. But I was a lonely laddie, a situation not made any easier when I got to Petworth station to be met by someone who thought it all wrong that a minister's son from Scotland should get a job (and they were hard to come by) that could have gone to a local lad. But it wasn't long before I realised why I'd been given the chance—because I'd learnt to work hard. Dear Eustace Mordaunt must have given me a good reference and I did work harder than most of the locals.

At first I worked on the Lavington Stud, but after six months I was moved down to the Westerlands Stud. The bothy at Lavington was very big as, in the days when Lord Woolavington was alive and lived at Lavington House, there had been a vast staff, many of whom were single and lived in the bothy. But by the time I got there the estate was owned by his daughter, Mrs MacDonald-Buchanan, who preferred their estate in Leicestershire, called Cottesbroke. Mrs MacDonald-Buchanan's husband, Sir Reginald, was a dedicated follower of the hunt, so where better to go than Leicestershire. The story goes that Lord Woolavington—as James Buchanan and selling whisky—went to the Argentine and fell in with a certain Mr MacDonald, who had been a cattle dealer in Ross-shire and had prospered well in the Argentine, a country second to none in which to rear cattle. MacDonald had two sons and Buchanan but the one daughter, so Buchanan offered to look after the two sons when they came to Britain for their education. The elder, Hector, was the manager of the stud before General Turner. The second son, Reggie, married Kathleen Buchanan, hence MacDonald-Buchanan. Hector was much loved by the stud hands at Lavington but died before I arrived. Reggie was said to be very short-tempered, but he was kind to me and we had a very happy reminiscent lunch at the Newmarket Thoroughbred Yearling Sales after the war.

Sadly the Estate was coming to the end of its spacious days by the time I joined the staff, but just previous to 1936 virtually the whole village of Graffham was employed on the Estate. There were two stud farms, Lavington and Westerlands (Westerlands is mentioned in Domesday Book), two farms, woods, gardens, excellent pheasant shooting: in fact a complete estate as they used to be, with all the resultant employment which sadly is so lacking in the countryside today. My great pal was Wally Clayton, who eventually retired as stud groom at Lavington having been responsible for such famous horses as Relko and Sing Sing. I was to find out very quickly that looking after thoroughbreds was a very different matter from seeing to a few shaggy Highland ponies. George Shaw, the old stud groom, naturally thought the 'Gineral', as he called the General, had employed someone who knew how to lay down a horse's box properly. As one of the stallion men said to me in a thick Yorkshire accent, 'Ye'r as green as bluidy grass, Ben', and how right he was.

Easton was the stallion standing at Lavington. Lord Woolavington had bred Captain Cuttle and Coronach, both by Hurry On and both to win the Derby. Then he bought Easton to try to win his third Derby, but Colombo beat Easton into second place. As thoroughbreds become yearlings on the first of January in the year succeeding their birth, if they are born on 31

Haymaking at Graffham in 1937, with the author, who knew how to build the load, on top of the lorry

December they become one year old the next day. It was natural that most owners tried to get early foals, and so the mares used to arrive early in the year. A mare's gestation period is eleven months and they are covered 10 days after foaling, so foaling and covering time were very busy ones on the stud. We had to walk the mares back from Petworth station and got the huge sum of 2*s*. 6*d*. for walking the five miles. Woe betide anyone who was found riding a mare! The trains were nearly always in the evening and we had to help the porter shunt off those heavy horse-boxes using a long pole. There was the railway tavern hard by the station, which was handy because we often had long waits. Beer was luckily only 4*d*. a pint so one couldn't drink the whole of the 2*s*. 6*d*. We carried storm lanterns in case an occasional car came along. Some of the younger mares which were just out of training could be quite flighty, but the old brood mares had all done it before.

In 2000 I drove from the defunct station, which, I'm glad to say, although now a private house, has kept its attractive frontage, down the road along which we used to lead the mares, and the traffic was horrendous. All mares are now moved in luxurious lorries by road. But how I would have loved to nick the lovely leather head-collars with which each horse-box was fitted. Those old railway horse-boxes had the most wonderful leather padding in them, but I suppose in the end they were all just destroyed.

I remember on one occasion we had a sick yearling that was very well bred, in fact the same breeding as Owen Tudor that was to win the Derby for the MacDonald-Buchanans. This sick yearling was to be given a helping of gruel four times a day, which contained Jersey cream, fresh farm eggs, brown sugar and brandy, all brought down from the house by the chauffeur. I was sitting up (another 2s. 6d.) with the yearling, along with the old vet, Spurgeon. I can't remember why George Shaw wasn't there but I do remember that when the colt died Spurgeon said, 'Well, Ben, he won't need any more of this', and he and I finished the brandy!

8
Loo Attendant

After a winter and spring the General decided that I should be sent to Westerlands Stud, but not before I had had some idyllic mornings exercising his hunter on the Downs. I am a fervid Scot but I have a very soft spot for the Sussex Downs. At that time they were completely unspoilt and made wonderful exercising gallops. One could see for miles north and south on a clear winter's day. I remember saying to a local farmer in the Graffham pub one night, 'If I farmed on the Downs I'd grow barley with all that chalk you have.' He scoffed at me, but I little realised how prophetic I was, because since the advent of the war thousands of acres of barley have been grown on the chalky downs of England.

The General thought that I would learn more from the stud groom at Westerlands, one Harry Hogarth, than I would from old George Shaw. In this he couldn't have been more wrong, because old George's second man, Steve Long, was a mine of information and had taken a liking to me, whereas Harry Hogarth and his wife took a dislike to me and he did his best to give me the dirtiest jobs possible and the ones that had nothing to do with the horses. On both Lavington and Westerlands the ordinary stud hands, of which I was one, were lent to the farms when the studs weren't busy: so I could be feeding Sussex bullocks, putting up nets for Southdown sheep on a turnip break, haymaking or harvesting—all great experience. The stallion men were much too grand to do anything like that, nor did they have to lead the mares back from the station. When the rest of us were painting in the summer (everything in black and white after 'me Lord's' famous brand of whisky) or creosoting or some other monotonous job, the stallion men always seemed to disappear to 'do the old 'oss'. Mrs Hogarth especially disliked me. She had a fairly attractive daughter, and whether she thought I might make a beeline for her or not I do not know, but I was told fairly firmly that as the latest-joined hand it was my job to empty the big pail that we had for the bothy 'loo'. As the way to the sandy wood in which we dug the hole meant passing her front door, it had to be done each Friday night, after dark. This was all right in December but when it came to June and my girl friend was waiting in the pub which was about to close then it wasn't so funny. I was still the latest joined hand two years later! (I saw the same wood in 2000, and can now see why the Chinese use human excrement

Bill, one of my fellow stud hands, with a mare and foal in the mare and foal yard at Westerlands Stud, 1938

for fertiliser—because the trees, though broad-leafed, were immense compared with their neighbours!)

One stallion at Westerlands was Coronach, by that time 'getting on', as we'd say, since he had won the Derby in 1926. I had the honour, and pleasure, of looking after him when his regular attendant was off sick. He had never been an outstanding breeder, although he bred a good filly in Italy called Corrida, but he was still being used by those who wanted Hurry On blood. The other stallion was Colorado Kid, looked after by an irrepressible Yorkshireman who shared the ancient bothy with me. He it was who called me 'bluidy green', but we became great pals. He was as bawdy as they come and I don't think Father and Mother would have approved of his language or his jokes, but he was solid gold *and* he could cook, which was pretty essential as all I could do was boil an egg. He had been a travelling stallion man in Northumberland, which means walking the stallion round a district and staying at different farms where mares congregated and were covered. I asked him which was his best season and he replied 'The one I travelled "Hustle Bustle",' which he pronounced 'Hoosle Boosle'. He said 'I had fifty mares for the horse and twenty for mysel'. That was Jack, rough as an uncut diamond but a damned good pal to someone who realised he had led a sheltered life.

Life on Westerlands was similar to Lavington, only with two stallions we had more visiting mares. The staff was the stud groom, the second man who came from Dorset and was as useless as Steve Long had been good, two stallion men, three stud hands of which I was the junior and therefore 'muggins', and a wonderful old carter who was responsible for lifting the horse dung from the paddocks each day. He it was who told me 'If you want to grow good grass, bhoy, ye must 'arrow and roll it' and to this day I harrow (to aerate it) and roll it after I put on the fertiliser to consolidate the roots. Bless you, Sid: I hope you have a good pair of horses where you are harrowing and rolling those Elysian fields. You'd be ashamed of the fields you once kept so beautifully: I saw them in 1983 and thought you would turn in your grave!

In the summertime, how I loved to listen to the nightingales, and there were dozens around Westerlands. But I'm told there are hardly any left now, which I'm willing to bet has to do with the rise in the raptor population. In the autumn all the paddocks, being fertilised with horse dung, were a mass of mushrooms: so much so that we had to mount a guard to stop wide-eyed guys from Portsmouth coming in the middle of the night to clean up a field. But they soon turned tail when a keeper fired a shot over their heads. We lived on mushrooms and bacon for weeks.

When there was a starlit night you could see the stars through the tiles of the bothy, and the only fall of snow we had in my three years there came through the tiles onto our beds. Such is the resilience of youth we just threw it off the bed clothes and then wondered when we came to bed the following night why the floor was awash! The tap was outside, and one of the wives of a married stud hand came in once a week to clean up. Bless her for all she did. We could have done better ourselves but she was needing the extra bob or two. I remember the eggs we bought from the Keeper's wife: they had the best yolks I have ever seen because the hens were (naturally) fed on pheasant feed, a legitimate perquisite, and she charged us 10d. per dozen. We always had beef on Sunday. Jack cooked it and I washed up. When we weren't busy—impossible at foaling time—I went to church and sang in the choir, but was mighty annoyed that because I was Church of Scotland I wasn't allowed to take communion although the C of E was willing to use my lungs. However, thank God (literally) it's all changed now.

Life where there is stock can never be humdrum, but the busiest time for us was always January to April when we really worked like slaves and loved it. I remember because of sickness among some of the staff Jack and I sat up with foaling mares two nights each in one week in addition to our normal ten-hour working day, and I had been to the station (five miles from Westerlands) twice for mares. On the Friday Jack decided we should go to a dance in Fittleworth, some twelve miles away, on our push bikes. All I remember about that occasion is that we put our ancient alarm clock inside a tin 'chanty' and the noise would 'awaken the dead', which we were next morning.

I had fondly imagined, in my conceited way, that I was either going to be trained to be a stud manager or at the least a stud groom. How green I was, because the stud managers, pre-war, were either friends of the owners and were supported entirely by their stud grooms, or were ex-Army cavalry or artillery officers (like the General) who knew quite a bit about horses, or were titled, or both. As for stud grooms, pre-war it was the greatest closed shop of all time and only sons of stud grooms (and in one case of which I knew, the son-in-law of a stud groom) got a super job.

Luckily for the thoroughbred breeding industry, this has all changed since the war, and I might, with my background of stud work, just have got a stud manager's job, but Mr Harry Hogarth made it crystal clear to me that there was no future for me in the stud world. In the Sixties, when I was staying with Lady Wyfold, a well known stud owner, in Glen Kinglass, Argyll, an estate which I managed for her, she showed me Harry Hogarth's obituary in *Sporting Life*. I didn't shed many tears.

9
Fun and Games

Work hard we did, and for long hours, but we played hard as well. I had never played much cricket at school but, as the General had played for the Gentlemen against the Players, when there was that distinction between the amateurs and the pros, and as he captained the Graffham side, it was obligatory to play. Woe betide any local umpire who gave the General out LBW, because the old man would argue violently and refuse to leave the wicket. There was the famous occasion when the local blacksmith was umpiring and gave the General out. He was firmly told: 'You'll never pare a mare's feet or shoe my hunter again if you dare to give me out LBW.' Strangely enough, the decision was altered. An occasion I relished was when I carried my bat for 25 and we beat the Fittleworth side. I always enjoyed playing at Eartham, where if someone hit a six the ball went out of sight down the southern slopes of the Downs and we all sat down and admired the view of Chichester harbour. Then there was football in the winter and, although I was no footballer with my size twelve feet more often getting in the way, it was one way of getting an hour or two off work, and those were few and far between.

As I've said already, we used to go miles for dances and at one of them I met a farmer's daugher whose dad had come from Scotland to Sussex. I stupidly told her that I played the bagpipes, and before I knew where I was I had to play them at the Chichester Burns Supper (there were a lot of Scots in Sussex). One thing led to another and I was invited to the farmer's house for supper. At the Burns Supper the farmer had done himself more than well on his native country's beverage, 'the Cratur'. I was therefore more than a little surprised on arriving at the farm to be told by 'himself' that madam was against the 'dram' and all we would get was home-made wine, but that he thought I would enjoy it. I chose the parsnip wine and it's the only time in my life I can't remember getting home. My push-bike was in a heap on the bothy kitchen floor when I got up with a splitting headache next morning. This was my first experience of local Sussex wines, but give me Scotch any time. I think the lady in question would have been wiser if she had allowed her husband to drink his native brew.

Sadly, none of that family are now left. Having been allowed to live a full life into my eighties, I go when I can to the Sussex Yeomanry reunion luncheons. Ken Grigor, son of the aforesaid, who joined the Yeomanry at my, shall we say, gentle urging, now no longer appears at these gatherings.

Robin Fisher, a nephew of John Ferguson of Glenartney and son of the famous 'Uncle Bob', had come south to manage a farm for a Mr Latilla near Horsham, and after I managed to buy a second-hand motorbike for the huge sum of £5 (more than two weeks' wages) I visited him as often as I could afford. He had been a more than useful fullback for Perthshire and with only one eye operating used to say, 'If I get them between my one eye and the touch line, they're couped.' And upside-down they were. He managed to get me the odd game of rugger and I love to tell the tale of a telegram received by me saying, 'Wanted for Trial on Saturday', and I asked Harry Hogarth for the day off. His reply was, 'Fine, but someone else will have your job on Monday', so that was virtually the end of my rugger-playing career, except for games at Hove at the outbreak of war and a marvellous game or two against the NZ Division in Cairo. Today the local papers would have banner headlines, 'Local Stud Worker Wanted for Rugby Trial'. Changed days indeed.

The Lavington estate had a famous pheasant shoot. The MacDonald-Buchanans lived there occasionally when first I went to work there in 1936, but after that they let the big house and the shoot to Captain Ewan Wallace. Captain Wallace would be best known as Minister of Transport at the beginning of the war or perhaps by others as father of Billy Wallace who was tipped by the media to marry Princess Margaret. But, for my money, he will always be remembered as having the best team of guns I have ever seen and ever will see. When Captain Wallace took the shoot he brought his own Ayrshire keeper with him, one Alastair Davidson, ex-Black Watch, a super piper, a teetotaller (unusual in the Black Watch and his profession), a stickler for perfection and someone who really knew how to show sport. Every beater only tapped the trees with hazel sticks—none of the shouts and whistles one hears nowadays at a shoot—and how well he showed his birds. Some of the old beaters wore smocks. The whole set-up was gloriously old-fashioned, with a horse and cart for the game and another on which there was a barrel of beer and bread and cheese for the beaters, but an ancient Austin estate van came out with the Toffs' lunch.

These shoots were some of the best organised operations it has ever been my luck to see. The guns were the best in the country and so they should have been as they spent five to six days a week shooting when pheasants, partridge and grouse were in season. They were Captain Wallace, the then Duke of Marlborough, Lord Sefton, Lord Duff Cooper who used to bring his

The author (centre) with two grooms at the Burton Stud, where Davy Jones, who should have won the National but didn't because of a broken bridle, was bred

gorgeous wife Diana (over whom we ordinary hobbledehoys used to swoon) and the rest of the guns were the local gentry, Lord Cowdray being a frequent visitor. As the General was Estate Manager, although a middling shot, he was often invited. All the rest were shooting with two guns, so he had to do the same: he took me along as his loader, a job I had done many times when ponyman on the grouse moors. One started down below the Downs, pushing the pheasants up on to them, and the final drive was in a chalk quarry with the birds being driven out over beech trees. I thought most of the birds were out of shot but I was wrong. These were the days before mass rearing was practised, but I remember sitting having a keeper's tea (I always made up to the housekeeper, who was invariably very fat and ugly but was in charge of the cake) and Captain Wallace poked his head round the door as he knew it had been a good day and said, 'What's the bag, Davidson?'. 'Nine hundred and ninety-nine', said Alastair. 'Have a heart,' said Captain Wallace, 'Can't you make it a thousand?' 'No, Sir,' said Alastair, 'Cos it's nine hundred and ninety-nine.' Dear honest Alastair, who went to his last job as head keeper with the Duke of Buccleuch and became a great friend of Robin Johnstone.

Owning a motorbike made such a difference to one's life. Ken Gilkes who was second man at the nearby Burton Stud invited me to go to London with him for his parents' silver wedding celebrations. Ken's father was Lord Derby's stud groom up in Yorkshire. I'll never forget that night. We parked our motorbikes outside Charing Cross station, had a wonderful meal at the old Lyons Corner house, where I was to have an historic meal twelve years later, and then saw the incomparable 'Crazy Gang'. From then on I was 'hooked', and until they died I never missed an opportunity of seeing them.

The Burton Stud had bred a good horse called 'Davy Jones' that was to be ridden by Lord Mildmay in the Grand National, and everyone in the Petworth area had their shirts on him: a locally bred horse and the most popular amateur 'jock' of his time—what more did one need? One of our duties at the stud was to mow the acres of grass with an antiquated mower which was pulled by two of us—we might as well have been donkeys—and was guided by a third member of the staff, usually the favoured stallion man. For once Harry relented and let us knock off to listen to the National on an antiquated crystal/whisker radio that Jack and I shared. The excitement was immense as Davy Jones cleared the last lengths in front and I had visions of being able to buy a new motorbike with my winnings. But anyone of my age-group will know the sad story of the broken reins and Davy Jones going back onto the jumping course instead of the straight. *C'est la vie*. It was to be 1981 before I was to get a new vehicle, although I had many second-hand ones in between. We didn't have much money, but by gosh we did have fun.

10

The Sussex Yeomanry

Having shot at Bisley for the school it was only natural that I should gravitate to the small-bore rifle club in Petworth. The leading light was a Captain Shackerley-Ackers, and he was desperately keen that I should use my training in the OTC and become a Territorial officer in the 4th/5th Royal Sussex Regiment, the local 'Terriers'. The thought of facing Mrs Hogarth in regimental 'blues' and the ribbing I'd get from my mates on the stud were enough to deter me, but even more was the fact that with my flat feet I was terrified of being a foot slogger. However, in order to get a respite from the stud and farm work, and get a holiday, I was determined to join the 'Terriers'. The obvious choice was the Sussex Yeomanry, a choice which I never regretted.

The local Troop was at Midhurst, and drills were held in the Cowdray Park Hall. Lord Cowdray was Troop Commander, Jay Gingell his farm manager was Troop Sergeant Major, and Wally Stringer the estate handyman was Troop Sergeant—a very nice, cosy and feudal set up! I was welcomed with open arms in 1937 and joined the Surrey & Sussex Yeomanry, in which I was to serve as Yeoman, Lance Bombardier, Bombardier, Sergeant, Troop Sergeant-Major, Battery Sergeant-Major and officer: something of which I am immensely proud and, as one of the few rankers who was commissioned into the same regiment, I proudly keep my rank. The Surrey & Sussex Yeomanry were amalgamated just before the war, so it was the Surrey Battery in which I served as an officer for all too short a time. The drills at Cowdray Hall were hairy, to say the least, as half of the troop never turned up for parades. Camp was the highlight of the year. Okehampton in Devon was one of the favourites, and I remember only too well the dear Sussex Yeomen who thought they knew about drinking being absolutely flattened by the 'scrumpy', the local cider which left the head clear but the body footless!

We trained on old First World War 18-pounders and 4.5 howitzers, but I was sad that by the time I joined the Yeomanry they had lost their horses. One of the nice things about getting to know the Cowdray Park staff was that I used to go and see them on a Saturday afternoon and watch the polo. As Prince Philip and Prince Charles weren't around then, it wasn't such an 'in' sport. We used to lie on our tummies on the grass and watch the one sport in which I would have liked to excel. One always had to get back to bring in mares or feed yearlings or do some other chore, but one was allowed the afternoon off. We had to get back to get in the yearlings during Goodwood Race Week. Mrs MacDonald-Buchanan always had a house party, and we managed to see a bit of the racing and then had to dash back to have the yearlings looking right for her guests. I loved Goodwood: it has such a lovely setting. I had never seen racing before, and the atmosphere completely captivated me. I have not been back to attend a race meeting there since then, but I've seen pictures of it on TV. Like many racecourses in the country it has been all jazzed up, and Trundle Hill, from which we used to watch the racing in comfort as there weren't many attending race meetings in the hard-up thirties, now resembles a sardine tin, the racegoers are so packed together.

Bookies may be a despised race by some but not by myself. There was a horse running at that time called after the shrub, Cotoneaster. The bookies were shouting the odds 'Two to one "Cotton Easter"!' and their other howler was the horse Hermione which they called 'Hermy-one'. But they were and are big-hearted chaps. I now have a twelfth share in a horse, and the bookie with whom I regularly lose my quid or two seems to know more about the horse's chances than I or my fellow syndicate members do, and the same goes for nearly every horse in every race. I don't know where they get their information.

Goodwood Races were great times for the London racing fraternity to come out in their charabancs to have a party. Charabancs were the old open buses with canvas hoods that had to be pulled over the open seats in inclement weather. There was no heating or air-conditioning then, you got whatever weather was on the menu! We Sussex Yeomen used to prepare for the Londoners by training at dart-playing like mad. Six of us used to lie in wait for the returning charabancs at the Cricketers' Arms under Duncton Hill, tenanted by a bad-tempered old rascal called 'Hoppy'. As the exalted Londoners got into the pub we local yokels used to ask rather timidly, 'Would you like a game of darts?' After that the execution took place, with cries from us as we won time after time, 'Chalk it up Hoppy!' We were strictly teetotal that night or nights, and the cockneys more than slightly inebriated, so it was the slaughter of the innocents. The money that was chalked up on Hoppy's board kept us in beer for weeks. (Hoppy's pub, the Cricketers, has been nicely renovated since then, while keeping its 'pub' character, and now serves excellent food instead of Hoppy's standard bread, cheese and onions.)

Goodwood Races and the Yeomanry have always been intertwined, as we always had an informal meeting of Yeomen there, but I always had to leave to show off the yearlings. Fred Darling was the number one trainer in those days, 'The master of Beckhampton', and he used to come and choose the yearlings that he thought were fit for him to train. The rest were sent to Victor Gilpin who trained locally; he may not have been in Fred's class as a trainer but at least he treated us stud hands as human beings *and* gave us a tip.

Probably the most remembered thing about Cowdray Hall was the great event in 1938 when everyone thought the balloon was going to go up. Chamberlain had come back with his famous (or is it now infamous?) 'Peace in our time' stuff. All sorts of bodies suddenly remembered they had joined the Yeomanry but never attended a parade, and they all flocked to the Hall that night. As Bombardier, I was calling the roll, detailing people to different gun crews, and was left with one not too large a man who had a riding mac tied in the middle with string (or it looked like it). On my asking his name he said 'Hislop'. His name wasn't on my list, so I said, 'When did you join?' and he answered, 'I can't remember. John Cowdray told me when the balloon went up I was to be an officer in the Sussex Yeomanry.' John Hislop was the legendary amateur jockey and—with his wife—breeder of Brigadier Gerard. Quick as a flash I said, 'Sorry, Sir, the officers are in the billiard room'.

Through the Yeomanry I got to know a family called Reid in Heyshott, the next village to Graffham. Colonel Miles, the father, was an ex-cavalry man and a great friend of General Turner. The Reids' two grooms were both laid low in spring 1939 with what I have always called the two doubles, double pneumonia and double hernia. At that time they had two useful hunters that they were preparing tor the Cowdray Point-to-Point, a lightweight called Mr Gaynus to be ridden by David Reid, then in his final year at Repton; and Kingfisher to be ridden by son John at Oxford. The General was asked to supply someone to ride exercise and I was the lucky guy.

What fun that spring was, and how I loved the Downs. There is nothing like good hill work to get a horse fit, and the Downs are ideal because they are made of chalk, which gives good footing, but they are not too steep. The great National Hunt trainer, Ryan Price, whom I was to meet later in connection with those horses, said to me, 'Coutts, remember you are doing more good to the horse's fitness bringing it down a hill than cantering up it', something I've never forgotten. Colonel Reid's butler, who was to become Mr David's batman in the Sussex Yeomanry, one Annetts, was more than good to me, and I shudder to think how much of the Colonel's whisky we consumed: but, as I've said before and will say again, if the wages are not high the perquisites must make up for it!

At the end of my period with the Reids I was told that David would be joining the Yeomanry, which he did, and we became great friends. After a brilliant banking career he has died. David's mother, who had always been kind to me when I worked at Hoyle, not only had the house opened up for my first wife and I to spend our honeymoon there, but this time gave me permission to help myself to anything I fancied in the extremely well-stocked cellar. As the year was 1944 the war was still on, and alcohol was extremely scarce. Frances Reid, like her son David, was taken far too early.

But quite my favourite story of this period in my life is that of Colonel Reid saying to me, 'Ben, I know you've made a good job of getting these horses fit, but I think I'll get the horse coper over to put them over a jump or two.' Ryan Price, God bless him, would not have been amused at being called the local 'horse coper', but between us we produced the two winners, lightweight and heavyweight in the Cowdray Point-to-Point of 1939, and I hadn't a bean on them, as I had left Westerlands to take up another job by then.

11
The Phoney War

By the time the war really did start in September 1939 I had been working, very unhappily, managing a small farm for a veneer-wood merchant. He was really only playing at farming, and I suspect only bought the farm so that his son could be in a reserved occupation when the war broke out. He didn't realise that farms, like all businesses, need capital, and he was cheese-paring in the extreme. The fences were non-existent and the hedges were so overgrown that they were no longer stock-proof, so that I spent half my time fetching stock back from my neighbours. He was so mean I had to borrow friends' implements to do the essential work on the farm. Even more annoyingly, as my wage was a pittance I was supposed to have the farm van for my private use, but his son kept taking it away at the weekends just when I wanted it and I was left stranded. Robin Johnstone very kindly sent old 'Joff' down to keep me company, but the old dog didn't like it and cleared out on me. Although the Sussex Police advertised his loss for weeks he was never found; I felt very bad about it and wondered how far he got on his long journey back to his beloved Ettrick.

The owner, his son and I were harvesting, with me building the load, when the postman arrived with the telegram saying I was to report forth-with to Chichester. I've never enjoyed receiving a telegram more, and I had the greatest pleasure in telling my boss exactly what he could do with his farm. I'll never forget his face as he kept saying, 'What am I going to do without you to keep us right?' To which I had great pleasure in replying, 'I couldn't care less.'

The Regiment, like many others, had to double in size, and so the 98th (Surrey & Sussex Yeomanry) Regiment had to find a cadre to form the 144th (Surrey & Sussex Yeomanry) Regiment. I was bitterly disappointed at being part of that cadre, as the 98th went off as part of the British Expeditionary Force, but, as they were all put in the 'bag', I think we were lucky. We started off in Horsham and then went to Hove County Cricket Ground, where we played at being soldiers with old civilian trucks and one or two ancient 18-pounders.

I distinctly remember being on duty as Sergeant of the guard when a distinguished looking gentleman, who said he was looking for his son, was detained by my guard. It was Harold Macmillan looking for his son Maurice who was a junior officer with us!

We were billeted with civilians who were very kind to us, but it was a boring winter with lengthy route marches, endless lectures and a lot of PT. The Regiment was made up to strength by an infusion of cockneys who were the very opposite to us slow moving countrymen, but it made a first-class unit with the quick-witted and quick-thinking cockneys and the solid, steady yeomen.

We used to play the game 'Do you know the muffin man?' almost every evening in different pubs. One sings it with a full pint of beer on one's head, and points at someone while singing: he in turn puts his pint on his head and points at someone else. The first one to drop his pint has to stand a round of drinks. So we five or six who had practised the game for weeks using water would, when we all had our pint securely on our heads, then turn on one poor unsuspecting 'civvy' who invariably dropped his amid shouts of 'pints all round!'.

Spring 1940 saw us getting a full complement of the split-new 25-pounder gun that was to be such a success, and with all the new vehicles that came with them we got down to proper training. Our Colonel and both Battery Commanders were all territorials, but the Majors were superseded by two regulars that spring, and what a difference they made to the unit. Major 'Bob' Mansergh, who commanded the Surrey Battery, was to finish the war with his knighthood and as Lieutenant General, and with the highest accolade that can be given to a gunner, i.e. the title of 'Master Gunner'. He did me the great honour subsequently of asking me to speak at one of those wonderful dinners at Woolwich, at which those in charge of the Officers' Mess pull the green baize table-cloths from underneath the wonderful collection of silver on the table—and there's lots of it—and the silver remains upright. I'd love to know the secret of how they did it, and I say 'did it' advisedly, as I'll bet they don't do it now.

After being fully equipped with our new guns we were made part of that sparse force that was supposed to guard the south coast against invasion. On reading the military history of this period, I think our regiment had about two counties to cover! But it was certainly the time when 'Winnie' made his great speech about 'fighting on the beaches' etc., and at the end of it, when the mike was turned off, he added, sotto voce, 'and cut stout sticks with which to beat them about the head, for it's all we've bloody well got'!

One of our stations was at Hambledon in Hampshire, and as one of our Majors had an estate there he got me to organise a harvest squad for him. Judging by the rundown appearance of the estate and the age of the tackle, he would never have had his harvest moved quicker. His old retainer said he'd never seen better stacks.

The two regular Majors came to us in the village of Dursley in Gloucestershire where we were scattered around the town, mostly in the large buildings owned by R A Lister, the well-known agricultural machinery manufacturers. The Dursley people were very kind to us, and we made a lot of friends. The local vet, Cecil Adams, who was also a first-class organist and a bon viveur, became a special buddy of mine. We organised a choir from the regiment that did a lot of its practising in the Hunter's Hall pub.

When we were in Dursley we had to play host to some of the survivors from Dunkirk. The first lot we got was a rabble from all different units who had left everything behind, but a whole week later we were hosts to a regular cavalry unit who had fought a rearguard action. They were white with fatigue, but every one of them carried their small arms. I remember our regular Majors lecturing us about the difference in the two lots of men and saying, as we were to find out, how essential discipline is to a fighting unit. Our days at Dursley were blissfully happy, as the people were kind to us and the regiment was being honed into a good, well-disciplined unit. I was approached to see if I wouldn't go to an OTCU to become an officer, but I decided I wanted to see action with the regiment of which I had become very fond. Rumours kept flying about as to where we were going, but with the fall of France we knew it couldn't be there for some years at least. We had been very lucky not to have been sent to France just before Dunkirk, as there had been talk of it.

At last, a year after the outbreak of war, we got our marching orders to go to Liverpool to embark. The ship on which we were meant to sail was bombed in the harbour, so we were sent to the racecourse at Aintree to wait for another one. My goodness, we were lucky, because the convoy we were meant to be a part of originally was decimated, and we would certainly have lost our precious guns if not ourselves. Sadly, much though I'd love to see the Grand National, now that I have the time and could scrape up the cash to see it, I can't face the crowds. There weren't any crowds at Aintree in 1940, but we were glad to be able to use the racecourse loos!

Eventually the ship, the *Highland Brigade*, that was to take us was ready, though we had to wait for her to offload her cargo of Argentine beef. She was still distinctly chilly when we embarked. The skipper was delighted that we weren't to be part of a convoy, as she was a fairly fast craft. I had never been to sea before and suddenly found that I was a natural. At one time in the Bay of Biscay there were only three on their feet in the Sergeants' Mess. Poor Major Munn, our Battery Commander, was a shockingly bad sailor. One day after we had got through the worst of the storm we were ordered to bring everyone on deck whether they could stand up or not. There were some pathetic sights: the poor Major was just about to salute the Battery Sergeant-Major when he had to put his hand to his mouth and make a rush to the handrail where he was gloriously and ignominiously sick in front of his whole unit. But it was the same Major George Munn who made us all keep a small haversack packed in case we were torpedoed. In the haversack were a waterbottle, iron rations, a field dressing and a whistle if we possessed one. I little thought on the way out that my packed haversack would be partly responsible for saving my life. As we got further south I was to realise for the first of many, many occasions, that my fair skin was not made for sunny climes as I burn hopelessly. One of the sergeants in the Surrey Battery, who had been a good amateur boxer, started a boxing class and I realised what a demanding sport it is. Once more my skin let me down as I became a mass of bruises.

At this time we didn't know whether we were going to the Middle East or the Far East, but when we got to Cape Town the rumour got round that we were bound for Port Suez and the Middle East.

I'll never forget that first sight of Cape Town. After the blackout in Britain it was magic to see the myriads of lights, and of course it was equally beautiful by day with Table Mountain standing majestically over it.

We had joined the convoy by this time and we were all ordered to stand off in the Bay as, sadly, an Australian Division had just been ashore and had beaten up the town. When eventually we got the OK to land, our regiment had the honour to be first ashore. I've never known a welcome like it, there were dozens and dozens of cars. Another Sergeant-Major and I were detailed to see that everyone was properly turned out, so we were last to leave ship. We thought all the cars would have gone, but not a bit of it. We went down the line saying how sorry we were etc until we found two smashing South African blondes. I could have done with more than two days in Cape Town! I little realised then that I would return one day to South Africa. As a farmer who loves the land and the people who tend it, no matter what race or colour, I think it is a wonderful part of the world, but like so many countries it has been devastated by greed, whether for power or money.

12
Sudan and Abyssinia

When we arrived in Egypt we went to the Artillery Base of Almaza outside Cairo. I had a drink with an old Regular Sergeant-Major who had spent most of his service in India, and I was enjoying watching the sun go down, when a bugler boy went past from another regiment. The RSM said, 'Isn't he nice?' Jack Kirkby had said I was green as grass, but here I was, a Sergeant-Major, and I'd never heard of homosexuality and was embarrassing the RSM by asking what was nice about the boy! However, very soon we were to see any amount of men going hand in hand as we were about to be posted to the Fifth Indian Division. As we were 'army' troops we could be shunted around wherever they were short of a regiment of artillery, and the Fifth Indian Division had to leave one of its artillery regiments in India because of an outbreak of some disease or other. Very soon we were off to the Sudan down that fantastic river, the Nile, and then in ancient steam trains. Every time the engine stopped for any time we flocked round it to get hot water for our 'char'. I had a fantastic wee batman who had been a lighterman on the Thames, and he could produce tea out of thin air. He used to get eggs from the 'Gyppies' and have them boiling in no time, with full co-operation from the engine driver.

In Khartoum the regiment divided, the Surrey Battery going to the Kassala front and the Sussex Battery to Gedaref. On our first night in Gedaref the Assistant District Commissioner invited the Battery Commander and the three Troop Commanders for drinks and dinner. The next morning I was sent for by the Battery Commander who said, 'You're in luck. The ADC went to school with you, one Bunty McDowall, and you're invited there for dinner tonight; but don't make too much of a habit of going, because I can do with a few hot baths and free whiskies.'

The Sudanese Administrative service was looked on as the 'tops' in the Thirties and used to take some of the best young men in our country. Brother Wally tried for it but didn't pass the medical; but Bunty McDowall had had a brilliant school career at Glasgow Academy, and was good scholastically and at all games. He gave me some wonderful evenings, always remembering to ask the Major once a week to keep him sweet.

That Eritrean campaign was quite extraordinary as we were fighting the Italians on two fronts, ours with a brigade of infantry and a battery of

25-pounders, and the main force at Kassala. It was high hill country but very wooded where we were, and the only time one saw the enemy was when one was in an observation post. The river Atbara ran close by and was used by us all for washing, but it was here I saw the Indians going down hand in hand to wash. In the Indian divisions each brigade had two Indian Battalions, one British, and the fourth and fifth Indian Divisions were to distinguish themselves before that campaign was over.

Our actual position was called Gallabat, and we were engaged in shelling a fort held by the Italians. One day the troop commander, who was occupying the Observation Post and directing the gunfire, sent word via his signaller that he wanted to see me. It transpired that he thought, rightly, that the signaller was 'duff' (no use) at the job, and he wanted me to show him how to send orders. It turned out that as it was his first time in action and the O.P. was under constant rifle fire the poor lad was terrified. It happened that our Battery Commander came into the O.P., and hearing me transmitting the orders down the phone said, 'Sergeant-Major, after the war you should take up broadcasting.' He little realised how prophetic his remark was to be, as I have now been broadcasting on agricultural and other matters for over fifty years.

After a short spell at Gedaref we were reunited with the Surrey Battery for the attack on the heights of Keren. It was here that the Camerons covered themselves with glory and had a ridge called after them. People were rather inclined to think of the 'Eyeties', as they called the Italians, as being sun-loving hopeless fighters, but as in many countries, my own especially, the hill men have always been 'bonnie fechters' and the Bersaglier and Alpini fought well. The Camerons took an awful pasting. I'll never forget the night that they were withdrawn and they came back through our waggon lines with a piper playing. Four or five lorryloads were all that came back, and stronger men than I were in tears. I'm a hopeless 'greetin' Geordie' at the best of times, so I was really blubbing. There is something haunting about pipe music, especially as the piper was playing the lament 'The Flowers of the Forest' and not their regimental march, 'The March of the Cameron Men'.

Keren was eventually taken and we moved on up to the capital of Eritrea, Asmara. It was here that we had a terrible outbreak of jaundice. The hospital was very makeshift and the food was the same as the ordinary rations: sausages swimming in fat and bacon ditto—quite the worst thing for jaundice. The one super thing we used to get was Israeli marmalade that really tasted of oranges. It was just after my spell of jaundice that we were reviewed by

*The author in 1940, at that time the youngest Sergeant Major in the 5th Indian Division
(if not the entire Middle East)*

the Army Commander General Platt who was called the 'Kaid', the name
given to the Commander of the Sudanese forces. Some of us had kept our
yellow and blue Yeomanry side hats, and it was decided that it was to be a
Sergeant-Majors' parade and that that rank was to wear them. After the
inspection the Kaid said some very complimentary things about the regiment and then looking directly at me he said, 'But it's the first time I've ever
seen a Sergeant-Major with the same colour of eyes as his side cap.' David
Reid, for whose father I had worked at Heyshott, was the Kaid's ADC and
had introduced me to him. David had joined the Sussex Yeomanry on the
outbreak of war.

Asmara was a rather lovely town, thanks to the Italian planners, with
broad streets and tree verges. My daughter Philippa, in her work for Save
the Children Fund, spent two years in the Sudan, two in Eritreia and two in
Ethiopia. She loved Asmara, and was in the process of organising a trip of
nostalgia for me, centred on Asmara, when the stupid war between the
Eritreians and Ethiopians broke out. According to her it was caused by a
dispute over an area of useless land, and she knew the region well as she had
done a report on it when in Ethiopia. As in so many wars, no one gained
anything, but the death-toll was enormous and Asmara, devastated once

51

again in the space of half a century, has to get back to the task of restoring the attractive city it was before the Second World War. Sadly I'm too old now to have that nostalgic visit, not only to Asmara, but to Keren and Massawa where we fought, to see again the war graves where some of my chums lie.

We went down into Abyssinia after the Eritrean campaign, and it is rather fun to think of being in the only campaign that ended in success because at that time the news for the Allies was nothing but doom and gloom. Apart from gaining a high regard for the Indian Regiments we admired the Rhodesian pilots who did our air observation work for us in ancient Lysanders, which seemed to us 'brown jobs' to be held together with wire. These lads always maintained that the reason they survived was that they were so slow the Italian fighters were past them before they could fire at them. In that campaign we had little or no air support, and how the British resources must have been stretched.

Another unit which fought alongside us and for whom we had the highest regard was the Sudan Defence Force or SDF. Their British officers were all Majors or Bimbashi and were handpicked. The Sudanese, all over six feet tall and black as ebony, made magnificent soldiers.

Both Eritrea and Abyssinia had one really good main road through them, as the Italians have always been great road builders since Roman times. I remember once going down the main road to rejoin the regiment at Amba Alagi, a wonderful fortress which was the last to fall and which ended the campaign. I had a puncture: this had been our second since leaving and so we set off for some nearby lights. Being in enemy country we went with drawn revolvers and felt absolute fools when we were greeted in word-perfect English by someone who turned out to be the local administrator. The war had passed him by and he didn't know what to do, but he was kindness itself and gave us food and wine, and got his servant to mend both punctures. We had a wonderful crack as he was a passionate polo player. But what interested me most was that he had had a course in road-building and engineering before being sent to Eritrea/Abyssinia, which I don't think would have happened to Bunty McDowall and his fellow DCs judging by the Sudan dirt tracks.

When the Duke of Aosta finally capitulated and the campaign came to an end, it was decided that I should go to Cairo for a course before rejoining the regiment as an officer.

13
Tobruk and Alexandria

By the time I caught up with the regiment they had been pulled out of the Fifth Indian Division and sent up to the garrison of Tobruk in the desert. Tobruk was at that time a legendary name as the garrison had held out against constant attacks by various German and Italian forces, and the war in the Western Desert ebbed and flowed past this besieged town. It was over-run at last when a South African Division was defending it, much to the annoyance of the 9th Australian Division which had held out for so long, and the other regiments like ours, which were proud of our part in repelling the constant attacks on the garrison. All felt that the South Africans gave in too easily.

All Tobruk's supplies had to be brought in by night, and I was taken in with other reinforcements in a K-type destroyer of the same type as the famous Kelly that Earl Mountbatten commanded. On board was a Dr Browning whom I had known in Glasgow Academy days, and I little realised how soon I was to see him again.

Unloading had to be done quickly because there were always troops being embarked and the harbour was forever being bombed. I don't know how many ships were sunk going to and from Tobruk, but it was an un-popular run. There was the famous 'Potato Jones' who ran the gauntlet so often he became a legend in the Middle East.

It was great to be back with the regiment again and I was posted to the Surrey Battery. Shortly after rejoining, a bit of stray sharpnel blew my nose completely off and for all intents and purposes my fighting days were over.

The next thing I knew, and it was two days later, was Dr Browning lean-ing over me and asking how I was. He kept telling me how lucky I was that my eyes hadn't received any permanent damage, but, as I couldn't see any-thing for days, I just had to believe him. I don't remember how long I was in that casualty clearing station as I was very heavily doped, but eventually I was put aboard a hospital ship with many others bound for the 8th General Hospital in Alexandria. On the way there the hospital ship, which I'm told had large crosses painted on each side, was strafed by enemy aircraft.

I was extremely lucky, because in Alexandria a team of four, comprising a plastic surgeon, a dental surgeon, an anaesthetist and a sister, had just been formed into a Maxillo-Facial Unit, and I was their first patient. Plastic surgery is common today, but without the experience gained in both world wars it would never have progressed as it has done. There was a super Yorkshire orderly and a year later when I was being discharged to be sent home as my blood had run thin or something, he said, 'Ee, I remember when they put you on the operating table the surgeon said, "We'll make you like Clark Gable", and you were no sooner under the anaesthetic than he said, "Now, where the bluidy 'ell do we start?"'

The slow process of building on a new nose started. In Alexandria I had ten operations. As there was time in between these, one could get out and see Alexandria and I became very friendly with a New Zealander who had a fractured jaw. Jim Wynyard was one of the nicest people it's ever been my pleasure to know, but unfortunately he went back into action and was killed. He and I were lucky enough to be befriended by an American judge and his wife. The Egyptians had a mixed Court of Appeal with two Americans, two British, two Dutch etc., and Judge Brinton, the American, was the senior judge. He and his wife, who was pro-British, were kindness itself and were always having Jim and me out to parties or to swim. They certainly made hospital life, which could have been dull, much more attractive. During our stay in hospital the Germans came very close to Alexandria and there was talk of the nurses being evacuated. The Egyptians mobbed the banks to get out their money and I've never seen sights like it. Our favourite restaurant was Pastroudis: the owner was very pro-British and said that as the Germans were obviously going to overrun the city we could eat and drink free. But after two days of our over-indulgence he said, 'Sorry, enough is enough: you drink too much.' Poor Jim had his jaws wired up so he was on a liquid diet. Mainly John Collins gins! On one occasion we were coming back together and on the wee steep hill approaching the hospital we found an Egyptian sitting on top of a huge loaded cart and belabouring a donkey. We decided to help the donkey and let it out of the shafts and put the man in them instead, but we had to run for it as a lot of his pals were watching. This was during the period that the Germans were close to Alex and there was a strong anti-British feeling.

When I was in hospital Randolph Churchill was admitted and we had a super sister on our ward called Kitty McShane. He was not an easy patient. Something Kitty did annoyed him and he said, 'I'll tell the Prime Minister on you.' Quick as a flash she replied, 'Nahas Pasha [the then Egyptian PM] will not be amused.'

I had my twenty-sixth birthday in Alexandria in 1942 and as the Brintons' daughter-in-law was also twenty-six on the same day they threw a super

On the beach at Alexandria with Bob Maxwell, the day before my tenth operation

party for us. One of the friends they invited was Lady Grizel Wolfe-Murray, wife of a Black Watch officer, whom I was to meet later in not such happy circumstances.

Thanks to the Brintons what might have been a very boring year was not so. They were fabulously wealthy and had their own indoor swimming pool. It was the only time in my life I shall ever have a large, smiling, Sudanese servant awaiting my exit from the pool with a huge bath towel, the like of which I've never seen since. They had many interesting friends among the civilian population of all nationalities. One of these was a Mr Finney who owned the national newspaper. The Judge was tremendously interested in everything: I never knew anyone who carried more general knowledge in his head than he did. He was also very physically fit and was a strict teetotaller although his household was most generous in its hospitality. One of his great interests was archaeology, and where better to live than Egypt if that is your hobby? He had a cottage in the desert at Sidi Bish, where before the war he used to go digging. Mrs B., on the other hand, was not a bit interested in that sort of thing. She was very social, an excellent hostess and very pro-British—so much so that after the Judge died she came over to London to see out the rest of her days in a London hotel. I was glad at this time to repay, in a small way, some of the kindness they had showed me in their home.

However the medicos decided that I wasn't fit enough to stand any more operations and that I should be sent back home to complete my nose. The dental surgeon of the team said to me, 'Try and get to Archie McIndoe at East Grinstead. He's the coming man in plastic surgery and he trained under the famous Sir Harold Gillies.' With only half a nose I was given a note for the doctor on the ship: among other instructions were 'regular douching with saline solution'. I little realised how regular that was to be.

The Mediterranean was, of course, closed to civilian shipping, and so after sad farewells to the Brintons I set off for Port Suez, to join the P & O ship the *Stratheden*. The passengers were a real mixture of time-expired regular soldiers and RAF personnel, women and children who had been evacuated from Malta, which was coming in for its heaviest bombardment at that time, and walking wounded like myself. Lady Grizel Wolfe-Murray was also on board as she was going home to have a baby. With her in the same cabin was one 'Freckles' Hawkins, a nurse who had served a long stint in the Middle East and whom I was to get to know well in later years. She was bringing home a baby girl for a Colonel and Mrs Redman, as Mrs Redman wished to stay on with her husband.

14
Atlantic Torpedo

The *Stratheden* was an extremely well-run ship and we had a happy voyage down to Durban. Just before we docked there was an announcement that the Captain had received sealed orders and all passengers had to disembark. One of the doctors on board thought I should go into a local hospital as my nose was giving a bit of trouble. While there I was introduced to a plastic surgeon who was very keen that I stay and recuperate in South Africa. I love that country dearly and I was sorely tempted, but the message from Eric Dalling that he reckoned that Archie McIndoe was the tops made me want to get home. Little did I realise at the time that, as a 'brown job' from the Army, I had about as much chance of getting to Archie, who was the RAF's consultant plastic surgeon, as a snowball has in hell.

Eventually all *Stratheden* passengers going to Britain—many were staying in South Africa—were embarked on an old Cunard liner called the *Laconia*. The *Laconia* had started the war as an armed merchant cruiser and still had her gun mounted on the stern. This had been her first trip since she had been given back from the Navy to her company. Most of the crew had been drawn from the Merchant Navy Pool in Liverpool, and with a few exceptions were not a patch on the *Stratheden* crew. Many of the officers were older and some had come out of retirement because of the war. Altogether from first going on board many of us had an eerie feeling about the ship. This was not helped by the fact that there were some hundreds of Italian prisoners-of-war below decks. We had a very energetic Major Creedon on board who was not at all enamoured with the Captain and the OC Troops, and he decided that we should form a voluntary guard in case of accidents. He felt the guarding of prisoners was not what it might have been; with women and children on board he feared the consequences, and how right he was.

Thanks to my conceit, in Alexandria I had had made for me a pair of 'winkle-picker' shoes to try to disguise my large size-twelve feet. All they succeeded in doing was to give me an ingrowing toenail which became very painful, and, on the advice of an army doctor who was coming home, I was to have it taken off during the long voyage home. My bosom pal was one Jock Miller, one of the civilian specialists attached to the RAF who had done his stint in the desert and was getting another posting. Somewhere off the west coast of Africa the doc thought it a good time to take off my toenail. I will forever thank George Munn for his haversack advice and I took it with me to the ship's sick-bay and also my old cavalry greatcoat, inside the lining of which I had stitched an English five pound note.

We were 200 miles off Ascension Island—thanks to the Falklands campaign, a namely place now but unknown to most people then—when womph! and again womph! we got two tin-fish in us. The U-boat commander said later that we were a sitting duck, because each evening we used to send a huge trail of smoke behind us. The ancient boilers were coal-fired.

Although one had always imagined the worst, the panic was unbelievable. When a ship is torpedoed all the bulkheads have to be opened and I found myself passing a bar, so I helped myself to two bottles of Johnnie Walker. This was manna from heaven, as for some reason whisky was scarce: we suspected that some senior officers used up the ration. It seems that some nights before we were torpedoed one of the Polish guards had accidentally let off a round of ammunition, with the result that every guard was afterwards only allowed one round per man, quite useless for stopping advancing hordes of POWs.

I eventually found Jock, but it was too late to go to our guard points. Already the prisoners were everywhere. As the ship was at 45° to port, the starboard lifeboats couldn't be lowered and everyone was trying to charge the port side: it was an awful and unforgettable scene. Some officers had a bit of control but all too few. There was a small contingent of Naval personnel coming home, I think because they were time-expired, under a young officer who was brilliant, a real leader. He did more in organising people trying to get into the lifeboats than any other. Sadly I heard later that he had perished after his arm had got smashed.

I'm afraid the young Merchant Navy men were not a good advert for the Red Duster, as they rushed to get into the boats. Not so the old salts, who remained true to the old Merchant Navy tradition and where possible made 'women and children first' their rule. However the P.O.W.s were the problem once they got free. That mixture of P.O.W.s, women and children and all the other personnel should never have been allowed on the same ship.

Jock and I did see Grizel, 'Freckles' with wee baby Sally Redman safely into a boat, but sadly Sally didn't survive the night and, although Freckles was one of very few who made land in a lifeboat, Grizel didn't survive. Their epic journey is brilliantly written up in *Atlantic Torpedo* by 'Freckles' herself. Jock and I had decided we would be safer on a raft as we had already seen two lifeboats turned turtle by too many people being in them and more hanging on to the side.

Looking down from the deck of an ocean-going liner to the sea is a most frightening sight, especially if the sea is full of screaming people, upturned boats, rafts and bric-a-brac. We went aft where things seemed to be quieter; Jock got a raft and between us we heaved it over the side, having first had the sense (Jock's not mine) to tie the rope to the rail. We then got some rope ladders and chucked them over. I don't think I've ever been so terrified in my life as, dressed in pyjamas with my old greatcoat on and my faithful haversack on my back, I followed Jock down that rope ladder. It seemed miles, but it was a case of either that or, like the captain and many, many others, we would go down with the ship. Jock let out a hearty swear as his bottle of whisky got broken on the way down.

When we reached the raft the *Laconia* was beginning to go under and we had a hectic time hacking at the rope that attached it to the ship's handrail. All we had was a useless wee knife that Jock had nicked from the dining room, designed, I would think, to peel fruit. At this point I thought Jock, the raft and I would go down with the ship, but at last, after endless sawing, the rope parted, and just in time too. It was then that I silently thanked my father and mother for making the whole family learn to swim; none of us were speed merchants but we all swam strongly. One has heard so much about the suction caused by a sinking ship that we both started swimming like mad and taking the raft with us. We hadn't got away a minute too soon, as the old girl started to go down by the bows. It's a terrifying sight seeing that huge hulk high above, and there is almost something obscene about a pair of propellers high in the air, for all the world like an old lady showing off her breasts in public.

Just after the ship went down there was an awful underwater explosion. For some reason unknown to us it caught Jock worse than it did me, although I felt it all right, but he was desperately sick. I had a quiet smile at the doctors' instructions 'frequent saline solution', as I now had the whole of the Atlantic in which to bathe my nose.

During that first night we collected various people on our raft, mostly Italian P.O.W.s who, poor devils, being ill-nourished and ill-clad, just drifted away. War is a terrible thing. I had nothing against those P.O.W.s, but it was a case of 'the de'il tak the hindmost', and everyone was looking out for Number One. There was one pathetic soul Jock and I did look after, a corpulent stoker who hailed from Liverpool. He had retired from Cunard before the war, but had volunteered to rejoin when the war started. He was unfit, ill-clad and far too old to be experiencing the situation in which he found himself. He had been hanging on to a spar and we pulled him onto the raft. In consultation with Jock I gave him a good slug of our precious whisky. He silently slipped overboard during the night. To my dying day I'll regret that neither Jock nor I could remember his name or find out an address to which we could have written, to say what guts he showed to the end. There aren't many today who would be willing, as old men, to volunteer to defend their country.

Talking of writing to relations who lost their loved ones in the sinking of the *Laconia*, on board was a Church of Scotland minister, a Mr Copeland, who lost an eye and had other wounds as a result of the torpedo striking the ship. When I eventually got home I wrote to his widow saying what a wonderful job he had done, as although he had those ghastly wounds he kept comforting others and helping them to get into the lifeboats, but refused to get into a lifeboat himself. In my letter I likened him to my hero, 'Titus' Oates, who I reckoned gave his life for others on the famous Scott expedition to the South Pole. Imagine my amazement and embarrassment when I got a stinker of a reply, accusing me of saying her husband had committed suicide! I have never thought Oates or Copeland did that. But it shook me, and I wrote no more letters of condolence.

It was very strange in that first night how we never came up against any of the other rafts or lifeboats, although near morning we did come up against a submerged lifeboat which, because of its buoyancy tanks, was still afloat and gave us more room than the raft.

Although we were close to the Equator and it was hot during the day we were desperately cold at night and I was mighty glad of my old greatcoat. As we weren't sure what the future had in store for us we decided to ration the water and the whisky very severely. On that first night the U-boat passed us at a very short distance, an eerie sight if ever there was one. It transpired later that the U-boat commander, when he found he had sunk a liner with women and children on board, and not an armoured merchant cruiser as he thought, took a lot of the lifeboats in tow and gathered them together after radioing Dakar to the Vichy French Navy to send out a ship to pick us up. A raft is very close to the water so we never saw anything else for days until suddenly we spotted another lifeboat.

15
Le Gloire and Casablanca

When our raft came alongside the lifeboat we found it was hopelessly over-crowded, but we entreated them to take us on board. I was never any good in the sun and walking around our submerged boat, the sun shining through the sea water, had given my legs a form of elephantiasis: they were huge and extremely painful. One good thing the sea water did for me was remove some nasty warts that I had had on my hands for years and they never returned. Some people in the lifeboat seemed to give up the ghost easily and would just let themselves gently over the side and disappear in the night. It turned out that the lifeboats hadn't been properly inspected: water was short and blankets were missing. Altogether, it was not a pleasant sinking. But help was at hand in the shape of a Vichy French cruiser *Le Gloire*. Those of you of my age group will remember that some of the French forces chucked in their hands with the Germans and were known as the Vichy French. Quite a number of their Navy stationed in Northern Africa had done so because they were smarting from a roasting they got from the Royal Navy at Dakar early in the war.

I felt that same feeling of awe when our lifeboat came alongside the cruiser as on the raft beside the *Laconia*. Even though the cruiser was almost stationary it was going too fast for us and one of our number got badly squashed. Altogether fourteen lifeboats were picked up. The French gave us brandy and tea but the matelots were not co-operative with us. The decks of French men-of-war are steel whereas ours are of wood, and with my huge and sore legs I couldn't walk to the loo but our far-from-helpful guard helped me there on my hands and knees with his bayonet! I didn't bother going again but got some sort of receptacle instead!

I understand we set sail for Dakar but were re-routed to Casablanca. I rather suspect this was because the French knew that something was afoot. We were a sorry-looking bunch and all too many well-known faces were missing. I was especially sorry for the women survivors, as their clothes were torn and their skins were horribly burned with the sun and salt water.

When we landed in Casablanca we were put into a makeshift prisoner-of-war camp. My nose started smelling rather nastily so I was sent to the local hospital where they kept me for the rest of my stay. The French doctor hadn't much English and my French is bad to say the least, but the French

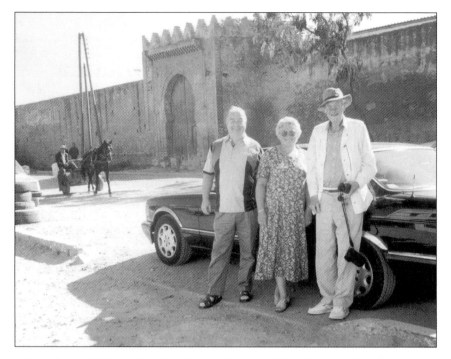

The author in 1999 revisiting the Medouna Prisoner-of-War Camp in Casablanca, where he was imprisoned in 1941 by the Vichy French

nurse had no English at all. I remember the shocked look on her face when I was going to pop the proffered thermometer into my mouth and I suddenly saw vaseline on it. Luckily I remembered how we took the horses' temperatures at the stud!

A young Canadian Air Force pilot was my room mate. He had been shot down while taking photos of the North African coast and had lost a leg. He was given a wooden 'peg-leg' such as Long John Silver wore. Alan had been told he was to be repatriated through the Red Cross in the South of France which at that time had not been occupied by the Germans. It transpired that the same thing was to happen to me and we looked forward eagerly to the day when we were to embark. The great day came, only to turn out to be a great disappointment, as the ship on which we were meant to travel was chock-a-block with passengers from Dakar and wouldn't embark anyone at Casablanca. The Allies had obviously fooled the Germans and Vichy French into thinking the North African landing was going into Dakar. *Le Gloire* wasn't allowed to take us there. And then they evacuated a lot of women and children from there.

So it was back to hospital for a few more days. By this time I'd been fitted out with the weirdest suit you've ever seen; I swear it was made out of sackcloth. Getting footwear to fit me was an even bigger problem, and I finished up with a pair of issue boots for their native Senegalese soldiers and they were like 'herring boxes without topsies'. Alan wasn't too badly dressed as he had got some Red Cross parcels. It was a funny set-up in Casablanca, because the Germans weren't officially meant to be there, but as portrayed in the super film of that name there was intrigue everywhere.

There is no doubt the Germans were stripping the country: the Messagerie Maritime boat on which we eventually travelled was full of fruit, vegetables and figs, which our informer told us were all bound for the German forces. Our informer was the Captain's cabin boy and was half French/half Australian. He was to be a friend indeed. As soon as we were on board we were sent for by the Captain who told us in no uncertain terms that he had no time for the British (and obviously Canadians too) and that he was sending us below and we would remain under lock and key until we got to Marseilles. But he didn't realise that the informer kept feeding us on grapes and other fruit, and the odd bottle of wine was pushed in the door with the instructions to throw the empty out of the porthole at night in case he was found out.

As we passed Gibraltar we saw a naval ship and longed for her to come over and release us. The next night there was the most awful bang and I was sure we had been torpedoed. Oh Lord, I thought, caught like rats in a trap and no sign of the informer. What seemed like an eternity went by when, with the boat at 45°, wonder of all wonders, we heard an English voice calling out, 'Where are you?' We weren't long in answering! Our good friend the informer had handed over the key to a young British Naval Officer. No, it wasn't the destroyer from Gibraltar that had rammed us but part of the Naval unit attending to the North African landings. It transpired that our Vichy captain wouldn't heave to when ordered, so to put him out of action the young British skipper just rammed him.

We were taken on board the *Princess Beatrix*, which was a Dutch seagoing car ferry that had been converted into a ship for carrying the landing craft that were being used to land the American troops. Alan and I had a front-row view and I was allowed to go ashore with a young Scottish naval officer who had gone to school with my youngest brother. This young officer wangled for me to join his landing craft, and it was an eye-opener to see how adept those young men were at operating them, when one realised they had only been in the Navy for a very short time. When we were ashore the whole crew of the landing craft and myself had a swim, in the nude, and in the warm Mediterranean water instead of the Atlantic cold comfort it was bliss.

The Commander of the *Beatrix* was a Commander Brunton, and he was kindness itself to us both but was a bit scathing about the American troops, who were certainly a bit green to say the least, and it was just as well they weren't hitting much resistance at that actual bay. So green were they that they stacked their rifles outside a café when they went in, and then wondered why they were missing when they came out! Alan at last realised why he had been taking aerial photographs of the coastline: the French had got it all wrong when they thought Dakar was the port we were after. It was Oran. With gin at 2d. a nip and with my old English fiver now coming into its own, Alan and I had a whale of a time.

But all good things come to an end. Commander Brunton sent for us and said that he had just received orders to go further along to Bugie, and as it was a hot spot we would be an encumbrance. But he would let us off at Oran.

16
The Homecoming

Alan and I felt a bit lonely on the Oran quay as everyone on the *Princess Beatrix* had been so kind to us. There was any amount of shipping around but we thought we ought to report to the Officer in Charge of the port. Just as we were wondering what to do next we were hailed by a gloriously gallus-looking Glaswegian, Glengarry on one side of his head, cigarette stuck in the corner of his mouth and driving a 5-cwt truck. He was obviously skiving and we looked a good excuse. We must have looked an oddly assorted couple, Alan with his peg-leg and I with my ill-fitting sackcloth suit and huge boots. He dumped us at the embarkation offices, and as it was upstairs I left Alan below. I had a job convincing the guard on duty that I was a British officer, but Alan had his papers and I was allowed upstairs.

For the first time in the war I realised what 'red tape' really meant: behind a desk sat a young Guards officer surrounded by piles of papers tied up with red tape. He looked up and asked me why the hell I was dressed up as I was. After a short preamble I asked if he could organise a trip home for Alan and myself, 'We're disembarking troops not embarking them. Don't you know there's a war on?' I'm usually a mild-spoken man but I was so infuriated that I whipped off the patch that covered the gaping hole that had once been my nose. It was a nasty mess and red raw. 'While you've been swanning it in Birdcage Walk, some of us have been through the mill, thanks for your help.' I strode out. I don't think I've ever seen anyone look either so pea-green or so embarrassed, and he obviously didn't like the look of my nose. He mumbled something about a camp outside Oran but I'd had enough. When I got back to Alan, who should pass back in his 5-cwt truck but the wee Jock, so we scrounged a lift back to the part of the harbour where the troop-carrying liners were berthed, which was different from where the *Princess Beatrix* had been.

Imagine my joy and surprise when the first ship that I saw was my old pal the *Stratheden*. I was given a hero's welcome and assured that Alan and I would get a safe and quick passage home. They were certain with my nose that I would be among the dead and missing from the *Laconia*. After 'Freckles' Hawkins had made land in her lifeboat, Grizel's death had been announced, since she was the Earl of Glasgow's daughter. The *Stratheden*

The Stratheden

crew just imagined that I would have bought it. What a lovely thought to be going home on such a superbly-run ship. How lucky Alan and I had been not to get onto that first boat out of Casablanca, as we would have missed the North African landings and would have run right into the occupation of Southern France, for the Germans took it over immediately the Allies landed in North Africa. Goodness knows what sort of trouble we would have run into. They always say it is better to be born lucky than good-looking and I've certainly had my share of luck. And talking of luck, the Paymaster on board was a Glasgow Academical and he gave us a sub.

The home-going convoy was a very fast one, but we had the boat practically to ourselves and I was able to find out that the sealed orders that the Skipper of the *Stratheden* received in Durban were to go to America to bring over the Americans for the North African landings. The crew in their turn wanted to hear all about the sinking and about many of the passengers whom they had got to know but who were no more. Although I felt absolutely safe on the *Stratheden* I wore my lifejacket night and day, much to the crew's amusement. In 1959 I was to return from the States in a P & O liner called the *Parthia* and there were two ex-*Stratheden* officers on board. They used to give me a drink or two and get me to tell the blue-rinsed American women my story.

There can be no landfall like the 'Tail of the Bank' on the Clyde. The morning we got in it was a sharp winter's morning with a wee touch of snow on the distant Argyll hills. I had a feeling then that I was going to make the hills of Scotland my home, as indeed they have been since the war.

We were no sooner disembarked at Greenock than I was whipped away to Buchanan Castle, which had been turned into a military hospital for the duration. Because I was the first back from the Oran area and had witnessed the landing, the Army Intelligence Service said I had to wait at Buchanan Castle until I was interrogated by someone from London, if you please. It turned out to be a complete waste of both of our time, as I knew it would be, because I hadn't seen any battle plans or actual fighting. But, red tape again.

I had heard that the Buchanan Arms Hotel at nearby Drymen was famous for its wild goose, so I asked the pretty sister if she would accompany me but she said she had strict orders that I wasn't to leave hospital. I took a big chance and asked the rather *passé* matron—I suppose she would be at least forty—whom I was sure hadn't been asked out by a male for years, if she would join me and the trick came off. She said we'd need to go through the woods so that no one saw us. The matron was a tough old bird but, thank God, the wild goose was a young one and very tasty.

While at Buchanan Castle I had to go in front of an Army Medical Board, the Chairman of which knew my father: we were at Drymen in close proximity to Milngavie. He and his colleagues said I was to be sent to the new plastic surgery unit at Bangour, near Edinburgh. I was adamant that, had they seen my medical papers, I was due to go to Archie McIndoe at East Grinstead; but as my medical papers were now fathoms deep in the South Atlantic I hadn't the proof etc. etc. The Lord forgive me for the most blatant lie I've ever told in my life, but it came off and was to have a marked effect on my future life. The Colonel was so impressed with my story that he decided to phone the Queen Victoria Hospital and find out if they knew anything about this crazy Scot who was sure he could get in where only RAF personnel were being treated. At that time, December 1942, the Plastic Unit was a small, hardworking team and everyone mucked in. I still can't believe my luck, but when the call came through Archie wasn't actually operating and happened to be passing the telephonist. He spoke to the Colonel asking what I needed. On hearing 'a new nose' he replied, 'I haven't done a nose for ages, send him on down.'

Just last year I visited the McIndoe Museum at East Grinstead, and in it is the antiquated and very small switchboard to which I owe so much. Of course now it has been replaced by a complete new room with every possible modern piece of equipment, which is only right and proper for the Blond-McIndoe Research Organisation, now recognised worldwide.

I was allowed a couple of days with Dad and Mum at Melrose. Because of poor communications they didn't know where I was and feared the worst. When I arrived their reactions were typical. Mother, who never could show her right feelings, said 'Well, you're home again', and Dad burst into tears. I know where I get the title 'Greetin' Geordie'.

Melrose was host to a Polish Division who were dying to go fighting but for some unknown reason were kept there too long for their or the locals' good. The local regiment, the King's Own Scottish Borderers, had been in action and had had their share of casualties, and this caused quite a lot of ill feeling. Dad and Mother did their bit in the local canteen and Father was part-time teaching at the local preparatory school, St Mary's. Of course, because a lot of his Elders were away at the war, just running his Church took a lot out of him. A good friend of mine post-war, mentioned else-where in this book, one Pat Wilson, has made a few bob out of buying and selling Highland estates. He always likes to tell me how my Dad was the person who corrected his maths papers at St Mary's, and Pat got something like 5% in his final exam. Talk about the blind leading the blind—Dad couldn't add two and two, an ability, or lack of it, he has passed on to the author of this book. Pat must have got over his problem, whereas Dad and his family never did. However Dad did pass on to us his good speaking voice, and this has been a boon to me.

17
East Grinstead

Archie, later Sir Archibald McIndoe, has become a name to conjure with in this country, and I'll never forget my first meeting with him in the famous Ward III, Queen Victoria Hospital, East Grinstead, Sussex. He came bustling in followed by the usual retinue, saying sharply to Sister Mealy, 'Is this the brown job who bullshitted his way into an RAF Hospital?' He took a good look at my nose, or rather lack of it, took out the plastic support that had held it up since it was put in in Alexandria, said to his assistant, 'Put that in the Museum', and to me, 'We're fellow Scots so there's no use operating on you until after New Year's over. You've had a fairly tough time, so take a fortnight's leave and report back here sober. Blokes with booze in their blood bleed like stuck pigs. And by the way, I'll need two years to put that lot right.' I've always maintained that, famous surgeon as he was, he was also a brilliant psychologist. It was exactly two years later that I walked out of Queen Victoria Hospital, discharged from the Army.

Before going back to Melrose I phoned Mother to see what Dad would like for a Christmas present. She said, 'Bring him a bottle of whisky, it's very, very scarce, unless you can get some from the NAAFI.' I remonstrated and said, 'But Dad doesn't drink', and she replied, 'Wait and see.' I was lucky in that I got a bottle of Antiquary, which was then a great favourite of mine; their old bottles had corks in them. Imagine my surprise when Dad got out the corkscrew, opened the bottle and threw the cork in the fire saying, 'We won't need that, there's not much in a bottle.' He was certainly right, we didn't! Little had I realised how much our parents gave up to educate us. Father and I patched up many old wounds over that dram. Whisky was in short supply, so I wrote to Johnnie Walker's saying how my life had been saved thanks to having a nip every night on the raft and the lifeboat, what ambrosia it was, etc. The reply came back something like this: they appreciated so much my kind remarks about their blend and they hoped that at the end of hostilities I would remember my experience and drink nothing else. No word of the bottle or two that I hoped would come for Dad and me. That blend has never been my pin-up since, although I know it's 'still going strong' and there is nothing wrong with the blend, it's excellent. I have had different treatment from other firms.

That leave was a particularly happy one. I was able to get to know and admire Dad as never before, and realise what a fantastic organiser and worker Mother was. For the first time I heard her speak at an open meeting and I know now that Father might have been the professional, but Mother was the natural speaker. As a believer in breeding I have a lot to thank them for in instilling in me some, and *only* some, of their ability at public speaking. I was also able to visit my beloved Ettrick after five years' absence. The weather was frosty, so we were able to curl on the Broadgairhill Pond. All the curling was outside then but now, of course, it has become a very fashionable sport at which the ladies excel as much as the men.

I went back to Broadgairhill in 2000, to find the curling pond grown over. This is partly because there hasn't been a real frost for years, and had there been one there wouldn't have been enough folk at the top of the valley to play. Those who are now there in their 'second homes' wouldn't know anything about the thrill of the 'roaring game', the shouts of 'Soop, soop!' [sweep] and the lovely drams and camaraderie at the end of a match, under starlit skies and a keen frost settling in. This is nostalgia, I know, but how sad it is that the next generation won't enjoy such wonderful days, as curling now, like most sports, has gone almost entirely professional.

Then, all too soon, it was back to East Grinstead and two years in hospital, during which I was to have fifteen operations. I was slowly, and only very slowly, accepted by the RAF inmates who found I wasn't as bad as they thought I might be. We had in the ward during my first six months some of the original 'Guinea Pigs', that famous club which was formed by some of the inmates of the 'Sty'. Peter Weeks, sadly gone, became a special friend, as did Geoffrey Page who wrote a book about his experiences. So did Bill Simpson, whose bestseller did nothing to hinder him getting a good PRO job. They were great chaps, and they just took over the town of East Grinstead.

Archie was desperately keen that we not only fraternised with the civvies but were seen by them, so that they got used to the pedicles, skin grafts, new eyelids, new noses, new ears, etc. My wound was as nothing compared to most, as it was clean, not a burn which most had. Burns must have been terribly sore, because all one's nerves come to the surface of the skin. The 'local' was the Whitehall, where mine host was a super chap, Bill Gardiner, who on Archie's instructions had mirrors all round so that we got used to seeing how ghastly we were.

Unfortunately for me my Battery Commander, George Munn, had his mother staying in East Grinstead. There would have been nothing wrong with that if she hadn't been the chairwoman of the governing body of the

Queen Victoria Hospital when Archie swept in, determined to take it over, which, being Archie, he did. Mrs Munn was *not* amused and I found myself in a very difficult position as piggy in the middle—with Mrs Munn coming to visit her son's ex-Sergeant-Major and decrying Archie in a loud voice in front of all the patients of Ward III, and Archie coming in later saying what an old bitch she was and didn't she realise how lucky it was that this cottage hospital had been to be chosen as *the* plastic unit for the RAF? I saw both points of view, so for once in my life remained silent.

Another frequent visitor I had was a Mrs Mann of the famous brewing family, whose son Tom was one of the best young officers we had in the Sussex Battery. Tom and I had run the Regimental rugby team in Hove and became great pals, as he loved the Highlands dearly. Many a night, both on the *Highland Brigade* and in Eritrea, we would jaw away about grouse-shooting, stalking, ponies—anything to do with the Highlands. Or it might be fox hunting that we discussed, but on this sport I had to listen more than speak. The Mann family are famous beaglers and fox hunters. The 'Bolebrooke' beagles, which they founded at their home in Bolebrooke, Sussex, are still to the fore. I think I'm right in saying that Tom's three brothers all became Masters of Foxhounds. Unfortunately Tom died in the Eritrean campaign of some awful complaint: his mother often said to me, 'If only he'd been killed in action.' Mrs Mann was loved by all at the hospital because she was one of the old school and, because of petrol rationing, she came in a pony and trap. Being of the old school, when she descended from the trap she would hail the nearest person in sight, whether it be nurse, orderly, yes, even a sister, and say in a dictatorial voice: 'Hold the pony while I visit a patient.' Half an hour later or even longer he or she was released from duty, but such was Mrs Mann's charm (helped by chocolates got from an American relation which were unobtainable in Britain) not one of the 'National Service' grooms ever complained. In fact they said she was a lady with manners, who always said thank you, and the pay was sweet! I'm glad that many years later I was able to repay some of her kindnesses; I was able to represent her when she wanted to buy a house in Newtonmore, Inverness-shire, near where I then farmed.

Hospital was monotonous, yet there was always something going on. You were either being prepared for an operation, which meant staying off the beer, or having continual dressings. Again I was sorry for the burns cases who made up most of the ward, as they had to go into the saline baths to get their dressings removed, whereas with me it was a matter of whipping off the Elastoplast (bloody sore) and putting on a fresh dressing. Sister Mealy had the most wonderfully soft hands and was known as one of the tops in her profession at applying dressings. I was glad that she was honoured by the Queen for her work.

With his anaesthetist, Jock Hunter, his Sister Jill Mullins, and lots of aspiring young plastic surgeons coming in to be trained, East Grinstead became, and is, a name to be conjured with, but in my day, fifty-eight years ago, there was but one 'boss', Archie.

18
Archie McIndoe

Archibald Hector McIndoe was a New Zealander who realised that, if he was to succeed in his chosen profession, he must go to a country which had more citizens on which to use his chosen skill of plastic surgery. He trained for a time under his cousin, the famous Sir Harold Gillies, who had made his name in the first war as Archie was to do in the second. According to his own account his best paying job was straightening Jewesses' noses for £100, which pre-war was big money. He was obviously one of the up-and-coming plastic surgeons at the outbreak of war and was chosen to set up the plastic surgery unit at East Grinstead. He was a glutton for work, but he was great fun at a party and could play as hard as he worked.

One of the many memories of his ability to play as well as work hard was the occasion when the East Grinstead cinema was hit by an enemy bomb. We had in the ward an American, Hank Mahn, who had lost his legs. Hank had been shot down over the channel, but managed to get on to his inflatable raft. He drifted on this for days, with his legs dangling over the side, and the enless immersion in salt water rotted them. He wasn't in East Grinstead for plastic surgery, it just happened to be the nearest hospital when they brought him home. He was a delightful man who became famous as the only person known to have survived this sort of ordeal. He did this by catching and killing a seagull that landed on his raft and living off its blood: he managed to swallow this without being desperately sick. Hank was an inveterate cinema-goer and, of course, someone had to push him there in his chair. On that occasion it was my turn, and thank goodness the film was so bad that Hank asked to leave early. We were halfway back to the hospital when we saw the plane circling the town, so low we saw the swastikas on her wings. We just couldn't believe our eyes or ears when *womph,* she let go her load. By the time we got back to the hospital it was going like a fair and trained plastic surgeons were back to ordinary operating. I was roped in to help the male orderlies. It was late at night before Archie did his final round, but I remember him saying, 'Now, let's have a party!' and party we did. What a man.

So dedicated was he to his work that, although he would say to Adonia, his first wife, that he would be back at eight, it was more often ten or eleven. Inevitably the marriage broke up. When I first went to the hospital,

Adonia and Venora, Archie's two daughters, were in America for safety's sake, but I was present at their very joyous homecoming—he loved them dearly. As well as a flat in London Archie had a small house just outside East Grinstead, and latterly he was very kind in asking me there on many occasions. There were four of us who were regular visitors: Paul Hart, Geoff Page, Robin Johnstone, a District Commissioner from Kenya, and myself. Years later I was to receive a letter from Robin saying, 'I have a certain Philip Coutts sitting in front of me. I think he will make an excellent Colonial officer.' Robin was on the selection committee choosing ex-servicemen for the service.

With his fantastic personality and charm it was natural that Archie was much sought after by the wealthy around East Grinstead. Some of the old school, like Mrs Munn, didn't approve of him moving in the Jewish fraternity so much; but it seemed obvious to me that he would, as he was very fond of music and played the piano well. He had a love of culture and all good things such as good food and drink. All these things were shared by his Jewish friends. Tilly Marks, one of the famous Marks & Spencer family, was especially fond of him and used to spend hours holding her hand on top of his while we all listened to gramophone music. If any of us was not due for, or recovering from, an operation Archie would take us along with him. Because of his popularity we, his patients, gained a tremendous amount of hospitality, and the beautiful country house of Saint Hill, owned by Neville and Elaine Blond, was handed over to us for any time we weren't actually wanted in hospital.

Figures from the world of the stage were also the great man's friends, and I remember Frances Day captivating us all in Ward III with her sexy voice rendering, 'But in the morning No No, No, No, No N... o.' We had regular stars to entertain us, all arranged by Archie. One of the patients on the ward was put in charge of the artist(e). It was my turn when Max Miller, the 'Cheekie Chappie' from Brighton, came up. He used to be thought of as very naughty, but compared with the stuff we get on TV today he was as clean as a choirboy. The star had to change in the saline bathroom, then go on to an improvised stage in the ward and, as there were no stage lights, the artist could see all the faces. I was in the wings (the saline bathroom) when Max came off the stage, and he said, 'I've only done half my show, but I can't do any more looking at those faces.' He himself looked a ghastly colour, but before he went he said, 'Bring the boys down to Brighton and I'll see them right.' This we duly did, and Max, who was well known for being mean, did us proud with a free first-class show and free food and drinks.

So far as my fifteen operations were concerned, one of the great things about the 'Maestro' was that he explained to you what he was going to do, which gave you more confidence, whereas in Alexandria they just bashed on without one knowing what was to come next. To fill in the hole at the top of the nose a rhinoplasty was made, which consists literally of scalping you, attaching the bottom piece to a bit of existing nose, leaving it like that for 10 days to allow the nerves and blood vessels to join up, then cutting off as much as was needed, flapping back that which wasn't and letting the hair grow through it. The result, with no bone to hold it up, was called 'Cyrano de Bergerac' by my pals. At that time it looked a mess but, my goodness, what a super job he made: people who don't know what happened just think I'm an ex-boxer. As my brothers have gone thin on the top, I've no doubts that regular shaving of my hair for operations helped me keep my thatch.

The bone for holding up the nose was taken from my two hips, an extremely painful operation, as they chip it off with chisels, but the resultant chipped bone is said to be stronger than the original bridge to one's nose.

The time at last came when, apart from trimming operations, the great man could do no more for me. 'You'll only get an office wallah's job and that won't suit you, so I'm going to have you discharged, but meantime I'm going to have you posted to the Army else you'll be put on half pay.' This was typical of Archie and typical of the Services. After a certain number of months in hospital you were put on half pay. So I had an instructor's job in Cromer until my discharge came through. While there I was on sick parade feeling awful: one man with an Africa Star, one man with sun-stroke. Yes, you've got it, his name was Coutts.

When I got back some of the final trimming was done, but he wanted to let it settle before the *coup de grace*. I came back from civvy street to meet the new lady in Archie's life, who was Connie Belcham. Connie was and is most attractive, and has exquisite taste. She it was who moved Archie into a beautifully decorated and furnished house in Forest Row.

These two had all too few years together: they were obviously blissfully happy, enjoyed the same things and had some super holidays in Kenya to-gether where they had a share in an estate and where Archie recharged his batteries. At one time he had asked me if I wouldn't like to go out there, but I declined. Robin Johnstone, who had gone into partnership with Archie, found that male wartime friendships can be very different in civvy street when the friends were both married men, so it finished rather acrimoni-ously and I was glad that I made up my mind to try to get a niche in farming

Sir Archibald McIndoe on the left, Geoffrey Page D.S.O, D.F.C. in the middle and the author on the right. Sir Archie visited his native country for the only time and did the author the honour of staying with him, to shoot white hares, in 1945

in Scotland. However Paul Hart, the last of our gang, whom I see regularly, always says I should have joined the company that Archie formed to buy that Kenyan estate, as none of the others, Archie and he, though a well-known bulb grower, knew anything about ordinary farming. But I still think my decision was right, as I would have had to come back to Scotland after Archie's death in 1960 to get back into the mainstream of Scottish farming. In fact I was making a niche for myself in farming broadcasting which has stood me in good stead over the years.

On my discharge papers the Maestro had written, 'This man will do much more good back in Agriculture than he will in the Army and I predict that he will make a name for himself'. You could have fooled me. Some years later in the Fifties Archie was in Argentina, partly for business and partly pleasure. He asked if he could visit an *estancia*, and was taken to the famous Sirryton herd owned by Senor Charlie Duggan. When they were looking at the stock bull, Archie, for something to say as he was no cattleman, asked, 'Do you happen to know a Scot called Ben Coutts?' Charlie replied, 'He bought this bull for me.' The reason was that there was a temporary embargo on the Argentine Peso: Charlie got me to buy the bull, and we took it to Millhills until the embargo was lifted. It's a small world.

When I was eventually discharged and I got my discharge money, £70, he it was who advised me to put it into Marks & Spencers, but I had no clothes and I was contemplating marriage. That £70 was all the money I had in the world, so my chance of making a fortune went west.

Geoff Page and Archie came to visit me at my first post-war job. We went white-hare shooting in the snow. The Maestro decided Scotland was too cold for him and so I saw him very few times after that. He was a very great man who was taken much too early: he had a very powerful influence on my life.

The greatness of the man was rightly honoured in millennium year, when English Heritage had a plaque put up outside the flat in Draycott Avenue where Archie lived from 1949 to 1955. Also that year Geoff Page died. He had a wonderful memorial service in St Clement's Danes, at which the Queen Mum and the Duke of Edinburgh were represented. The Queen Mum's representative was there because Geoff had been responsible for having a suitable war memorial in honour of the Battle of Britain pilots erected at Dover; the Queen Mum was patron and unveiled it on a fearful day. The wather was so bad that the fighters, which were to have flown over, couldn't take off and the tea marquee took to the air instead! The Duke was represented as Patron of the Guinea Pig Club, of which Geoff was one of the few remaining members. So of the three in the photo opposite who went to shoot white hares in 1945, I'm the only survivor.

19

Strathallan Estate

On one of my sick leaves I stayed with a friend at Amulree, high up in the Perthshire hills. She had a war widow and her little daughter staying with her. I was ready to settle down and she wanted a father for Sara and to stay in Scotland. Lest it sound a marriage of convenience, I don't want to give that impression, but as subsequent events were to prove neither of us was the great love of the other's life. We were together for twenty-two years, but differences of religion, politics, art, music and each liking different types of people were more than the marriage could stand.

But back in 1944 Creina stood by me and we started looking for a job. Although I'd been a farm worker I was ignorant about the managerial side. Again luck was on my side. The owner of the Strathallan Estate in lovely Strathearn was taking a tenant farm back into his own hands, and was advertising for a manager. I was told, long after, by Sir James that there were many more capable and more qualified than I who put in for the post, but he felt slightly guilty that he himself hadn't gone off to the RAF. He held a pilot's licence, so once more I was in luck. He felt that by appointing a wounded officer he was doing a bit more for the war effort, which he also did as a very able member of the War Agricultural Committee. He had a first-class brain.

The Strathallan Estate at that time was a model of how to run an estate: half was tenanted and half in the owner's hands with managers in each. There was also excellent shooting: grouse, pheasant, partridge and wild greylag geese. There were salmon in the Earn and Sir James was an adept fisherman. The woods, too, were well managed and the local blacksmith was in the centre of the estate with the joiner next door. Luckily for me Sir James' adviser, and later to become his Estate Manager, one Bob Duncan, was the local Agricultural Officer for Perthshire and so he knew of all the farm workers who were on the move. In the war years a man had to notify the War Agricultural Executive Committee and had to have a good reason for moving before permission was granted. Bob found me a first-class grieve (or farm foreman as he would be called in England).

What a lot I was to learn from Geordie Wilkie during my three years at Lawhill. Lawhill House had been the old shooting lodge on the north side of the estate, and has a glorious view of the Ochil hills, facing due south, but the rooms were huge and how we were ever to furnish them goodness only knows. Creina had some furniture, but I had none, and I remember the first encounter with the tenant's widow, a Mrs Wilson. She was furious that her son didn't want the farm, and without her knowing about it had handed it back to the Laird. Sir James was a very shy man and, as Mrs Wilson tore him off a strip, he gently pushed me in front of him, saying 'Captain Coutts is a wounded officer and I'm sure you'd like him to be happy in Lawhill.' She then rounded on me saying, 'You'll have to take over that mirror [a huge ornate thing over the fireplace] and that drawing room rug as they are too big for the house into which I'm moving.' I'm sure the valuation was honest, but bang went most of my £70 before Creina and I ever set up house. I have the carpet to this day, 57 years later! Not only do I still have it, but it has been lifted and relaid five times—in Dalpatrick, where I stayed to manage the Millhills Estate; Gaskbeg, my farm in the upper Spey Valley; Cuil, when I managed the Ardkinglas Estate; and Woodburn Farm after I married Sal. Now it's at Woodburn Croft, where the carpet and I will end our days. I don't think a modern carpet would last half as long, so perhaps it wasn't so dear after all. The mirror is still in the same place on the wall in Lawhill. Sir James' grandson, who farms that end of the estate, lives there. When visiting him recently I pulled his leg and told him he ought to be buying it back from me!

Sir James' system of management was simple; he saw his managers in the spring and discussed the cropping with them so that there was no cross cropping or what one sees today, interminable barley, barley, barley, so he was able to keep his land in good heart and the managers couldn't take the goodness out of the ground. He then saw us again in the autumn and discussed the stock sales. He didn't want his managers—and there were six of us—to deal in stock, so when it came to buying hill sheep for fattening on our good strath farms he arranged with a curling friend of his in Glen Devon to buy them privately. This farmer, Jimmie Cram, used to have them beautifully 'drawn' in their sizes, and then the haggling started. We had all been attending sales in the previous weeks to get the feel of the market. After the conclusion of his sale, and although we weren't forced to buy them, we were expected to buy them, we had a gargantuan meal and then went to the local pub, the Tormaukin, which in those days had an old black coal-burning range, in front of which was ensconced the local minister. He could sink more whisky than any layman I've ever seen. I don't know what sort of a preacher he was, but he was dearly beloved of his flock, most of whom were shepherds and sheep farmers. Tormaukin (the old name for a white mountain hare) is now an extremely up-market pub. As I and a good friend of mine frequently use it on our way back from seeing a racing establishment which trains a horse in which we each have a twelfth share, we put the Tormaukin up for the Best Pub of the Year Award 2000. This it duly won, and we were treated to free lunch and drinks on the house!

Sir James kept his finger on the pulse of his farms by making his managers fill in time-sheets for all employees. The time-sheets were picked up on the Friday night when the wages were delivered by his faithful secretary, Miss Walker, who cycled with them. My old cattleman, who was very religious, put on his time sheet, 'Look up Hebrews, Chapter 13, verse 8, which says "the same yesterday, to-day and forever".' A very true picture of a cattleman's life. It was from this old man, Findlay Bruce, that I learned the art of feeding fattening cattle to the second. No matter who I had round to buy cattle there was no way we could see them until Findlay pulled out his ancient turnip watch, with its old celluloid dust covering, and said, 'You can go in now', and as the cattle got to their feet and stretched he would say with pleasure, 'That's when they put the meat on.' He was a fund of cattle knowledge and was always proud of the days when he had his own cow and had to graze it on what he called 'the long meadow' (the public road) as he wasn't allowed access to the fields. Why he was proud was that the boss's wife liked his milk better than that from the 'hoose coo', obviously because Findlay's cow would get an abundance of herbs on the roadside.

Lawhill was a mixed farm with arable crops, beef cattle and fattening sheep. Until his dying day Sir James was a dedicated potato man and all his farms had as large an acreage of seed potatoes as he thought wise, which in those years was every seventh year or longer. Lawhill was one of the better farms on the Estate and because of that grew wheat.

Lifting potatoes in the forties and fifties, yes, and even afterwards, was done by hand. When I was at Lawhill the war was still going on in the Far East, and labour was hard to come by. I had an ancient ex-Army lorry which Sir James told me to drive to the Raploch District of Stirling, where I was to contact a certain lady, whose name escapes me after all these years. She always had a fag hanging out of her mouth and was never fully dressed—she usually wore a woolly nightdress covered by a huge dressing-gown and on her feet were what used to be called 'baffies' (warm bedroom slippers) in my young days. She would direct the assembled mob of tattie-howkers, and there were any amount who wanted the extra cash and some tatties to take home, to the various lorries which were waiting for them, and I was only one of half a dozen. I used to wonder why (a) I always got the best squad, and (b) when I returned them at night I had to hand over to her the payment due to them. It transpired that she had lost a son at Dunkirk and so favoured me as being a wounded soldier. With regard to (b), it turned out that she was the local moneylender, and thus knew how much each member of the squad was due to be paid!

The first thing I had to do was organise the threshing of the wheat stacks which in these days was in the May succeeding the crop. The wheat was always in 2½ cwt sacks and had to be carried up to the grain loft. I decided, even with my long back, if I was ever to become respected by my neighbours, that was the job for me. It just about ruined me for life, but to this day one old neighbour says it turned me from being an ignorant Army officer into 'one of them'. But the job I really liked at a threshing day was forking off the stack and laying sheaf after sheaf the right way and right beside the cutter's hand, so all she had to do was slit the binder string with a very sharp knife. But woe betide you if you got one wrong. The stacking in those days was immaculate. Geordie Wilkie and Wat Bonthorne, my second man, didn't get on, with the result that we had a stackyard of which the whole Estate could be proud, as they spent hours of their own time patting them into shape and made a beautiful job of their thatching. Oh, how much we miss in craftmanship in modern farming: our workers now are craftsmen but their crafts of welding, maintenance of tractors and machinery, drilling, crop spraying etc. don't give the same universal pleasure as the old skills of stooking, stacking, horse ploughing, hedging by hand and all the rest.

Sir James, as President of the Royal Caledonian Curling Club, was an ardent supporter of the game and I was 'made', as they say, with the local Strathallan Meath Moss Curling Club, the second oldest in Scotland. In those days we had a very strong club and I often think Sir James would rather his employees curled than worked, in winter at any rate. Many a good game we had, and many a good friend I made while curling: 'the fun was guid', as one worthy put it.

It was at Lawhill that Archie McIndoe came to see me and I wished to impress him. Looking back now I realise what a nerve I had to ask the great man to stay in that draughty house. There was no central heating then, only open coal fires, from which most of the heat went up the chimney! As whisky was almost unobtainable I asked Jim if he could help me. He had always drunk Matthew Gloag's Famous Grouse, and gave me a note of introduction for which I expected at the most one bottle. When I was offered three I nearly fell down, but it did that firm no harm in the years to come.

There was the great story of Jim on his annual visit to fish at Aboyne, staying at a hotel owned by a group that had awful whisky. The only place he could send a telegram was from the hotel, so he despatched to the faithful Miss Walker the words, 'Send a covey to Aboyne Station', and a dozen duly came up to be smuggled into his room (Grouse whisky of course).

The Strathallan managers got £5 per week with the usual perks of house, milk and potatoes. This would seem ridiculous now, but at that time was the going rate. On top of this Sir James went 50/50 on the profits after deducting 5 per cent on his capital invested. But Jim realised that stock, if anything, was my metier, and as his good friend and neighbour was in all sorts of trouble with his manager I was recommended to manage the Millhills Estate near Crieff for Duncan Stewart.

Fifty years on I am now back worshipping as a member of the Trinity Gask Church which is next door to Lawhill. When I come out of the church of an autumn day and look round that beautiful countryside I feel sad that our farming technology and know-how may have increased our yields, but at the expense of the one thing that matters in life, people. Where I employed seven men there is but one now and the cottages are mostly filled by those who have no real interest in the community.

20

Duncan Stewart

Duncan Stewart OBE, of Millhills, would in his day be one of the most brilliant stockmen that Scotland possessed. He was grandson of a crofter on Loch Tayside of which he was justly proud, but his father had left the croft to found D & J McCallum Whisky, whose blend was called McCallum's Perfection; there was the old Highland gag, 'Some say McCallum Mhor [the rallying cry of the McCallum Clan] but I say "More McCallum".' The sale of this whisky had been extremely successful, especially in Australia, and Duncan's father had bought the estate of Millhills three miles out of Crieff in Perthshire. Not only did he do that but he brought out of Ross-shire practically a whole family of Gordons: one to be his manager, one to be his head cattleman, an inspired choice, and one to run his household.

Willie, the manager, had died and by all accounts had done not too badly as manager; the Millhills Beef Shorthorns were a name to be conjured with and were being exported all over the world, with fat tips and insurance agencies to be picked up by some. Willie's son, also called Willie, was made manager but didn't fit the bill, and Jim recommended me for the job. Jim and Duncan were partners in a big hill project of which more later, and as well as that Jim also had a Beef Shorthorn herd and leant heavily on Duncan for advice on buying stock bulls etc. so they saw a lot of each other. John Gordon the cattleman was still with the Estate, but up with the Highland Cattle fold at Fordie, Comrie. He was a wonderful character: he had an enviable record, having brought out no fewer than three champions at the Perth Beef Shorthorn sales and two at the Highland Bull Sales in Oban. To his dying day he always swore that he got diddled out of his third, and with this I totally agree.

At the time I went to Duncan Stewart's there were 1000 acres of arable land. He had four farms of his own and rented a large part of the neighbouring Dollerie Estate. There were the two hill farms of Balmuick and Brae of Fordie as well, where he ran not only Blackfaced sheep but his Highland cattle fold and a cross-Highland herd of cattle. As Duncan still had interests in the whisky business and in pubs in Edinburgh, my job was a daunting one, but he told me when he engaged me that he wanted dedication and honesty and I hope I gave those qualities to him. I went from Lawhill to Millhills in 1947, the year of the big storm, but as the house in which I was to live was still occupied by some of the Gordons I stayed on at Lawhill and travelled the four-odd miles.

It was from Lawhill that I set out to go to the Oban Bull Sales just before the big storm broke, and brother Frank took me to Crieff station as Creina was expecting our second child. Frank was to come back and collect me three days later. The lovely railway line from Crieff to Oban, which I had travelled on so many years before, looked all the more lovely as we had heard rumours that it was to be axed. John Gordon got rough justice with his bull: the judge, one Mr Inglis and factor to the Duke of Atholl, had been out of touch with cattle all during the war years, and if you're judging cattle you must keep your eye in. The result was John was beaten in his class but all of us were delighted that our bull made top price. The weather in Oban had been quite lovely but with a hard, hard frost, most unusual in the far west. John and his pal Jock Burns, Sir James' cattleman, loved their drams and made a holiday of the Bull Sales. They were therefore in good form when we boarded the train for home. At Tyndrum old Jock was waxing eloquent about what an awful job Inglis had made of the judging etc., and as he was pouring another dram he didn't see Inglis passing along the corridor. Seeing us there Inglis was about to open the door and I kicked Jock hard on the shins, whereupon Jock said, 'I was just talking about you, Mr Inglis', who, of course thinking it must have been complimentary, said, 'How nice of you, Gordon.' We fell about laughing, but the bottle got passed round again and peace was restored. Tyndrum has always been a bad place for snow: Inglis had got stuck there and decided to abandon his car and take the train. It would be many weeks before he saw his car again.

We had a slow journey back to Crieff with frozen points at Balquhidder junction, but we eventually got back almost three hours late and stepped out into a raging snowstorm. Duncan's chauffeur was there with his old Ford V8 shooting brake which had a high clearance, but Cook, the chauffeur, said conditions were very bad. Duncan said I could go with him to Millhills where Sir James was going for the night, but I demurred as I thought brother Frank might eventually appear. I tried to phone but the lines were down. The stationmaster was wanting to shut up shop, so I went up to my friends at the George Hotel who hadn't a soul in the house. Next morning the wind had died down and the sun came out. One was able to see the drifts which were very deep. I went down to an old boy, Ritson, who kept a riding stable and asked if I could hire a horse and he said, 'All six of them.' He said the hire of it would be to feed it until the grass came: I had that horse until May! That spring of 1947 was the worst I can remember. The snow never let up.

The author among the famous Millhills Beef Shorthorn herd, which he had the privilege of managing from 1947 to 1951

Duncan was of a very shy nature and got me to do a lot of front-running for him, like attending meetings on his behalf; he even made me deliver some speeches for him, as his nerves would get in such a state that his duodenal ulcer would start up and he would have to go to bed. He was most willing to teach me all he knew about cattle breeding, and his knowledge, especially about pedigrees, was considerable. Scotch Beef Shorthorns ruled the roost in these days, and the Millhills herd held the record for the breed for Millhills Comet, which made 6,000 guineas in 1920. This record was held until it was broken in 1946 by Pittodrie Upright and Uprise at 14,500 and 14,000 guineas respectively. The annoying thing was that in 1946 Millhills had a very good young calf called Climax which was Reserve Junior Champion, and had he been Champion he would have been the top price because the American who bought Upright said he was going to buy the Champion whatever he made. The runner-up was Col Hardie of Ballathie, who as head of British Oxygen was not without a bob or two.

In those days I used to go round the three farms to see the three grieves and the three head cattlemen before seven to discuss the day's work or, sometimes, to give a direct order. We had the most marvellous squad of men, and so many of them that everything was kept spick-and-span: woe betide anyone found dropping matches in any of the yards, which were swept daily. There was one outstanding grieve called Jock Myles, he was on the home farm, and like Geordie Wilkie before him taught me a lot. The knowledge of these men was terrific: they could gauge to a bushel how much corn a stack would thresh. If I wanted a field split into different crops— say, yellow turnips, swedes and kale—they were almost shocked when I used to pace it out, they just knew! They weren't only knowledgeable, they were so nice to work with. Many and many a well-known farmer and estate factor can thank his success in no small measure to the grieves and stock-men; I for one have been proud to work with them.

At nine I had to be up at the office to report to the boss when he was at home. He was a stickler for time. Depending on what I had to report to him we usually went to see the cattle which had always been his love and were to remain so to his dying day. In those days it was nothing for us to bring out thirty to forty bulls for sale. As all were individually fed in boxes and strawed up to their knees you can imagine the amount of work it took, and we had eight cattlemen. Jock Myles used to say wryly, 'The rest of us on the arable side are just their wet nurses seeing they hae plenty o' a' thing!'

Perth was the Mecca of the Bull Sales, and still is, but the breeds have changed and so have the buyers. Just after the war the accent was on an exporter's bull: this was the barrelly wee fellow, very near the ground and all too often over-fat, having had at least one, if nor more, foster mother as well as his own mother to suck. When I was at Millhills the Shorthorns had it all their own way. Calrossie, Millhills, Cruggleton and many others were send-ing dozens of bulls to the Argentine, USA, Canada, Australia and New Zealand: we were the stud farm of the world. Then the Aberdeen-Angus got their turn and today, because the breeders of both these breeds forgot the home customers, the overseas buyers have forsaken us. With the de-mand for big cattle and lean beef, the Charolais, Simmental and Limousin reign supreme.

When I managed Millhills in the forties, Woodburn was part of the estate and tenanted, though adjacent to the 'big hoose' and steading. I am now retired to the Woodburn Farm Cottage, which I call Woodburn Croft as it has two acres and stables. I pass Millhills every day going for my paper. Sadly, because of the change in farming practices, the lovely bull-boxes that I had to have painted every year are now falling apart, and the courtyard which was swept every day, and on which I once paraded the white shorthorn heifers in front of Greer Garson, the actress, is now overgrown with weeds. Having said that, the present incumbent is farming the estate extremely well as an arable unit, but that was never my idea of farming. Gavin Catto, who started life like me as a farm worker, and finished as one of the most respected members of staff in the Scottish Agricultural Colleges, and who, with his lovely voice, was a constant and much-loved broadcaster, said to me when I went to Gaskbeg after my time at Millhills: 'If you want to do well, Ben, grow guid gress [grass] and also ken a guid baste [beast] to graze it'. Sadly, in the modern age of farming, there are few who now follow his advice; but there may come a day when they have to.

21
Characters in the Cattle World

I don't know what it is about stock but they always seem to have characters as much as their owners and/or their attendants. Can it be the hours and hours spent getting the pedigrees right before arranging the matings, and the constant attention that stock require? Or is it that all good stockmen are dedicated? Whatever it is, characters abound in the stock world.

I well remember standing beside Lord Lovat, recently returned from the war: the occasion was a Shorthorn meeting in the Station Hotel, Perth. He was dressed in his old patched Fraser tartan kilt and in tartan stockings with even more patches in them, and a pair of old slip-slops on his feet. He had a large glass of whisky in his hand. Surveying the company with that almost supercilious, but yet humorous look as only 'Shemi' can do, he said to me, 'Ben, what's happened to all the characters nowadays?' I replied, 'Sir, I'm standing not 1,000 miles away from one right now'. Shemi was and has been very good to me, and like all successful men he has his enemies, but no one will say anything against him in my company.

I once did an advisory job for him. When I said that as I was Duncan Stewart's employee I couldn't take a fee, he said, 'Well, you'll come and stay at Beaufort Castle for the Inverness Highland Show.' Sure enough he remembered. The Queen Mother, whom I was to get to know many years later, was also going to be one of the guests, but she was laid low with a heavy cold. At the same time Lord Trent, the head of Boots, was there and he produced this huge round white cheese as a present for our host. I asked Lady Lovat what it was and she said it was a Brie. I said that was impossible as Brie was a wee triangular cheese! We live and learn.

Then there was Captain John McGillivray of Calrossie who could be a real bully, but I got on well with him. He was a kenspeckle figure: always wearing a green pork-pie hat, tight-fitting breeches, green stockings, highly polished black shoes and with a pipe always in his mouth. Calrossie stock were highly sought after, and during my stay at Millhills, much to Duncan's fury, Calrossie usually had the top average. We were using a big bull called Kinsman, whose stock were not wanted by the exporters and so weren't selling too well in Perth. I suggested that he allow me to take three of them to the Inverness Bull Sale, as one of our cattlemen had heard big bulls sold well there. So off I set, only to be confronted by the Captain in the swing doors of the Inverness Station Hotel with the remark, 'What are you doing here, Coutts, Inverness is my market?' To which I replied, 'In that case, Captain, just stay away from Perth, that's ours.' From that day until he died we got on like a house on fire. When I went to Inverness-shire to farm, Captain John lent me a caravan, on the lovely beach beside his farm, rent-free, and I was ordered, but ordered, to go up each evening and have a dram (if not more than one) of a certain ambrosia called St Mary's Seal. I've never seen it before or since, but it was great stuff. Captain John's favourite topic was his days with Highland cattle at Garvald and the time he had to walk some cows all the way from Tomatin to Blair Atholl for the use of some famous bull. Stirring stuff, and we had a lot in common.

Bertie Marshall with, also, his pork-pie hat, but instead of knee-breeches a loud checked suit and a bow tie, was for all the world like a bookmaker and a successful one at that. He, too, was kind to me. He was a great worthy and one of the 'tops' in the Clydesdale world, and once said to me 'Never show a man a horse you want to sell him until you've given him twa big drams and the light's starting to fade, that's when horses look best.' Bertie was a well-known exporter of cattle to the Argentine, and of course at that job all the cattle had to be well insured. He was at Liverpool supervising the loading of the bulls when one broke away and fell between the ship and the quay. Bertie ambled over, saw there was no way the bull could be extricated, took his pipe out of his mouth and said, 'Ah weel, that's the first yin sold.' I had to organise, while at Millhills, the dispersal sale of Colonel William Stirling's Keir Herd of Shorthorns at Dunblane, and was going round getting buyers. I asked Bertie if he would come. His reply was Bertie to the tee: 'Laddie, I'll mak' them a trade.' He was sitting up on the bales puffing at his pipe and I hadn't the heart to tell him there was meant to be 'No Smoking'. He had come early and rightly demanded a dram, which I had the hardest job forcing out of the Estate Factor, but after two or three he carried out his promise to me and 'made them a trade': a fantastic trade to be honest.

During the exporting boom the man who would make and lose more money than most would be Moubray Alexander. He was by far the ablest at knowing the sort of bull the Argentinians required, and one knew that if Moubray was decrying a bull in our string then that was the one he wanted to buy. In the Forties and early Fifties all the big strings of bulls were exercised on the cobble stones of Caledonian Road outside MacDonald Fraser's Mart, and those of us who did the exercising used to get up at 4.30-5 am to do it. There was always great rivalry between Gordon Blackstock, the Calrossie manager, Gerry Rankin, the Cruggleton manager, and myself, the

Millhills manager, about who was to get out first, but whatever time you got out Moubray was always there. He had to see a beast walk right before he'd buy it, and oh, how I wish some of our modern whizz-kid breeders would follow his example. Moubray was always a handy man to have running up a bull, and as Duncan had been in partnership with him at one time he occasionally helped us.

Dr Jimmie Durno of Uppermill, Aberdeenshire, is one of the names to be conjured with in Scottish agriculture. After he died his herd was run by his daughter Mary and went from strength to strength. Sadly Mary has also gone, and in a typically self-effacing way had ordered a completely private funeral, so that none of her old buddies had a chance of bidding her a fond farewell. She was a tremendous supporter of the Shorthorn breed, great fun and a character. Her father was always kind to lads like me coming into farming, and did me the honour of coming to visit me in my first farm in Inverness-shire. He was not only a great breeder of Shorthorns but the top agriculturist in Aberdeenshire of his day, hence his Doctorate from Aberdeen University. He was a terrific supporter of the Highland Show and would be proud to know his daughter became its President. As Chairman of Directors at the famous washed-out show in Aberdeen in 1951 he was doing his duty and the rounds of the stock exhibits. The rain was coming down in stair-rods as he jumped in beside a Border Leicester shepherd who just, and no more, moved his pipe to say, 'Aye, aye, Mr Durno, that's a shower 'll play bugger with your show.' The understatement of the year!

Lovat Fraser, who was a fellow Merchistonian with Duncan Stewart, was the chief auctioneer in those halcyon days of expensive bulls overseas. Strangely enough, like Duncan, he was highly nervous and this probably helped his selling, which for me was the tops. I will always call him the 'Prince of Auctioneers', as he was so distinguished-looking and knew his buyers so well: whether they were wee farmers from the Highlands who could be coaxed another guinea or two, or whether they were rich overseas buyers who could be sprung 100 guineas at a time! I often thought the odd fly on the wall did a bit of bidding without knowing it! He once said to me, 'Ben, my job is to know who my bidders are and what they can afford; your job is to produce the cattle to the best of your ability.' He was a pin-up character of mine, and even more so when he recommended me for a top job in Australia with Sir Roy McCaughy. But Creina wouldn't go: perhaps she was right.

Captain John had two brothers breeding Shorthorns: Kenny and Findlay. It was widely rumoured that Kenny had more than a little to do with the mating of the Calrossie herd. Whether this is true I know not, but I always remember my first meeting with him. The annual visit to each other's herds to see the opposition, and perhaps pick a future stock bull, happened in January which can be tricky weatherwise, and Duncan again had duodenal trouble and sent me with our neighbour, Douglas Dron of Crieffvechter, in charge. Douglas had a lovely little Canadian, Mr Jones, staying with him who, bald as an egg, looked for all the world like Humpty Dumpty. He was over to buy a stock bull for the herd owned by Massey-Harris. We got stuck in snow drifts in Drumochter Pass, and only got out because this wee guy Jones told us all how to exert our pressure on the stuck car in front of us, a huge Bentley driven by a well-known Border sheep farmer. I've never seen a man who knew more about weight-lifting, and so he should: it transpired that he had been Amateur Weight-lifting Champion of Canada. Thanks to him we eventually got through and to Kirton, Kenny's farm. His first remark to Douglas was 'They tell me Duncan Stewart has appointed a useless ex-Army officer as his manager'. He could well have been right, but he looked mighty embarrassed when Douglas had to introduce me. The happy sequel to that story is that Douglas won the Championship with Crieffvechter Empire and my friend Humpty Dumpty bought him to go to Canada.

After we got out of the snowdrift in the Drumochter Pass we stopped for supper at the Dalwhinnie Hotel, which was to become a great 'howff' of mine in later years. We had some excellent venison served to us by an extremely good-looking local lass. When the Canadian had to make his speech at the Shorthorn dinner he said, 'You Scots keep banging on about good heads [on your cattle] but I've only seen two, one was on a Highland bull that Ben Coutts showed me at Brae of Fordie, and the other was on a wee lassie at Dalwhinnie Hotel.'

There were many more characters, too many to mention, but sadly today they are becoming fewer, because life has become so much more hectic. Owners don't spend as much time wandering through their stock, as the computer now rules their lives. In the forties and early fifties there was no TV, so people made their own amusement or spent most of their time with their stock. That old saying, 'What is this world, so full of care, there is no time to stand and stare', was never more true than in farming at the beginning of this new millennium.

22

Ben Challum

Duncan Stewart and Jim Roberts, in conjunction with Sir William McNair Snadden, the local MP, and Dr Joe Edwards (who had been a contemporary of Duncan's at some time but in the late Forties was high up in the Milk Marketing Board) had got together and bought a huge slice of land from the Breadalbane family. At one time, 'From Kenmore [Perthshire] to Ben More [Mull] the land is a' the Marquises' but by the war it was down to so little. Duncan was no fool and knew a good thing when he saw it: he got the others with him to buy what they called Ben Challum Ltd, which was the larger part of Glenlochay, Killin, with Ben Challum towering over it, hence the name; Kirkton, Crianlarich, which although miles round by road is just over the top of Ben Challum; and Arrivam at Tyndrum which was over the border in Argyll and not in Perthshire like the rest. The whole carried 8,000 breeding ewes with three different managing shepherds, and this too was my responsibility along with Millhills.

Before I even came to work for him Duncan had done a tremendous job in reseeding the downfall in Glenlochay and changing the stock from heavy-coated Perthshire sheep (that couldn't milk a cat) to south country type sheep that were short-coated and could milk their offsping. I loved my job in the hills and probably went there more than I should, but I made many friends there that I still enjoy meeting. We were the first estate in Perthshire to benefit from the then new Hill Farming Act scheme. We made one cardinal mistake in that we built new houses at the top of the Glen because we all remembered the days of cheap labour, which were still with us, and each man was meant to be as near his ewes as possible. Nowadays the cottages have to be as near civilisation as possible and the men get expensive Landrovers, Suzukis, you name them, to get to their sheep. The Shepherd/Manager in Glenlochay was a wee spitfire of a man called Willie Hunter. He was a fantastic worker and like all of his kind found it hard to keep labour, so I, as often as not, was the go-between and had to sort out the problems, but he did a fantastic job for the Company. He it was who introduced me to the Newton Stewart Mart, where James Craig held sway in the sheep world of the south west, as Lovat Fraser held sway with the bulls in Perth. Many years later when I was farming on my own, but had been down to Newton Stewart for rams in the interceding years, not only for myself but buying for

Ben Wilson (a famous ram breeder from Lanarkshire when the Lanark men would not touch Newton Stewart rams) and had gone rather more than my usual money on a ram, Jim Craig said, 'Is that for Ben Challum, Ben Coutts or maybe Ben Wilson?'

The day-to-day running on the estate was done by the shepherd/managers, but the four directors had quarterly meetings and used to formulate policy. I attended these meetings and therefore knew the way their thoughts were going and had to see that their plans were put into practice. In Glenlochay and Kirkton we had some downfall land which could be improved with drainage, lime and slag and reseeding and, most important of all, fencing. If one reseeds on the open hill without fencing, the sheep not only draw to it like bees to honey and eat it out but they usually get a heavy worm burden.

The four directors were ideal for each other. Duncan was the stockman, Sir James had great arable knowledge and as a member of the Agricultural Council had up-to-date knowledge of new grass seeds, fertilisers, etc. and generally what was going on in the research world. Joe Edwards was full of new ideas, some completely unworkable—like his wish to introduce Brown Swiss cows to an area that has 90 inches of rain and is snowy in winter, and where our cows were outwintered! But Joe kept us up to the mark by injecting new ideas. Sir William McNair Snadden had the very useful contacts of Parliament and he and Duncan had much to do with the introduction of the hill cattle subsidy that has done so much to improve the hill farms of this country: unless there are cattle to graze down the rough grasses the sheep can't get the benefit of the reseeded pasture. It was also Sir William who persuaded the then Secretary of State, the Rt Hon. Hector McNeil, to visit Glenlochay to see what we were doing and that the Government grants weren't being wasted.

Looking back, it's fantastic the amount of labour we employed. The old way of shepherding was one man to a 'hirsel' of 500 ewes, which meant eight shepherds in Glenlochay for a start, plus a tractorman/lorrydriver. The same number of sheep and more cattle are looked after by half that number or less today. Without the hill, ewe and cow subsidies there would be no one in the Highlands today, so Duncan Stewart and his team did a good job back in the Forties.

The great time at Ben Challum was the lamb markings, when the glens were gathered in June, hirsel by hirsel, to clip the yeld sheep and mark the lambs. Each farm has its own 'lug' mark and all lambs gathered are so marked, and the male lambs, except those being kept for rams, are castrated. You can imagine the rivalry between shepherds to see who had the highest percentage.

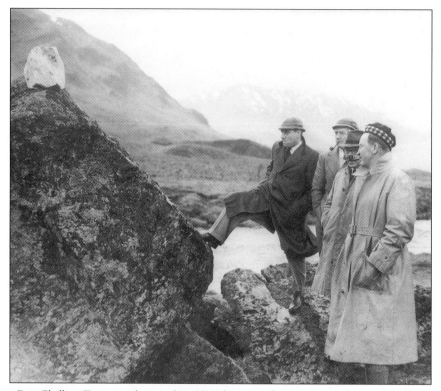

Ben Challum Estate was honoured in 1948 by a visit from the then Secretary of State for Scotland, Hector MacNeill. He is on the left of the group; next to him with pipe is Duncan Stewart. The author is the one in the tartan bonnet. The photo was taken at the herring-stone in Glenlochy, where in days gone by fishermen would swap their herrings for butter, turnips etc. from the local crofters

Of course a lot has to do with the ground, but a good man can make a tremendous difference.

Then we had an annual 'round up' of the cattle which had to be tested free of tuberculosis. This meant giving two shots of serum, one for avian and one mammalian. We had no fancy cattle crates in those days, so we used to put them in our strongest stone-walled sheep fank and lasso them! Many lumps of skin came off many knuckles before the day was out. On these occasions we were helped by Tim Norman, Duncan's stepson. Tim had served in the Gurkhas during the war and was quite fearless: he used to lasso animals better than most wild-west film stars. I was, and am, very fond of him, but I reckoned he wasn't cut out to be a farmer and said so to Duncan, who didn't agree. He gave Tim Brae of Fordie, with its lovely house, and

Balmuick. But I was proved right in the end of the day, as Tim chucked up farming and made an outstanding success as a restaurateur in his Timothy's restaurants, firstly in Cupar, then Perth.

We had a marvellous Crieff vet called Jack Ferguson whom I took up to do the testing and castrating. Tough though he was, he always said that that day was the most tiring in the year for him. Although practically a teetotaller, he always let me stop at the Lochearnhead Hotel for a refresh. I had met Jack when I was a boy, when he had taken away a huge dead Clydesdale foal by having to cut it away section by section: he was working for over four hours, and he told me all those years later that he had never been paid for the job.

The summer or 'milk' clippings—'milk' because it was the milk ewes— were happy times, because of necessity the job had to be done on dry days: no huge sheds then, although they were just coming in, as were shearing machines. I remember the old shepherds shaking their heads and saying of the machines, 'They'll never do: they shear far too close to the skin and the ewes will die of the cold.' Today no one would dream of going back to hand shearing. The sad thing is that wool prices have remained static and over-heads have soared, so that it would pay one to breed sheep with no wool if they'd survive the Scottish weather.

Then, of course, came the lamb sales when the wether lambs, unwanted ewe lambs and finally the draft ewes are sold. With the large number of sheep to sell, plus calves and supervising harvest operations, autumn was a hectic time for me. Stirling was our centre and once more there was friendly rivalry between the shepherds as to whose lambs would fetch most money. In those days, before the advent of vast areas being planted by the Forestry Commission, the sales of sheep were huge and a lot of time was wasted for me, as it was natural that if I had, say, three lots of lambs in, then one would be near the beginning, one the middle and one could be sold as late as six o'clock at night. It was around this period that I met Captain Bennet Evans from Wales who, like myself, was to be a founder member of the Hill Farm Research Organisation. He it was who sold all his sheep on one day on his farm, and I was so fired with the idea that I put it to my directors but, although I never succeeded in pulling it off for Ben Challum, I was able to organise one later for another estate.

The directors gave a super party for all employees and their wives and for all neighbours who had helped during the year. They always had a guest speaker, and I remember one of the best and one of the wittiest was Professor John Greig, who had conquered one of the hill sheep's biggest killers,

'Louping Ill'. There was an entertaining room upstairs at the end of a long passage of bedrooms; I was told to take anyone there who might be a bit dry because the dancing was all heavy stuff: quadrilles (jig time), Duke of Perth, Strip the Willow etc, and old fashioned waltzes were considered respites! It was near the end, if not after the end, of the night and I was going in front of a famous Wattie Burton who enjoyed his dram when I heard a slight noise behind me, an arm shot out of a bedroom door, Wattie disappeared and was not seen again that night. Later I heard that Mrs B. thought he had had enough!

Wattie Burton's farm of Cononish is now expertly farmed by his son John, who decided to go in for Swaledale sheep of which he has become one of the principal breeders, but at the time of writing gold has been found on the farm and all locals are wondering if Cononish is to be another Klondyke?

These were happy occasions and helped greatly to keep the district together, though I little thought in the Forties that I would be guest speaker when Willie Hunter eventually retired in the late Sixties.

23
Gaskbeg

Two things combined to make me want to leave Millhills and Duncan Stewart: firstly, he always hoped that his son would give up motor racing and come back to take over the estate, and secondly, Creina, a socialist, was never happy with my not being my own boss. Farms at that time were easier to come by than they are today, in fact I was offered the tenancy of two, but cash was the snag. Then Duncan, decent soul, said he would guarantee my overdraft. Lovat Fraser, head of MacDonald Frasers the auctioneers, also said he would help if I bought and sold all my stock through their mart. With these promises we moved to Gaskbeg in November 1951, after five very happy and instructive years. Creina was glad to move: not only because she was a restless character who always needed a new challenge in life, but after producing Hamish and Shaun at Lawhill, she had had a very nasty time with twins who arrived 10 weeks too early. The girl died at birth, but Donald, the boy, survived after weeks in an oxygen tent, and apart from the fact that he couldn't walk until he was two, is certainly all right today. Shaun had been born in the middle of the worst of the 1947 snowstorms, this at a time when people had their babies at home. I remember going to Auchterarder in a clapped-out old ARP ambulance that served as my farm car in those days. It was a low-slung Humber Snipe (yes, we drove British vehicles then!), the 1947 storm was at its height, and although we got stuck in drifts twice I managed to dig us out each time until eventually we bogged down on a brae half a mile from Lawhill. Miss Phimister, the Orcadian-born midwife, was the heaviest 'bag of tatties' I ever carried for half a mile!

Gaskbeg was on the Ardverikie Estate belonging to Sir John Ramsden up at the head of the Spey at Lagganbridge. Ardverikie was and is a famous deer forest, was nearly sold to Queen Victoria when she bought Balmoral and in shape the two houses resemble each other. It has now become well known as the shooting lodge used in the TV comedy 'Monarch of the Glen'. I use the term comedy advisedly—speaking as someone who has factored many Highland estates, the Producer or Director of this programme has simply no idea how far away from the mark they are in their portrayal of Highland estate life. I found the same thing when I was Agricultural Adviser to the 'Strathblair' series. We would set up a genuine agricultural scene but

The farmer of Gaskbeg, Lagganbridge, Inverness-shire

the Director would ignore it and do his own thing, so as to make the scene more photogenic or whatever.

Gaskbeg had been a 'namely' farm in its day but had had a tenant previous to myself who had let it go down badly, so it was a wonderful opportunity as the farm could only go one way, up. There was only half the number of sheep to take over, which was good because I hadn't the cash. The bad thing was that most of the 250 were old ewes: given a bad winter I could lose a lot. Just before I left Ben Challum, Duncan had had a contretemps with the shepherd/manager at Arrivain, one George Menzies. George would keep his sister and sick brother on the pay roll; Duncan reckoned they were just hangers-on so I was ordered to tell George that they must go. Whereupon George, who had quite a temper, told me that if they went so did he, and at the May term (28 May). This coincided with my taking over Gaskbeg, and as I knew him to be a good sheep man and first-class with dogs I offered him the shepherd's job there. I felt his wife, who was much younger than George, might be a problem and so it proved. She and Creina never got on; she was a handsome woman from a first-class shepherding family, but was scatter-brained. Dad once said of her, seeing her dressed for church, 'She scrubs up well, Ben.' Sadly, later on the scatterbrained wife left George for the 'bright lights' of Aviemore when the ski-ing centre got going. Even sadder, their second son, who had inherited the scatterbrains, did away with himself.

But between us George and I got Gaskbeg going again. Although he went into residence in May I couldn't leave Millhills until November. Just after I arrived, there was the famous occasion when we had a sudden snow-storm and George and I went to the hill to gather the ewes into safe areas. After doing what we could, because of where the snow had fallen we decided to come down behind our neighbour's farm; he was single but had a housekeeper who knew George but not me. Obviously there had been speculation about this Captain Coutts who had done quite a bit of farming broadcasting since 1947, but was also known to be a keen churchgoer and an elder to boot. So the housekeeper, after introductions, looked at me and said, 'Will you have a cup of tea?' Then at George, to whom she said, 'Or a dram?' George's reply was classic: he said 'A kent a man yince that had baith and he's still alive'.

Gaskbeg had a middling hill which carried 550 Blackfaced ewes, but it had excellent gravelly 'haugh' land running down to the Spey. I will never know to my dying day whether it was the water, the soil, the locals' ability at breeding cattle and showing them, or perhaps that wonderfully clear air that one notices when one passes over the Drumochter Pass, or that most cattle were fed on draff, the by-product of whisky—but whatever, Speyside cattle were famous in those days and bred no fewer than six Supreme Champions at the prestigious Smithfield Show in London. So with this good bit of arable 'haugh' land I decided to start a really good herd of breeding cows. Duncan, in his usual magnanimous way, gave me on leaving his service a beautiful silver-mounted evening dress sporran which I still cherish, but also Millhills Heroic, a Shorthorn bull. Speyside abounded in those days in good commercial Aberdeen-Angus cattle, big and useful; if only that society had stuck to that type they wouldn't be in the sore straits they are today. So it was these cattle that I sought as female stock, breeding suckled calves to be sold at Grantown-on-Spey or Kingussie at six months of age, so that one only had to winter the mother.

The Aberdeen-Angus breed at that time were the native cattle of Speyside, and there were herds from Gaskbeg and Cluny at the top of the Spey and right down the length of this lovely river. I think I'd be right in saying that Ballindalloch, the oldest herd in the country, and two or three more are all that are left. What has changed is that in the Fifties the herds, apart from two or three, were owned by wee farmers who were stocksmen, knew their cattle and were good judges of stock. They had been brought up in a hard school, where most of any ready cash came from letting out the farmhouse to the summer 'veesitors', while the farming family stayed in a tin shack for the summer. One such was Jimmy Gordon of Lower Dellifure. He told me that since he was, as a youth, a good fiddler, he made the odd bob or two playing at dances. On one occasion after a late night he slept in ('yoking time', i.e. when you yoked your horse, was 7 a.m. in those days). When he eventually came downstairs he found that the family had finished their 'parritch and babs', which constituted their breakfast, and were all off to work except his father, old Angus. He took his pipe out of his mouth and said, 'Jimmy, it's either the fiddle or the how [hoe for singling turnips], and if it's the fiddle you can leave the house now, and don't come back.' Jimmy said to me, 'I hung up that fiddle for five years, and never played it until Dad died.' Today Jimmy, who was a brilliant fiddler, would make more money at it than that farm was worth. But luckily, as well as this talent, he was a first-class judge of cattle and a fine public speaker.

Winter was a long-drawn-out affair. In our first winter of 1951/52 I took snow in the back door from November until the end of April, just the sort of winter George and I didn't want for our old ewes. We made the most lovely bog hay when we were there, something you seldom see nowadays because the push for more production has caused so many of us to reseed with modern grasses, whereas 'bog hay' is made from natural grasses, weeds to many, and containing lots of herbs. George once said, 'You could eat it yersel, it smells that good.' No balers then: it was terrific when we got a buck rake for the old Ferguson tractor to push the hay into the coles, which were all built by hand forks and tied down against the wind with ropes made from the hay itself by continuous twisting.

As well as building up the cattle and sheep stocks I decided to go in for seed potato production, which was unknown up there at that time, but it was ideally suited for it. Being at 1,000 feet above sea level, the aphids wouldn't like it much, the ground was free-draining, the arable land that I was breaking in had never seen a potato so there was no chance of eelworm infection, and there was abundant local labour—wives and school children all looking for a bob or two to augment the poor wages they then had.

So with all these pros for growing spuds I asked a potato merchant friend of mine to come to look at the soil. He had never been at Laggan before, which you approach from Dalwhinnie, rising steeply over the hill through peat bogs and heather before eventually descending into this fertile strip. Bobby Hamilton had got the mileage from Dalwhinnie to Gaskbeg, and when there were but two miles to go he had to get out to attend to the needs of nature. He was surrounded by heather and peat. He said to his wife, 'I always thought Ben was a sensible sort of guy, but I now think he must be crackers to think of growing tatties up here.' After seeing the ground he completely changed his mind and we had a very good partnership. The seed was so clean he was able to pay me a bonus for it. Because our growing season was so short there was never a big crop. Back in the early Fifties I would be one of the first growers of that well known variety Record, so successful in the chipping world.

Another innovation that I brought into the district was the combine harvester. I had a friend, Pat Wilson in Perthshire, who was then hard up and wanted to use his combine after he had finished in his own area, and he contacted me about the possibility of doing some work in Speyside. I had just grown rather a good crop on an area that had never been ploughed in living memory, and as it was a fair distance from the farm and 20 acres, which was more than I and my two men could handle, I thought the combine was just the job. To make it worth Pat's while, however, I had to organise other farmers down the valley near Newtonmore, Kingussie etc. also to use the combine. This I was able to do after a lot of persuasion. The next thing was a phone call from Pat in Blair Atholl; he needed fuel which I went down with. He eventually arrived in the most awful greasy old overalls to stay the night and start next day. I remember two old crofters sitting on the flood bank waiting for something awful to happen to the combine: they thought I had done a disservice to the district by bringing it in and spoiling the old way of life, and they kept saying, 'It's impossible', as they saw me leave with the grain in a trailer and the straw spouted out behind. Dear Calum and Jock (both now dead) you were right, but none of us can stop the march of progress, a lot of it not for the better. As for Pat, he has done more than well for himself; he has bought and sold estates to great advantage and now can spend his time, instead of driving combines, shooting pheasants from 1 October to 1 February and is among the best shots in Scotland, if not the best. The rest of the year there is always some roe to stalk. I don't know how many hundred trophies surround his domain and of course there are always hinds and stags to be culled in his various forests, but his start was a hard one, and like me he's none the worse for it.

24
Outside Interests

When I went to Gaskbeg I was not only my own boss but aged thirty-five which is, I think, about right for taking an interest in public affairs. I had been brought up by Dad to believe that the future of the Church of Scotland depended very much on the laity, and, apart from my years in Sussex, I have been a keen Church supporter; at Laggan we had a good minister under whom I enjoyed serving as an Elder and later as his Session Clerk.

The family all went to the local school and took their lunch with them. The gravedigger told the apocryphal story of hearing Hamish, looking at his lunch 'piece' as he passed the church gate, saying, 'Bloody cheese again, you'd think we were mice.' The village of Lagganbridge was a thriving one then, and many a good night we had at village whist drives and dances. Creina was always keen on doing something new and once she'd accomplished it she would drop it, but always being musical she formed a local band and was greatly helped by a young tractorman who was a really good accordionist. Since those days the village has gone from strength to strength, with many incomers contributing to its well-being. They have just had a book published about the district, and have a spanking new village hall and a very good shop which is run by the community.

For my part it was the period that I did my stint for the National Farmers Union and was sent from our branch to represent them at Area level in Inverness: they in turn sent me to Edinburgh on the National Council. Unfortunately, as in all walks of life, one gets people outside the Union who moan about how little they do etc., but I think it is essential for every farmer to be a member and where possible do their whack on committees etc., otherwise they never appreciate the problems. Membership of the Hill Farming Research Organisation was challenging in its early days, and as we had responsibility for three Research farms, one in the hills of Aberdeenshire, one in the Borders and one in Argyll, it meant quite a bit of travelling. Being on that board and on the NFU Council gave me a wonderful opportunity to meet the top farming brains and personalities.

Jim Wilson, the famous sheepdog handler, was to win three International shields outright, i.e. nine International wins altogether, a feat I think that will never be repeated. He was a great friend of mine. He used to come to stay with us on his way north to judge or demonstrate on the Northern

Circuit of dog trials. He it was who persuaded me to start the Laggan Trials, as the big haugh on Gaskbeg was ideal for the job. Creina had a good bitch which she was keen to run: sheepdog trials were another of the many things she wanted to do: as I'm the worst handler of a dog there ever was she could easily beat me.

The trials were duly instituted, and I'm glad to say are still going strong. I went around the local gentry to raise the necessary money without which I couldn't run them, and they all said they'd come, especially as the famous trials champion Jim Wilson was to give a demonstration. Jim's great show was to have three dogs lying in line and have a fourth dog put the sheep round them in a figure of eight. But when he arrived to stay with us the night before, he bore the bad news that he only had three dogs as his good bitch was on season. 'I'll find a fourth', he said, 'as two or three of my cast-offs are up here in the north.'

I was doing course direction and Jim was judging, when a local had a particularly bad run with a red dog that lifted its leg on a molehill, chased a rabbit and nearly put the sheep in the Spey. When the man eventually gave up Jim called him over and said, 'Put the dog in the back of the car.' I just about fainted, as the haughs were now crowded with people waiting for the great man and this was our first ever trial. The time came and the great man took the red dog's head between his hands and said, 'You're back with me Glen' and gave the dog a good old talking to, all the time shaking the dog's head. I was in a state of collapse by now but I need not have worried, as it was Glen he sent out to collect the sheep and he had one of the best outruns, lift and fetch of the day. He also used Glen to put the sheep through the other three dogs which he did perfectly. What a man: he never struck a dog in his life, and they worshipped him. Jim was also a master breeder of sheep who helped me greatly with the Gaskbeg stock.

Jim very kindly presented me with Glen when he was finished with him that day, as after the appalling run he had done with his current owner, a Speyside hotelier, the hotelier had asked Jim to take him back. Glen's fault for trial work was that he would 'tak a hod' [take a hold] of a sheep. This was more than helpful to me when I wanted to catch a lambing ewe, but in a dog trial means elimination. He was by a long way the best dog I was lucky enough to handle, and the Laggan shepherds nicknamed him 'Sputnik', as he could gather a whole hirsel on his own. He had a great barrel of a chest, which gave plenty of room for lungs and a big heart.

The local mart at Kingussie was seasonal and was run from Perth by MacDonald Fraser & Co. Lovat's brother Harry was responsible for it, and as nothing had been done to it for years it was falling into a very bad state of repair. I went to Harry and said that the condition of the mart made it impossible to show one's sheep properly. Harry said that as the firm weren't making any money out of the mart they would rather let it go. I went back to the NFU branch and reported that I had had no success at all, so we decided to go to the opposition, the Aberdeen and Northern Marts, and see what they could do. We formed a local small company of which I was made chairman, and for a time it flourished. We built cover for the buyers and concreted most of the essential passages and pens but, as time has gone on and as has happened in so many walks of life, things have tended to get larger and many farmers tend to take their stock to larger sales. I was desperately keen to keep it going for the crofters, of whom there were many in that area fifty years ago, but if they got the chance of a shilling more in Inverness or Perth, they were off! However I am glad to say that in this year 2000 it is going stronger than ever, and I think the late Harry Fraser would have been sorry he let it slip through his fingers, especially into the hands of his *bête noir*, Aberdeen and Northern Marts.

We felt it our duty to take 'mud students', or persons who wanted some practical experience in farming before taking over on their own, and I'm proud to say some have done well. Angus Pelham-Burn was chairman of the Aberdeen and Northern Marts as well as being chairman of the Bank of Scotland and Jeremy Dewhurst at the time of writing is president of the Scotch Beef Shorthorn Cattle Society. One of the most interesting we had, but only for summer holidays, was Max Hastings. I had done a TV show with his father, MacDonald Hastings. He said he was having marital problems and asked if I could take his son for the summer holidays. I don't think I've ever had to answer so many questions in my life, but I'm sure the fact that he was the first journalist to walk into the pub in Port Stanley had a lot to do with his Lagganbridge training. He has been Editor of *The Daily Telegraph* and is now Editor of the London *Evening Standard*. Although he wasn't actually working for me, Queen Elizabeth the Queen Mother's Factor, and also now the Factor at Balmoral, was employed at Gaskbeg. Martin Leslie, like myself, had set out to be a vet, but also, like myself, came a cropper and spent a summer helping the famous Ewan Ormiston at Newtonmore with his ponies. Gaskbeg House was being used for a film about an American boy in the Highlands and ponies were needed. Martin was in charge of them.

But the student of whom we saw most was John Russell. John had a good Oxford degree and had gravitated into the BBC in Edinburgh, and for some unknown reason was made producer of the farming programme to which I was a regular contributor. He suddenly realised how little he knew about the farming side and, much to his good wife Hope's amazement, he threw up his BBC job to come to Gaskbeg. Hope had brought a bit of cash to their marriage but not a lot, and she was very worried, as was I, how they were going to live, as John was a big spender. Like many Scots who have been brought up in England he was more Scottish than the local residents: wore the kilt always (in fact I sometimes wondered if he took it off at night), learned to speak the Gaelic in double quick time, learnt to sheep-shear and, most important of all, was dearly loved by one and all. When I left Gaskbeg I got him a farm manager's job, but unfortunately he was made redundant, and rather than leave the district which he had come to love, he took a crash course in teaching and came back to Kingussie as an English teacher and again threw himself into every conceivable activity. He died far too young, but the fantastic turn-out on a snowy day at Alvie showed the high respect in which the district held him.

25
Agricultural Shows

Duncan Stewart had never approved of showing unless it was attached to a sale, and looked on shows as a complete waste of time and money. I, being gregarious, enjoyed them and nothing has changed me, although in later years I got more than my share of them.

With my own stock at Gaskbeg I was able to start showing, both locally and nationally, and once you start to show you are often asked to judge at shows. My aim at Gaskbeg was to breed good suckled calves for the autumn markets, but a win with one at a summer show often enhanced their value.

My best year was in 1952 when I had a good heifer calf by Millhills Heroic, my Shorthorn bull, out of a pure Aberdeen-Angus cow. I showed her at Grantown-on-Spey and was second with her. A well known feeder, Alec Stobo, pestered me to sell her as he wanted to show her at the following year's Fat Stock shows. I was keen to keep her for the forthcoming Lochaber Show as it was their first and I had promised them an entry. Alec said the heifer, which he named Highland Princess, could stay in my ownership until the autumn as he wouldn't need her until then: she duly won the first Lochaber Show. I had the great pleasure of going back in 1982 to judge a much bigger and improved entry at their 30th Show. Alec had engaged one of the top feeders of the time, one Alec Ogg, to come to give the finishing touches to the heifer. Rumour had it she was looking well for the Scottish National Fatstock Club Show in 1954. I hadn't seen her since she left Gaskbeg and I must say I was delighted with her. I remember that day because I was doing the cattle commentary, and after she had won her class she had to go on and win the heifer championship and then take on the champion steer for the overall championship. I'm told the tone of my voice didn't alter, but I can't believe it as she went on to win the Championship. I received a very nice medal as the breeder.

There was a big party waiting for Creina and myself at Perth on our way home to Gaskbeg and we left all too late. When we got to Blair Atholl there was a slight flurry of snow but it was obviously hard, hard frost. The road over from Dalwhinnie was tortuous and runs high. As we were just getting over the top, *Womph*! We were bang into a snow drift with no chance of getting out. So off we had to set in the 'wee sma' oors' of the morning in the bitter cold and through quite deep snow. Anyone who has done it will know how tiring that can be. Poor Creina was ill shod for the exercise: it was before the days of tights and she had on silk stockings (which my mother said I would never be able to afford!). We had a good three miles to trudge but there was a phone box after two miles and I reckoned I could summon help from it. The last half mile was hard going for Creina, and I had to partly carry her. We eventually made the phone box, and although it was 3 a.m. I knew our local GP would come out. Dr MacKay and his wife were two of the best, and the right sorts for a country practice: he was piping and Gaelic daft and a strict Wee Free, but his wife had a wonderful twinkle and they offset each other wonderfully. I was no sooner through on the phone than he said, 'Hold on there, Ben, and get Creina into the PO box, and I'll be right with you.' What a topper he was, but that night cost Creina dear, as she was in bed with frostbite for all too long. I, on the other hand, was off to the Smithfield Show to do the sheep commentary. In hindsight I left Creina far too often while I went gadding to shows, sales, meetings etc. No wonder she got fed up in the end.

That was a great Smithfield for me. Highland Princess went the whole way and won again to complete the famous double. Alec Stobo, a most generous man, not only threw a monumental party to all and sundry in London, but considered that he had paid me too little for the heifer, so he sent me a silver cigar box, suitably inscribed, which sits in a place of honour on my mantelpiece. When I look at it, as I often do, I not only recall those two super shows but often wonder in this commercial world we now live in how many buyers would be as generous as that.

At Gaskbeg I had a small Highland fold, again helped by Duncan, which I grazed on the western, boggy, bit of the farm. I bought a promising bull calf from Fordie called 'Kinloch of Fordie' and, also in 1954, although I didn't manage to win the Championship in Oban, I was reserve and made the top price, 360 guineas, a princely sum in those days. It was the same year in which I was the Highland Cattle Society's President. My only claim to fame was that my first Vice-President was Sir Charles MacLean of Duart, who had to give up the job on his appointment as Chief Scout. 'Chips', as we called him, is now Lord MacLean KT and was the Lord Chamberlain to HM The Queen. The next to be appointed was Michael Noble, later to become the MP for Argyll, then Secretary of State for Scotland and then Lord Glenkinglas. All their President could get was an MBE.

There were so many Highland bulls in those days that we had the show one day and the sale the next, and had a wonderful ceilidh on the night of the sale. Along with the two mentioned above, the so-called cattlemen's

The Gaskbeg stock bull 'Glasgach of Duart', winner of Dundee Highland Show as male champion

ceilidh was star-studded, with the Dukes of Argyll and Montrose (the latter a very good Gaelic singer) and his factor, the legendary Johnnie Bannerman who was to become Lord Bannerman. Not a bad line-up for a ceilidh and, much more important, we had the Jocks who all did their bit. We still have these nights in Oban, but the turnout is small compared with the Fifties because Highland cattle, although they will always be wanted, have lost ground because of the demand for heavier, quicker-maturing cattle.

The sale in October 1987 was a fizzer and I hoped at the time that it signalled a return to good honest cattle that have longevity, can use their legs properly, can use roughage as part of their feed and are easy to keep. Part of the reason for that good sale was the demand from overseas, especially Germany. Sadly the overseas demand came to an abrupt halt after Stephen Dorrell's dramatic statement in the House of Commons that there was a connection between B.S.E. and C.J.D. I personally have never been convinced of that theory, as at least one vegetarian has had C.J.D. When I went to Germany in the Nineties to judge Highland cattle, after the sale and a few drams one German breeder confided to me that we were daft admitting we had B.S.E.—they just dug a big hole and called it J.C.B.! But goodness me, what a mess this has landed them in eventually. When it was proved in 2000 that they had B.S.E. in their cattle the German people virtually stopped eating meat, even their beloved German sausage.

One of the best shows I ever judged at was the South Uist Show in the early Fifties. A fair party had gone on all too late in the Lochboisdale Hotel the night before, and I was told to be outside the hotel at 8.30 the next morning to be picked up and taken to the show. Well after 9.00 a very West Highland-speaking gentleman pulled up in an ancient Austin and enquired if I was Ben Coutts. Answering in the affirmative I got in and we drove to Daliburgh. There he got out at the Post Office and took down a show notice which had all the classes for which one was eligible to enter. I wondered what his reason was for doing this but was soon to find out. We got to the show field which had a beast or two, a bell tent inside which was a crate of whisky and little else, and the so-called judging ring which consisted of the local tug-o'-war team's rope suspended on a few stobs, or so it seemed to me. What amazed me was that the judging area was not flat, which is essential to see a beast properly: although it wasn't Ben Nevis there was a virtual hill in the middle. Two hours later I started judging one of the best classes of Highland cattle I've ever seen, and I've judged the Highland, the Royal, the Yorkshire, Scottish National and Smithfield and many others. What made me howl with laughter was my steward producing the show notice he had pulled down in the P.O. and reading out, first in Gaelic and then in English, what the classes were to be. No beasts were led. They had now their fore, now their hind feet on the hill, so it was not my easiest judging assignment. But my classic memory is that after judging a heifer class I came back to my steward and said 'That one, that one and that one' (as they had no numbers on, one had to point them out with a stick). After going up to give out the tickets he came back to say 'What's wrong with the third?' To which I replied 'She's a good beast, but I think she's had a calf, therefore she's not a heifer, but why are you so interested?' 'She's mine,' he said. End of conversation.

Shows have given me many friends, and I'm proud at the time of writing that I am about to be Vice-President of my third Scottish local Agricultural Show. Firstly Speyside Farmers' Club in Grantown-on-Spey, second the wonderful sounding Glenorchy & Innishail Agricultural and Horticultural Society held in Dalmally, Argyll, and now the Ardoch Agricultural Society at Braco, Perthshire, who claim to be the second oldest in Scotland. I'm also Vice-President of the prestigious Royal Smithfield Club. Showing is a disease, but a very happy one. Friends are made (and sometimes lost when one puts down the beast belonging to the friend who thinks it should have won), and happy exchanges of farming experiences and gossip take place. At the bigger shows like the Highland, the Royal and the Smithfield, implements and machinery are displayed and their attributes demonstrated by enthusiastic salesmen, and quite a bit of business has been transacted over the years. But it's the wee country shows that I've enjoyed most, which sadly are having to adapt rapidly because of rural depopulation. I fear some will go to the wall— those that have too many chiefs and not enough Indians on their committees, or those which have spent excessive amounts on the afternoon's entertainment, i.e. more than the amount taken at the gate. Some will have to amalgamate and employ a professional secretary, as the days of the local banker or solicitor doing it for peanuts are long gone. No longer will livestock-judging be the main attraction, although the livestock parade will always be a central part of the afternoon's programme. More and more shows are slowly—very slowly—realising how important the so-called 'light-legged' horse section has become, as there are more horses in Great Britain today than in the days when horses carted all our coal, food etc. and tilled the land. The shows that have cashed in on the 'light-legged' horse classes are doing well, and are assured of a future, as are those that are homespun and authentic.

One thing that has changed dramatically for the better is the catering, thank goodness. For years dear old Strachan Kerr were the only caterers around, and I shudder to think what the modern Food Hygiene people would have thought of the state of their kitchens. However the reason that there are so many old codgers like me still alive, who showed and judged in the years just after the war, is because we built up an immunity against those bugs that are absent from all the pasteurised, homogenised etc. food that one gets today! But now there are outside caterers who serve a diversity of excellent dishes compared with the monotonous mince and tatties one used to be offered at show after show. Having said that, at some shows one can still be offered a cold meal of overdone roast beef curled up at the edges, with lettuce that was obviously left over from the last show! By far the best catering at local shows is done by the local ladies. It's always fresh, always wholesome and always served with a smile. The latter is something the run-of-the-mill waiter or waitress in Scottish restaurants could learn from these lovely show ladies, it costs nothing but it means so much.

Showing and judging have given me more pleasure than money could ever do. I thought in my eighties I wouldn't be asked to judge again, but

The author in the middle of judging 80 Aberdeen-Angus heifers at Carrick-on-Shannon, Ireland. At 82 years of age he was highly privileged to have been asked, and even more pleased that the heifer he made champion was the popular choice of the onlookers; but after half a century of judging he decided that this would be his last time of doing it

when I was 82 I was asked to judge the Aberdeen-Angus heifers at the Carrick-on-Shannon spring sale in Ireland. The reason for this is that they wanted to honour me as the first Scot to buy a bull at their sale back in 1971, since when there have been many Scots over to buy bulls. In 1971 there were ten heifers on parade, straight out of the bogs with hairy coats and heads unclipped, in fact I don't think one had ever seen a dandy brush, far less felt what one was like when applied to its body! Imagine my horror when I was invited back to be told I had 80 manicured heifers to judge, as a quarter of a century on the men from the bogs had learnt how to 'bring out' their cattle.

As usual in that lovely Emerald Isle everything was running late ('when the Lord made time he made plenty of it') and I was left with only an hour to do the job. Thanks to an excellent young steward I finished with one minute to spare. Better still, the spectators agreed with the beast I made Champion, which is high praise. I always remember when I took a team of young farmers up to Calrossie to teach them about stock judging, and the redoubtable Captain MacGillivray said to the assembled company: 'Once you've made up your mind and placed your beasts, and before you give out the rosettes, just back gently to the crowd, and they'll bloody soon tell you if you've done right.' So I reckoned that, as I'd done right on this occasion, I'd pull down the curtain on fifty happy years of judging shows.

26
Other Estates

I realised later that I should have set up an estate management office in Newtonmore or Kingussie. In the Fifties only Ardverikie Estate had a resident Factor and most of the other surrounding estates were managed from either Perth, Inverness, Pitlochry or even Edinburgh, and there was a great opening for a local man. The snag was, and still is with me, that I hate office work and it would have been necessary for me to take in a partner (which in those days meant someone sharing a business rather than sharing a bed!), but as most of those high-lying estates are not viable one couldn't charge enough to warrant another salary. What I did have for a time was an excellent secretary who came from Aviemore through snowstorms, the lot, but unfortunately she had to move.

The reason I took her on was that I had been asked to factor the neighbouring estate of Cluny. Cluny Castle was the old ancestral home of the McPhersons, but like many clan chiefs they had fallen on hard times and had to sell to a Captain Lindsay who was chairman of Morgan Crucibles. He was a kind and generous employer and we got on well together. The Estate was a good one of its sort with an excellent hill for sheep, grouse and deer. There was some good arable land which could fatten off the lambs. We decided, as Aberdeen-Angus cattle were taking over from the Shorthorns in popularity, to install a herd and we had some immediate successes, the top-price bull being 2,200 guineas. The sheep did well too, as I had moved George Menzies down to Cluny because he wanted two of his boys employed and there wasn't a job for them at Gaskbeg.

Captain Lindsay and I used to run a harvest-home in the village hall for all our neighbours and our employees. At one of them a good-looking lass in the village who was being chased by most of the single lads decided she had better sit on old George's knee. I was passing with a tray of drinks and heard George say, 'I doot you'll need to get off lass, I'm not as old as I thoucht I was.' There was a vacant cottage which Captain Lindsay very kindly had me do up for my parents which was typically generous of him.

There were also some crofters on the Estate and I was responsible for the upkeep of their buildings. Crofters have always been cosseted in Scotland, I think. The idea of crofting is one that appeals to many urban dwellers. The reality is that, in all too many cases, the crofters have lived in their crofts for a minimal rent—in my factoring days as little as £5 a year—and yet for this the landlord has to keep the homestead 'wind and watertight', a very costly business in the windy, wet West Highlands. Meantime the crofter often had a lucrative part-time job.

The grouse in that Badenoch area of Speyside were particularly good at that time and I was given more invitations to shoot than I could cope with. Sir Ewan MacPherson-Grant owned not only Ballindalloch down the Spey, but also the estates of Glentromie and Gaick. These he decided to sell: the purchaser was a Mrs Hone who wanted them for her two sons Tom and Barry. Someone had mentioned my name as a possible factor and I accepted with pleasure and had some happy years looking after these places. The farm on the estate was one of the best on upper Speyside, called Ruthven, and the lambs from it topped the Kingussie lamb sales more than once.

Some of the MacPherson clan thought they still had the right to fish the Gaick Loch, as they had been allowed to do in Sir Ewan's day. After Mrs Hone bought Gaick, one of them, an M.P., much to the annoyance of the resident stalker, kept coming to the Loch. This lasted until I put a chain and strong padlock on the gate where the estate marched with the neighbouring estate, and after he'd had a nineteen mile walk there and back to Newtonmore where he'd left his car, we didn't see him again.

Gaick at the head of the glen is my favourite Highland estate. It is right up at the end of what used to be a very bad road and is miles from anywhere. There is an old fashioned, but adequate, lodge, with a lovely view over the loch but above all it is surrounded on three sides by heather-clad hills, and no matter which way the wind is blowing one can go out from one side in the morning and stalk right round in a horseshoe shape until evening.

One of the old fashioned features of the lodge is the original 'water closet' behind it: the privy is built over the burn, and is a two-seater at that! I always think that one would have to be very friendly to sit beside someone in a loo, except in wartime when we all got dysentery at some time or other. You were glad just to get to the slit trench that served as a latrine before you soiled your pants, and then it wouldn't have mattered to you even if you'd had a German as a companion! I always thought we must have looked like a lot of old roosters on these occasions, as the 'seat' was just a pole, for all the world like a hen's perch in a hen house.

It was at Gaick that a famous local worthy, Ewan Ormiston, was born. His father had been a stalker at Gaick. Ewen was a crack shot with both gun and rifle and went off to the First War to come back from the Lovat Scouts with a Military Medal. He had a hotel and a butcher's shop in Newtonmore, but was best known for arranging shooting and stalking parties. He also had a large number of Highland ponies which he hired out, as did Glenartney, and he it was who originated pony trekking, although many others laid claim to that honour. There is no doubt that the advent of pony trekking is the reason why the Highland Pony Society is going so strong today. Ewen was a born raconteur and used to pull my leg about being an estate factor; he said that his father was once asked by an English tenant if there was any problem with vermin on Gaick and old Ormiston had replied, 'Oh, there are a puckle hoodie crows and a factor!'

Among Ewen's guests at his Balavil Hotel was Colonel Peter and Charlie Krindler of the famous and prestigious 21 Club in New York, and between them they hatched up the idea of rushing grouse, shot first thing on 'the Glorious Twelfth', down to Prestwick from whence they were flown to New York to be eaten in the 21 next day. I shudder to think how much they cost at the 21. Ewen had lots and lots of contacts, so he had lots of hotels wanting grouse on the 12th to serve that night, with the result that a van used to go round collecting the birds from all the surrounding estates early on that day. At Glentromie we used to shoot quite close to the road so that we would be able to hand over the birds easily. I remember the awful occasion when we had but one brace to hand over: it transpired that an eagle had been quartering the moor, which means bye-bye to any grouse flying.

The Hone family were new to grouse shooting, as were many of their guests, who were delighted to take advice from old Duggie McNiven, the head keeper. Some, as in all walks of like, were not so cooperative, and one particularly annoyed me because he was always on the phone—there was only one, and I needed it for arranging beaters, getting wages organised, game collected, etc. When he left he said, 'Thanks for everything; as you're the factor I can't tip you, but put some money in my firm.' As we hadn't seen eye to eye I didn't. The man was John, now Sir John, Clark, and his firm was and is Plessey; congratulations John, you were right and I was wrong and obviously am not destined to make money.

I was also asked to factor Corrybrough Estate down at Tomatin. This was another excellent hill estate, but unlike the others I managed it was badly run down, the owners were short of capital and a lot of money was needed to put it right. From a grouse-shooting point of view Corrybrough was a topper, as the land was shaped rather like a big bowl. Grouse fly along the contour from which they were put up, not veering to left or right, so that on a hill that has a bowl shape they can be driven over butts and then back round again, and they won't try to disappear over the top of the hill on to someone else's ground. Allargue at the head of Strathdon, a very small estate owned by the Forbes family, is another which is fortunate to be shaped like a bowl. In the late Sir John Forbes' day I was lucky enough to be able to shoot there, as I had invited him to help out the Hones at Glentromie. When I see the price of a day's grouse now, I realise what a lucky laddie I was when factoring estates, to get all that shooting for free!

My good friend George Mackie, from his excellent farm of Ballinshoe at Kirriemuir, decided to put some of his profits from his arable land into a hill farm (no better way of spending it, and all too often losing it!). He bought the estate of Braeroy up the glen from Roy Bridge and asked me to help him. I told him that along with his head shepherd Campbell we ought to walk the Marches. This we duly did on one of the Highlands' unusually hot days. When we got back George produced the bottle and said, 'You'll have a dram, Campbell', to which the reply came, 'The wife'll have the tea ready, but if you insist Mr Mackie.' A few minutes later another dram was proferred and the answer was the same, 'The wife'll have the tea ready, but if you insist.' Eventually the bottle was finished after the same questions and answers, and as Campbell got to his feet he said, 'Isn't it a good thing I wasn't born a woman. I could never say No!'

George eventually sold the estate lock, stock and barrel. To his dying day George, who rather fancies himself as a connoisseur of the arts, will regret that in doing so he included a valuable picture that the new incumbent then sold, thus recovering a large part of the price of the estate!

It was at this time that one of my neighbours was offered the east end of the Ardverikie Estate; as he didn't want the north side of the Spey comprising Gaskbeg, Blargie and Coul he offered them to me for £5,000! I phoned my bank manager in Crieff to see about an overdraft and set off early on a very snowy day because both of my men were sick and I had to feed the beasts before leaving. It was a nasty journey both there and back, and not made any more pleasant by being told by the bank manager that the powers that be at headquarters had looked up the map, seen the land was at 1,000 feet above sea level, so weren't interested, and anyway, I had an overdraft of £170! I know this was in the Fifties, but even then the asking price was peanuts. Even forgetting the farms, there were nine cottages on the land, and what would they be worth now? Changed days, they chuck money at you today if you're mug enough to take it.

So the tenant of Coul bought that farm and Blargie in which was an old chap who conveniently died the next year, leaving his farm to be added to

Coul. It was rumoured at the time that the timber was valued at £7,000, but whether true or false the whole thing was a bargain. The new owner was one Jimmy Wilson, whose son Donnie is still going strong (aged 80). They eventually sold Coul to an ex-student of mine and went to live in Blargie. Donnie dines out on the story of the eight weeks in 1963 when the main water to the house froze at 4 feet underground, and he had to make a hole in the ice of the wee loch behind the house. The ice was 14 inches thick! From that hole they pumped up water with an old Army stirrup-pump to the main tank in the house. We were tough in those days!

Other neighbours of mine, the Boswell Browns, decided they wanted to be landowners and bought Gaskbeg, as I was better off as a tenant than as landlord unless I was thinking of selling. But the B–Bs found being landlords wasn't all beer and skittles: there were still some items of capital expenditure under the Hill Farming Act to be completed.

The crux came in 1959 when I decided that the family should have a better education and Creina felt she had had enough of constant snows; she had worked hard but was looking for pastures new. So in the spring of 1959 we bought the farm and in the autumn we sold it, to give me the first capital I had ever had. I immediately spent it on the family's education, following Father's lead.

27
America, 1959

In our final year at Gaskbeg I had been chosen for an American scholarship by the English Speaking Union, combined with a Nuffield Scholarship, and Creina said she would hold the fort while I was away. There were still liners going to the States in those days, and so that students could mix with Americans before reaching the States the ESU liked students to go over by boat and come back by plane. In my case, because of pressure of work, it had to be the other way round, and just as well as it turned out. One started off in New York where an itinerary was worked out for you and I was to go south first, then out to the West Coast and back through the Mid-West.

While the itinerary was being fixed I went down to Washington and stayed with a niece of Mrs Brinton, whose husband was a high-ranking army officer. They both entertained me very well and he showed me round part of the American services headquarters, the Pentagon. The size is unbelievable, it's so huge. The story is told about a woman who stopped an Army officer and said, 'Quick, get me out of here, I'm going to have a baby.' 'Madam,' he said, 'you shouldn't have come in here in that condition', and she replied, 'But I wasn't in that condition when I came in!' I also saw the wonderful cherry blossom and when I went to church, a Presbyterian church, who should be there but the President himself, Dwight Eisenhower, which was one up on my Church of England pals who were bumming about the British Ambassador being at their service.

Back in New York I was just about set to go off on my tour and took one of the girls from the ESU office, who had done a fantastic job fixing the trip, out to dinner. She didn't hear what I said to the taximan and she had a fit when we rolled up at the 21 Club. She refused to get out of the taxi because she knew the amount of money we all had to spend and that there was no way I could afford what was then the most expensive restaurant in New York. I still didn't tell her my contact but dragged her unwillingly from the taxi. Imagine her relief when she met the Colonel and found that I had an open invitation to dine with him any time I was in New York. As I always wear the kilt on overseas trips I was introduced all round, and one would have thought I owned the whole of Inverness-shire instead of one wee farm, so lavish was he in my praise. But what a meal and what wines! I did get a quick look at the menu and just about died when I saw the prices.

I was desperately keen to get down to Kingsville to see the famous King Ranch, and that was duly organised, but I was told that Bob Kleburg, the owner, wouldn't be able to see me personally as he would have just completed his annual sale of his world famous Santa Gertrudis cattle and his equally famous quarter-horses. The cattle had been bred by him with the help of a well known veterinary geneticist and were three-eighths Beef Shorthorn and five-eighths Braman—the former for the fleshing qualities and the latter for heat resistance. The quarter-horses are reckoned to be the fastest over a quarter of a mile and, of course, when ranching cattle the initial speed is what is wanted.

I duly arrived at Kingsville having been in different places on the way down, but none have struck in my memory as did this visit. There were agricultural colleges where I had to lecture on Scottish hill farming, or I had to speak at ESU branches. Bob's PRO, one John Cypher, met me off the plane—you fly everywhere out there—and we got on immediately. He reiterated how sad Bob was that he was just too tired to see anyone etc., but that he, John, was in charge of me and that he would show me as much as he could. He was amazed that I should be wearing a kilt and said, 'I must take you down town tonight.' I had visions of lovely dancing girls or something, but how wrong I was to be. He pushed me through one of these swing doors you see in bars in western movies. I saw a long bar with a cowboy sitting at each end, and as I entered one put his hand onto his obvious six-shooter and I've never retreated out of a bar so quickly in my life! John was shaking with laugher. He took me in and introduced me to the 'boys'. I can't remember how many shootings they have a month in Kingsville, but they never even make the front page in the local newspaper. Half of their problems seemed to stem from the number of Mexicans who illegally come over the border, and the fact that every male in Texas carries a revolver of some sort, it's a Texan cult.

My guest house was absolutely wonderful and the couple who ran it had taken out my dirty clothes, there was a bottle of whisky and a carafe of iced water by my bed, and everything was wonderfully cool. As always the heat was troubling me. I wish I'd been born with a tougher skin. Next morning John and I set off to see some of the most impressive set-up it has ever been my pleasure to visit. In the afternoon we were both to have a siesta and he was to call for me after he had done some work. After my siesta I went for a stroll. A large Cadillac stopped and a charming lady poked her head out of the window and asked what my tartan was and what was I doing in those parts. We chatted for a few minutes, she drove on, I continued to stroll for a bit and when I got back to the guest house the whole place was in an uproar. The car lady was none other than Bob's wife Helen who was furious that, as they had only one couple in the house, I should be in the guest house, and even by the time I got back my case had been moved. The next few days were magic: Bob was terribly apologetic but said he was deaved with people wanting to see him and tried to keep them at arm's length, nor would I blame him as he was world famous in the cattle world. Each day when he had time he discussed the breeding of his cattle or showed me some of them. He was, although stout, extremely good on a horse and showed me just what a good shot he was by shooting a snake with his revolver while in the saddle! Or we might go out in one of his aircraft (he had many) and dive-bomb some of his grading up herds, as he used his home base on which to breed his Santa Gertrudis bulls and then sent so many out to his outlying stations, some of them hundreds of miles away. It was not only stock breeding in which he had proved his worth. He had cleared hundreds of square miles of their local bush called the 'Mesquite' and re-seeded it. One day we were out looking at one of the huge bulldozers he used for the job and I stepped back into a cactus bush. Then, if not before, realised the kilt is not the garb for Texas, but without it I wouldn't have had those idyllic days and evenings. For in the evenings Bob, Helen and I would sit round the swimming pool and 'dram' and jaw away about cattle. Sadly neither are with us today, but I'm proud to own a Texan belt with a Texan silver buckle which he gave to me when I left, and I'm prouder still that through my introducing Michael Noble to him Bob got some really good grouse shooting.

Also staying at the King Ranch were a well-known portrait painter and his wife, who were obviously not getting on at all well and hardly spoke to each other at the super dinners we enjoyed. I understand they parted afterwards, but not before the painter had completed a first-class portrait of Bob, in the background of which he included a bird native to Texas that Bob called a 'shite hawk'. I sometimes wonder if, like Annigoni's painting of the Queen commissioned by the Guild of Fishmongers, which has a salmon in the background, there was some connection between the bird in Bob's picture and the couple that gave it.

Dallas was unheard of in this country in 1959, as JR had to wait twenty years plus for his soap-opera debut, but I was offered a very large sum of money by an oil magnate in Dallas to get Charolais cattle from France to Scotland and thence to Dallas, as he couldn't import them direct. Two things stopped me: firstly I wasn't fit by the end of the trip (to put it mildly: I damn near died), so when I got home what with that and the sale of Gaskbeg I had other things on my mind; but secondly, from the Charolais I saw in Texas I thought the breed had no future. How wrong I have been proved to be!

My next stop was right on the border of Texas and Mexico with a family of Scottish origin called Warnock who had one of the biggest sheep flocks in the USA: I can't for the life of me remember how many tens of thousands. But what I do remember is how desperately hot it was and that is where I started my diarrhoea problems, which were to get more acute and at last take over the trip. While at the Warnocks we went over the Rio Grande into Mexico as there were gaming halls set up there for the rich Texans. The difference in the standard of living was frightening: one left tarmac roads and brilliantly-lit houses and went over to huge pot holes and houses with just a candle or two in them.

From Texas I went through Montana to San Francisco, my pin-up city in the world: not only did I meet up with the rest of the students but with an old pal of mine, Jock Moncrieff, with whom I had an uproarious night. The lady singer got stroppy because I was singing Scots songs, and we filled the bar as everyone told their Scottish pals. Jock says to this day that the reason the singer got stroppy was not that I was singing against her but that when she did her striptease act I got on the stage and followed suit, and my kilt was more popular than her lamé dress for covering up my figure. Luckily I have never been a true Highlander. I'm sure Jock is right as he tells the story so well, but my memories of the evening are dim to say the least!

My lasting memory of that city was of the Top of the Mark where they have a bar on the top of the Mark Hopkins Hotel, and you look out over the famous Golden Gate bridge and the whole of the town. Some of us wanted to go to church and some didn't, so we decided to meet in the Top of the Mark for gin and tonics after service. We decided to go to the C of E service where the Bishop of California was preaching. After the service he was pleading for people to stay for communion. He said, 'I know your excuses: mother-in-law is waiting, the chicken's in the oven and must be taken out, or I've got friends to meet for a gin and tonic in the Top of the Mark.' I have never ducked my head under a pew so quickly in my life: having done some lay preaching in my life I knew he wouldn't be seeing anyone, but he drew a bow at a venture and scored a bull. We stayed.

I went to Salt Lake City and lectured to the ESU there and then on to Colorado Springs, where a charming RAF couple looked after me, but it was the end of the road for me as my complaint was so bad I was put into hospital and had to have a specialist see me. It wasn't until 1979, thanks to

Connie McIndoe, that it was discovered that I had diverticulitis, but obviously this was the start of it. I will never forget my stay in Colorado Springs, as most of it was spent in hospital. The treatment I got was not what we are used to here in Great Britain, and even in 1959 it was fearfully expensive. As I was having constant dysentery I was extremely weak and was 'bedded' straight away. This was on a Thursday, and the nurses went on strike from the Friday to the Monday. As I was so weak I couldn't get up to go to the loo, and so had to lie in my excrement all weekend. When the English Speaking Union officials came in to see me on the Monday I thought the roof would take off from the rest of the building, as I've never heard such a row. After I was bathed and put into clean clothes I saw their top man dealing with stomach problems, who put me on pills that allowed me to walk again, but it meant the finish of my trip. I'll never forget him saying to me, 'When you get home again, Captain Coutts, sue that hospital.' To this I replied, 'We don't do that in Britain.' That was in 1959, but just look at what happens here now in 2001!

To any ESU readers I apologise for the useless student I turned out to be and especially that the bill for my medical care was £1,000 (luckily this was fully insured). I came home on the *Parthia* to find pals from my *Laconia* days, and was able to recuperate from what was literally a wasting disease. *Parthia* was a sister ship of the *Laconia* on which I'd been torpedoed. A couple of the *Laconia* officers, who like me had survived the sinking, were part of the crew, and we spent happy hours together talking of that terrible night. Happy, not in the sense of thinking of all the misery and death and the many things that Cunard could have done to lessen the suffering, but happy that we were still in the 'breathing business' and able to enjoy a wee dram. I was so lucky to be able to enjoy a voyage on one of the last of the ocean-going liners, on which the staff knew what the word service means.

28
Ardkinglas

Before deciding to sell Gaskbeg I had been offered the Factor's job at the Ardkinglas Estate in Argyll. This estate was owned by Michael Noble in conjunction with his brother John: Michael did the farming side and John the estate. With Michael becoming firstly the MP for Argyll and then Secretary of State for Scotland they had agreed to take me on.

It was a lovely estate to manage; it is still scenically lovely, but like too many Highland estates it has been drastically altered because of money difficulties, taxation and succession problems. When I went there in 1959 there were 4,000 breeding Blackfaced ewes, a fold of 50 pedigree Highland cows and a herd of 30 cross-Highland cows. There were nine employees on the farm and one who milked the Jersey cows for the estate's milk and did jobs around the big hoose. There were two masons, two joiners, two sawmillers, two gardeners and two keepers, which made for a thriving community with a full school, a good membership of Cairndow's lovely hexagonal church and a good-going local pub. How things have changed. Sadly now there are only a few ewes left and one shepherd and the estate has been split up. Having said that, the remaining estate side has gone from strength to strength thanks to Johnny, John's son, whose joiners are turning out the most delightful wood articles from the famous Ardkinglas trees, and the trees themselves are being replaced in a big planting programme. This is one excellent diversification from sheep. But when I was back in that lovely wee church to say good-bye to my good friend and master, the late Lord Glenkinglas, I had a few minutes to contemplate the changes that have happened over the years, and though some have been excellent, not all of them were for the better of district or the Highlands I fear.

When I arrived at the estate in 1959 I had quite an uphill task getting the estate and farm staff to pull together, as they had been run as two separate entities. There always has been rivalry between personal staff (butlers, house-staff, gardeners, grooms, etc) and outside staff (shepherds, cattlemen, sawmillers etc.), as the latter always think the former are spoilt and the former, who have never had a union, always think the latter are overpaid.

They were a happy bunch of men to work with, but West Highlanders don't have, shall we say, that sense of urgency that I was used to with my Speyside men. I always thought it was a matter of the climate, but having

The author, then Factor for the Rt Hon. Michael Noble, Secretary of State for Scotland, with the Ardkinglas male champion Highland bull at the 1962 Highland Show

worked there for five years of my life I now know it to be so. When I went there I went charging around getting shepherds organised for the gatherings, taking the sheep off the hill. By my last year I was lying in my bed saying to myself, 'You're the Factor, Coutts, let the head shepherd organise his men.' I remember tearing a strip off one employee for being constantly late and he disarmingly said in a lovely Highland voice, 'Do you know, Captain, the wife chust said the other morning the Captain will have something to say to you one of these days'. Oh! the charm of those folk.

Ardkinglas house, where John lived, is beautifully situated looking down Loch Fyne. It was built by Sir Robert Lorimer on the site of an old Campbell castle and is a real gem. I used to report there every morning and let John know what the farm staff were up to, and he kept his eye on the estate staff. But my favourite memories of the big house were when Michael had his daughters' coming-out dances held there, at which I was the MC. The house was floodlit and couldn't have looked more lovely. The gardens, both there and at Strone where Michael lived, were famous for their azaleas and rhododendrons, and in the Ardkinglas garden is the tallest tree in Britain.

But it was the farming side that attracted me. Michael had been so busy with his Parliamentary duties that he had left everything to his head shepherd, and suffice it to say that I didn't manage to get many improvements carried out until we dispensed with his services and appointed Donald McPherson, who should have been in charge years before. He did such a good job, after having been on the estate all his life, that I managed to get him a B.E.M.

One of the snags with a large stock of ewes is to get the right type of ram to suit them, and as the previous head shepherd had been buying in every market in the country it was decided we should go to one of the top breeders and ask him to keep his second-best cut for us. We argued that they were bred the same way as his best ones which, of course, he would want to sell in his usual market of Lanark, Newton Stewart, Perth, Stirling or wherever. We plumped for my old friend Jim Wilson, whose Whitehope rams were selling very well—they were the 'bare-coated' type of Blackface. For the uninitiated, the Blackfaced breed are the most numerous in Great Britain, and within the breed, because of the different terrains in which they are bred, they have different types. The bare-coated type, which came from the Galloway hills originally, are usually the ones which leave the best milking ewes and, as wool prices have remained static, the weight of wool is no longer so important. It is more important to have a good milky ewe. As we needed about 150 rams, allowing for deaths and casualties, the reader can understand how important it was to buy the right sheep. Duncan Stewart's great saying was, 'Ben, don't buy old so-and-so's rams, they are so well fed they'll fall in the first open ditch because they'll think it's a food trough.'

The Ardkinglas Estate runs from sea level (as Loch Fyne is tidal) up to Ben Ime, which is over 3,000 feet above sea level, and I enjoyed nothing better than the mornings in June when we were gathering for the lamb markings. Each hirsel was of some 500 ewes. Half the shepherds went out one side and half the other to surround the hirsel, because if an old Blackfaced ewe means to evade capture it takes a damned good dog to stop her. To be out on these high tops of a June morning with the whole of Scotland, in all its majesty, spread out beneath you, is pure magic. No wonder the Psalmist wrote, 'I to the hills'.

When you get near to the sheep fank (the pen in which the sheep are handled) the hirsel is cut into two or three cuts, as it is impossible to get 500 ewes and their lambs into a fank in one drove. Even then little bunches of lambs keep making a break for freedom. Once in the fank, at the marking gathering, comes the lengthy business of mothering up the neighbours' lambs. On the big Highland sheep farms there are no march or boundary fences, for two reasons: they would be far too costly to erect and a good snowfall just about flattens them. Luckily most hill ewes have a wonderful 'hefting' instinct, i.e. they graze mostly in a confined area and are seldom far from it. A ewe lamb born on a certain spot will graze in that area and will 'heft' to it, and in turn her ewe lamb will do the same. Having said that, as in the human race, there are always rogues that stray and become lost sheep, so when one gathers a hirsel one invariably has some of the neighbours' ewes gathered in as well. As one is about to mark his lambs with a lug mark, which each farm has and which is an identifying ear mark, it is imperative that one doesn't mark one's neighbour's lambs, which would be sheep-stealing. Hence the 'mothering up', which can be a long and tiring proceeding when one is longing to get on with one's own marking, and usually on the same day shearing the ewe hoggs and yeld ewes (the ones that haven't had lambs, or have lost them). Some shepherds are wonderful 'kenners'—they recognise and remember sheep which to the layman all look alike. If one is lucky and the neighbour's ewe comes in in front of a shepherd that was a good 'kenner' then he would remember the lamb. For my part I always carried a coloured marking stick and caught up the lamb and put a mark on it.

Then the clippings in July were always great fun, as shepherds vied with each other who could shear the fastest. Nowadays all the shearing is done with contract shearers, so that the social element has rather gone out of the occasion. Shepherds do fantastically long hours at that time of year, starting off at crack of dawn to gather, a day's work in itself, then sorting out different classes of sheep and the clipping and often not finishing until dark, only to start again the next day to do the same all over again at another hirsel. Now that there are so many large sheds the threat of rain is not so serious, but with Argyll's famous 100-plus inches of rain in the year I've seen hours and hours spent herding ewes on any little knoll to dry them with the slightest breeze that was blowing—one can't pack a wet sheep fleece for obvious reasons. It's interesting that all the old stone-walled sheep fanks were always sited beside a small knoll where sheep could be dried out.

When I went to Ardkinglas first, I was never home from mid-August onwards. The lambs and then the draft ewes had to be sold. As transport has always been the bugbear of the Highlands, and one which successive governments have done nothing to alleviate, we tried to transport as many of our sheep as possible with our own lorry. We had thousands of sheep to sell

A typical scene from the Fifties, a flock of Blackfaced ewes being gathered. It is one that might not be seen so frequently in the coming years, thanks to changes in farming practice

and the lorry only held 100 at a time, so you will realise that I spent an awful lot of time away from home. The big snag about this was not the travelling time but the waste of time hanging around waiting for one's sheep to be sold. It was because of this that I suggested to John and Michael that we should hold our own sale on the estate. Although this was a novel idea in the Highlands, as I wrote earlier, I had a good friend in Wales, a Captain Bennett Evans Pynlimmon, who had run a successful sale on his own farm. He had used the slogan, 'Pasture lamb is fatter but mountain lamb is sweeter', to advertise his venture.

A sheep sale takes a lot of organisation, as sheep have to be drawn into their different classes: top lambs, mid lambs, shott lambs, ewe lambs etc, and then have to be kept separately, so it is essential to have some good in-bye land on which to keep them which is properly fenced. A good large building is also essential in which to hold the sale ring. Both of these requisites were available at Ardkinglas, and I'm proud to say that twenty years later the sale was still being carried on, but as large areas of land had been afforested on Ardkinglas with a resultant drop in the sheep stock, two neighbours had joined the sale to keep up the numbers required to tempt the buyers to come. I will never forget to my dying day the first sale, as it was one of those wet autumns that only Argyll can produce and the timing of gathering the sheep stock was crucial to the sale. If one gathered too soon one would overstock the arable fields and the lambs, as a result, wouldn't look so well. If one left it too late then the sale day would be past. For five days the mist was down on every hill and not one man or dog went to a single hirsel. I stood watching the rain with eight disconsolate shepherds round me. They had never been too keen on the sale in the first place, because it stopped them getting their days off at the market and meeting all their pals, so you can imagine my name was mud. All came right in the end, and by dint of using two squads, one to gather the sheep and one to handle them in the fank, we managed to have the sheep ready with but a few hours to spare. That first sale was a cracker, and as Michael was Secretary of State it hit the headlines.

If I were younger I would be in the forefront of any group or association telling the consumer what a clean, sweet, tasty morsel a gigot or chop of a hill lamb can be. It is reared on the open hill with no chance of contamination with all those so-called horrible things like artificial fertilisers etc. What better slogan than my Welsh friend's 'Pasture lamb is fatter but mountain lamb is sweeter'? The hill farmer can't diversify, so needs the extra bawbees his quality product can bring in.

The large building in which we held the sale ring is now famous countrywide, if not worldwide, as the H.Q. of the Loch Fyne Oyster Bar Company. What a marvellous job Johnny Noble has done in revitalising this area, where he now employs more people than were employed in the days when the Estate was centred mainly on agriculture. When I sit in the restaurant at a table which has fitted into it the lovely wooden 'trevises', as we called the old partitions we had between the cows in the old Clachan building—which, when the cattleman was off sick in 1962, I had to milk and then muck out—I say to myself, 'It's better to tuck in than muck out!'

Ardkinglas was not only a good sheep farm, it also had some excellent sport. The rivers Fyne and Kinglas were both more than useful 'spate' fishing rivers, especially the former, and as the family couldn't always fish it themselves we used to let a lot of fishing. We always managed a day or two grouse shooting and Anne, Michael's wife, used to sit beside a hill burn after lunch and pluck the morning's bag, into the burn, so that we could have grouse for the evening meal on the 12th. Unfortunately, as on so many West Highland estates, the grouse are now almost non-existent, mainly because of the increase in vermin, especially the 'hoodie' crow which not only is a ravenous egg eater but will gouge the eye out a sheep that is couped on its back, or take the tongue out of a new born lamb if it doesn't get to its feet quickly. And yet some do-gooders want hoodies protected, little realising how many wee birds' eggs they take. I hate them and would sanction any means of persecuting them: they have caused me endless problems. They only have one enemy and that is man.

The stalking on the estate was also good, although the stags were not numerous, as it was primarily a hind forest. There were always one or two stags of twenty stone shot around 25 September. These were obviously beasts that had wintered down in the hazel woods around Lochgoilhead, as they were seen to cross the Rest and Be Thankful road to the hind forest.

What fun we used to have both at Strone and in the village. Michael had a more than useful voice and knew all the *Songs of the North* by heart. With one of his daughters playing the piano we had some super evenings. The whole family had a wonderful sense of humour and had nicknames for almost everyone. 'Snaillie' was the oddman who wasn't exactly greased lightning, 'Donald the Cook' was the shepherd who was famous for getting out of the hard work in the fank by announcing he 'would just put on the fire for the tea' and would disappear for an hour. 'The Stuffed Eagle' was a neighbour with a prominent proboscis, who always pronounced 'stuffed' as 'stiffed'. I got away lightly by being 'Daaad', as Donald, my youngest, had a very Scottish voice and pronounced Dad that way.

The village too had all sorts of things on the go. They had two excellent rinks of curlers and we had some marvellous matches against Inveraray when the curling pond froze; if not, we went to Glasgow to curl inside. (In Glasgow one of our great adversaries was the infamous Captain McRae with Otter Ferry Rink. He it was who made such a nuisance of himself as a POW of the Turks in the First War that they released him. He also flew an aircraft home to Balemore and crash-landed it on his lawn. And he it was who, as owner of a distillery, planted a bottle of whisky at the end of each rink: and opposing skips wondered why their side were playing so badly!) In 1963 we curled for 6 to 8 weeks on a curling pond, now overgrown, which was right beside Loch Fyne. Loch Fyne is a salt loch which, with the fresh water coming in from the Fyne and Kinglas rivers, was frozen a foot or two from the shore.

We have had a few nights of frosts below −10° in this year of 2001, but 1963 was the last year of what I call a real frost. That was the year that the water supply of an old mucker of mine, Neil Usher, had packed up, and he had, with his wife, to fill the house tank with buckets from the burn, some twenty-odd buckets each time, 'and one always spilled over my head, Ben,' he said. So as not to use up water flushing the loo he was answering the call of nature in the snow, when he was literally blown over by a grouse travelling at 60 m.p.h. being chased by a peregrine falcon! Oh, that one of our modern nature T.V. shows had been there to film that.

As Michael was busy in Parliament I had to represent him at the Captain's funeral. As he was a Kintail McRae, the body had to be transported from Otter Ferry to Kintail over four ferries. You can imagine how the end of the cortège were speeding to try to keep up. When eventually I reached the graveyard all was finished and the Captain was interred. I said to his chauffeur, an old friend, 'What would the Captain think of going at that speed?' He replied, 'He'd like the speed fine, but he's never passed so many pubs in his life'!

Carpet 'bools' were also popular and there were concerts galore. As in so many Highland villages many cottages are now summer holiday homes or are occupied by incomers and the life of the village is not as it was, but one can't turn back the clock. Like Laggan, the village now has a new hall, and both the rural communities with which I've been connected are going strong, thanks to those same people we used to call 'white settlers'. They are more willing in many cases to become involved in running affairs than some residents of the old school. Things are changing dramatically in Highland communities, and if I were, as I used to be, part of the village organising committee, I'd be all for anyone who was willing to put his or her shoulder to the wheel. But old ideas die hard, and some oldies hate the thought of change.

Sara married when we were at Cairndow, and we had a reception at our house for our immediate friends which was well done by my good friend Donald Ross from L'Aperitif in Edinburgh, and at night we had a dance in the Cairndow Hall with free drink for all the estate employees. Such was their capacity for whisky, which they could hold well, that the Hall occasion cost more than the official reception by miles.

After five years I was sad to leave Ardkinglas and especially Michael, as he had been more than generous to me. Among other things he was an acknowledged wine connoisseur, and he not only taught me a lot about wine but gave me regular presents of burgundy right up to his death in 1984. Michael said that he was leaving me some of his burgundy in his will, but I've never seen it!

Relationships between Creina and myself had worsened. She was able to get away from Cairndow to enjoy orchestral music and study art. As both were alien to me we decided that, as the family were all away from home, we should part.

29

Uganda

During my last year at Ardkinglas I decided to get away for a bit to consider the future of my marriage. As my brother Fleming, known as Wally in East Africa, was Governor General in Uganda I decided to give him a visit. He had asked me more than once to go and have a look at some of the livestock programmes they were carrying out. My youngest brother Philip was also there and it was a wonderful chance to see them. I had no feelings of scrounging, as both their families had stayed with us on different occasions. The story is told of Alastair, Philip's boy, being cajoled by his mother to sup up his soup, but the lad would keep staring at me and his mother said, 'Why do you keep staring like that?' and he replied, 'But Uncle Ben doesn't drink like a fish.'

I decided to visit the Brintons on the way out, and it was wonderful to see them again. They had retired to Cairo, but they took me up the desert to their cottage at Burg el Arab. It was just after a shower and the desert was a mass of wild flowers. One wonders how they last so long in the sand without rain. We also went for a day trip up the Nile, and although I had passed that way on my way to the Sudan, I was now looking at that most fantastic piece of arable land, the Nile delta, through the eyes of a farmer and not of a soldier. Astonishing to think that for thousands of years that small, but fertile, patch has been tilled in much the same manner and has fed that huge nation. On the third day we went racing: the horses were all Arabs, 'little white mice' the Judge called them. He took me to his club. Although strictly teetotal himself he was not against drinking. I was able to sample once more those wonderful John Collins, which seem to taste so super in Egypt, and to sit watching the native dhows slip past, again something that seems to have been part of Egypt's history since biblical times. Of all the foreign countries I've visited, which must be some twenty or more, Egypt has the greatest contrast of old and new side by side, with its donkeys and dhows right next to its Hilton Hotel and Cadillacs. I was glad I stopped off at Cairo as I wasn't to see the Judge again, and when I was wounded and thought I would never be 100 per cent fit again the Judge's wise advice was more than welcome.

On my arrival at Uganda for the first (and probably the last) time the red carpet was laid out for me. As Fleming was the Queen's representative and he was there to meet me he walked on the red carpet, most impressive.

BOTHY TO BIG BEN

The airport at Entebbe was to become famous in later years when the Israelis made their fantastically successful raid on it, a raid that must go down in history as one of the most brilliant of its kind in planning and execution. (The whole exercise is thrillingly written up by my friend Max Hastings in a book with the title *Yoni*, of which I'm proud to possess a signed copy.) When I saw it it was extremely well kept, as were all the buildings and hotels back in 1963, but I fear things are not the same now. Government House was a lovely building, spacious and airy. The staff were kindness itself, and having been in service myself I know one can enjoy serving people without being servile. Fleming was virtually having a year's holiday, as Independence had been declared and he, having been the last Governor of Uganda, was left for a year as Governor General, so that he had any amount of time to show me round. Jinty, his wife, was kindness itself and was sad to hear that things weren't going well with my marriage.

It seemed so strange that when we went anywhere everyone had to bow or curtsey but, of course, my brother and sister-in-law were the Queen's representatives. As for going into a hotel for a beer, as I suggested on my first day out, hands were raised in horror at the mere suggestion, and the country cousin was severely told off by the Governor General.

A happy compromise was reached when it was arranged that Fleming should visit an area right up in the north of Uganda with a view to the area's potential as a game park. This idea had been mooted by none other than Milton Obote. Fleming knew that once out of Kampala we could act as normal brothers. He also managed to wangle it that Philip could accompany us. Philip had joined the Uganda Colonial Service straight after the war, only to find, to his embarrassment, that his big brother was promoted from being second-in-command in Kenya to being Governor in Uganda.

The area to be visited, graced by the lovely name of Opottiepot, was on the northern tip of Uganda and bordered Kenya and the Sudan. It was swarming with game. The Governor's private plane was only meant to carry two passengers, and how it managed to take off carrying three six-foot-three Couttses is still a mystery to those who watched it. On the way north we had to touch down as the Governor General wanted me to inspect a beef scheme that had recently been initiated, and he had to inspect the Uganda Rifles Regiment who were on exercise. The Sergeant-Major I shall never forget: he was one Idi Amin who was to make world-wide notoriety in later years. Brother Philip tells the story of how he was scraping the barrel to field a rugby fifteen, and as Amin's company were stationed where Philip was then District Commissioner he decided he was the right sort of build to teach to become a lock forward. Much to Philip's chagrin, Idi scored a try over his own line!

The beef set-up was one that could be followed in many parts of the world because of its simplicity. There was a young Scottish vet, newly out of college. There was a set of weighing scales. There was a tin trunk such as was used by officers in the First World War for their kit. This held the money, and on top of it sat a Ugandan Rifleman with a loaded rifle. He and the box were enclosed in a barbed wire hut which was roofed with straw. The tribesmen, mostly completely naked or at best wearing a loin cloth, big handsome chaps as hill men so often are, came in with their one steer. After this the procedure was as in any market in the world: the most awful haggling went on as to the price for the steer. The young and very inexperienced vet stated the government price. The stockman would then take away his beast and try to sell him at the local market (and have a few kaffir beers at the same time). The vet had his orders when to shut up shop and just prior to that there would be a queue waiting to sell their cattle to the Government. I felt I could be home in Scotland, where farmers so often refuse a bid only to bring back the cattle at the end of the sale and take less money for them.

What impressed me was the type of cattle. I have been in so many countries that I can't remember all the names of the breeds, but they were big with great tops and real backsides and docile. All these cattle were for export: and now I understand Uganda is importing beef. Woe is me is all I can say. That was a unique scheme that worked well in a district renowned for its stock and stockmen. But talking of the latter, I wouldn't like to pick a fight with them: they were big, proud, fit men.

A contingent of the Uganda Rifles accompanied us on the last stage of the journey to Opottiepot and the camps they set up were quite excellent. One wanted for nothing, and I can see why so many people with the necessary money enjoy going on safari. The evenings were the happiest time. After the heat of the day there was the magic of the African night with all the different animal noises, for the countryside came to life at night. The Colonel and his second-in-command both brought their wives with them. Which was a pity, not that we chauvinists wanted to tell dirty stories, but the bush is a man's world and it meant two camps virtually. If there were to be women there, we Coutts brothers would rather have had the two Coutts wives as companions, for they are excellent company. Notwithstanding, the three of us used to get together last thing at night and jaw about family matters, school memories etc. Because of the war we hadn't seen each other for over twenty years.

On arrival at Opottiepot we were met by the local game warden, a charming young man whose knowledge of the district and game was first class. He was also to prove to be a very brave man without taking any foolish chances. There was a hut in which we ate and our tents were pitched around it. The 'loo' was an old thunderbox, which made me feel quite at home, but I don't know how the Colonel's lady felt, or the Governor General.

The next few days were some of the most enthralling and exciting days I've ever spent. As that particular district was so out of the way it was completely unspoilt, and the only big snag from Uganda's point of view was the poaching that went on. Hence the presence of the Uganda Rifles, who were scouring the country looking for the poachers. They sooner or later gave their position away with their camp fires, as they were forever having a 'brew up' (or its equivalent in Uganda).

We were shown every possible species that there was, but the highlight for me was undoubtedly the elephants and their young. We were taken far too close for my liking, but we all had complete faith in the Game Warden and he always proved right, but I still shudder to think what happens when the Land Rover engine stalls. Stampeding water buffalo was another awe-inspiring sight, and I understand they never deviate, so woe betide anyone or anything that gets in their path. I thought we were uncomfortably close. Poor Philip got a nasty touch of malaria so didn't get as much fun out of the trip as Fleming and I did.

I suppose it is natural for every one of us to enjoy being spoilt, but I have never enjoyed it more than on that trip. We were a happy bunch although, as I say, we would rather have been 'men only', as every safari was mapped out so that it wouldn't be too tiring for the girls, and when one went to the 'loo' one had to hold out a red flag to show that it was occupied. All in all it was a trip to remember, and anyone who hasn't been lucky enough to sit under the African stars discussing the day's safari, planning the next one and listening to the animal cries and shrieks has missed something. But for most it is out of their financial range, and I was a lucky laddie.

Sir Walter Fleming Coutts duly wrote his report, saying what a wonderful area Opottiepot would be for a Game Reserve, but it was not to be. Milton Obote left the country for a conference and Idi Amin took over, with the disastrous results known world-wide. Uganda was known as the Rose of Africa and with good reason. Although I wasn't there long enough to get to know it intimately, I hope and pray it regains some of its former standing in that vast continent. Happily things have recently changed for the better, and now Uganda is one of the most stable of the African countries.

I'm only sad that neither of my brothers who worked for and loved that country so dearly are alive to see that improvement today. In other parts of Africa things don't look so good: the eternal tribal warfare continues. Who am I, a Scot, to criticise? Our country was torn apart by clan strife for all too long, and yet some people think they can sort out Africa's problems overnight.

30
IWS Nuffield Scholarship

With the impending break-up of my marriage I felt unsettled and, although I had been to Uganda in 1963 for a holiday, I felt that when I left Ardkinglas in 1964 (the Noble brothers and I had agreed my term of office should be for a five-year period) I wanted time to think about my future.

I saw an advertisement in the *Farmers' Weekly* seeking a Nuffield Scholar, to be backed by the International Wool Secretariat, to spend two months in Australia, one in New Zealand and one in South Africa, studying their wool production and at the same time lecturing in these countries on the student's own type of farming. The advertisement stated that the student should be between the ages of 21 and 35; I was then 48 but I thought I'd have a bash, wrote away and was thoroughly surprised to be called to London for an interview. I've always been a jammy rascal, but on this occasion I was jammier than usual: the chairman of the interviewing board was an ex-Sussex Yeoman. And I was jammy twice over: I think I'm the only person ever to be awarded two Nuffield scholarships. But I have always worked on the theory that 'bullshit baffles brains'!

This break was exactly what was needed for me, and I threw myself into the tour with all the enthusiasm I have been lucky enough to have been given. The plane journey to Australia, as anyone knows who has done it, is long and tiring so I stopped off at Singapore to see Sara and to be present at her second son's christening. The plan was that I should do one month in Australia, go to New Zealand, then back to Australia and finally fly out to South Africa from Perth.

I arrived in Sydney, second to San Francisco as a favourite city, and, as it was a Sunday, I had the day to myself and I had some mail waiting for me. Among it was one from Al Gardiner whose acquaintance I had made on the *Princess Beatrix* at the North Africa landings. In his letter he said he had seen me on a TV programme which had been relayed to Australia, and if ever I happened to be there would I call him up. So I lifted the phone and called him; he thought I was speaking from Scotland. He asked me to a barbecue lunch, I said I'd like to go to a Presbyterian church, and after a pause he said there was one outside the station at Woronga and he would meet me outside after the service. When we got back to his house he had a drink waiting for him and when he asked me what I'd have I said, 'Same as you, Al.' 'But it's a pink gin,' he said. 'I know', said I, 'that's why I want it.' 'But you've just been to the Scots Presbyterian church and I thought you must have gone teetotal since the war, as that gang won't allow drink on the Sabbath.' We all fell about laughing. That was a most auspicous reunion: years later Al and his wife were to be more than kind to my son Shaun when he had an extremely nasty fall from a horse and was sent to Woronga Hospital for treatment.

The Australian Wool Board was in charge of my itinerary and, like all people in all countries, they want one to see nothing but the best. I feel this is a pity; when I get foreigners to Scotland I invariably try to show them some of the less favoured areas, otherwise they go away with the impression that farming, as carried out in the favoured eastern arable counties, is typical of Scotland.

Naturally I was shown the wool grading system and the intricacies of the wool trade, but it was when I went out to the stations that I really felt at home. I loved my stay in Tasmania where some really good reclamation work has been undertaken. While I was there I managed to put a young man in touch with Frank Young, the noted Galloway breeder, to their mutual advantage, and some good Galloway stock made their way out there. Naturally I spent a lot of time in New South Wales and one of my fond memories is the quaint sounding Goonoogoonoo, pronounced Gunnagnu, where Trevor Smidt was the manager. He took me all over in his private aeroplane and we had a day at the Tamworth Show together where I've never seen so many private aeroplanes. At these shows the Wool Board always had a stand, and Les Batten, who had been kindness itself in organising the Australian trip, was there with his team of shearers.

In this country we produce sheep for lamb and mutton, but in Australia wool is king, hence the reason for the Merino being worshipped as a breed. We judge our sheep on body conformation, they judge theirs on wool classification. While staying at the Uadry Stud I was shown a ram that had cost a vast amount of money and the stud manager was extolling his wonderful wool. 'But he's wrong on his hind legs,' I said. 'If you feed him too much he won't be able to tup a ewe.' I thought Tom was going to have apoplexy, but we came to like and respect each other. Before the advent of the Australian dollar, when their currency was pounds, shillings and pence, the Australian shilling had a Merino ram's head on it and the Uadry men were justly proud that the ram was bred on their stud. By the time I was there they were not the top stud, but in all pedigree stock breeding the place at the top keeps changing as new and younger stockmen battle to climb the ladder. It's very hard to stay at the top.

It used to amuse me that the idea of the average Australian flockmaster was that we 'Pommy' farmers looked after a mere hundred ewes. When I said I was responsible for 6,000 (as on leaving home I was managing 2,000 for Lady Wyfold as well as the Ardkinglas stock) they viewed me in a very different light, in fact almost with deference if I was asked to speak publicly, for the average Australian sheep farmer is a wonderfully hard worker but not usually a polished public speaker. I was sorry not to be able to visit the Northern Territory where my son Shaun has made his home, but distances are so huge. As it was, a great deal of time was taken up in travelling. One of the worst journeys I had was on a small gauge railway to Uadry. It took nearly all day and I was sitting on a wooden seat. As the temperature was in the hundreds my story of 'I wish I hadna goed' was much in my mind. One was literally tossed from side to side.

I did, however, visit a stud in Queensland managed by a Mr Simpson. By an extraordinary coincidence his son Rupert was to be Secretary of the Australian Aberdeen-Angus Society at the same time as I was Secretary of the parent Society in Scotland. The heat, as always, was my bogey. I had to spend all too much time getting out of the sun, and I was mighty glad to be presented with a big 'Aussie' hat belonging to the Wool Classer at Uadry. When the sun shines, as it occasionally does in Perthshire, I still wear it with pride.

I found New Zealand so Scottish, especially in the South, that it was unbelievable. Wearing a kilt once more proved the best possible passport. As in Australia so in New Zealand—the Wool Board members took me in hand and played pass the parcel. What hosts they were!

I was staying for a few days with a wonderful family called the McHardys. The guest room was across the lawn from the big house: I was told to have a rest and to turn up in time for the evening meal. When I came into the big room I came to a dead stop and pointing to the portrait above the fireplace said, 'Douglas, did your family happen to come from Strathdon in Aberdeenshire?' He answered 'Yes, but how in all the world did you know?' I was looking at the spitting image of one of my dearest friends, Robbie McHardy, who had been my shepherd at Gaskbeg and even yet does an odd day's work for me. It was the old Highland story repeating itself: one member or more going overseas and one staying at home. Douglas McHardy was a highly thought of Wool Board member who ran an excellent farm. Robbie could have done the same thing had it been his grandfather who went to New Zealand and not Douglas's. Robbie is one of nature's gentlemen.

Many of the New Zealanders I met I was to meet again, as many sheep farmers kept Aberdeen-Angus cattle as well.

A must for me was a visit to Te Awamutu to visit the Wynyard family, where only one son remained: three were sacrificed in New Zealand's Divisional Cavalry, including my dear friend Jim. How many New Zealand families were decimated, a thing that is often forgotten in this country. Another wartime association that I had to renew was with Kel Nelson, who was always bumming about the marvellous fishing he could get on Lake Taupo, far better than anything in Scotland. I stayed with him and we fished for two days and never even saw a rise.

At this time my son Shaun came to New Zealand on what turned out to be the last boat of pedigree cattle that came from Great Britain to the Antipodes. I luckily told him to have a year training under New Zealand farmers and then to think again, but that I thought he shouldn't think of coming back to Scotland as I saw no future for him in farming: I had no farm and no capital to hand him. The lovely story he tells is of the first station on which he managed to get a job. He was asked if he could ride: like his father, he was an adept liar and said 'Yes'.

He set off on his horse but hadn't cinched his girths up tight enough and finished up underneath his horse plus the saddle. I am proud to think that he overcame this initial failure and went on to be put in charge of the Mount Isa Mineral Company property with its 17,000 breeding cows, and before that proved his worth in rough-riding competitions in the Northern Territory in Australia. He has been there so long that with his musical ear he has picked up the accent, so that now he sounds more Aussie than a genuine 'Oz'. Sadly, after his successful running of the Mount Isa property, as in all too many walks of life the accountants came in to assess the situation. Whereas he had a station full of staff, about 15 from memory, many of them married, which meant there was a school and a resident cook, the accountants reckoned that it would make more money if the station was run with a reduced staff. What happened? The number of children at the school dropped to such a level that it was closed, and as Shaun had an 'afterthought' of a daughter he gave in his notice and moved to Katherine, where his daughter is being well-educated. He has been head-hunted for other jobs, but why do accountants always look at the bottom line, and ignore human beings?

One of the most treasured memories of my visit to New Zealand was to that great stockman and character Jack Evans. I had met him at the Perth Bull Sales many years before, and a visit to Palmerston North was a must as he was Dalgety's Chief Stock Buyer. It was Christmas time and I was expected to go to the famous Manitou Race meeting: they knew I had a background of racehorse breeding. Jack, the crafty old fox that he was, sent me to the meeting with his Company's racing manager, excusing himself on other duties. I got back in, can we say, extremely good fettle: wearing the kilt I had presented most of the cups during the afternoon, as they were mostly sponsored by a certain brand of whisky with which I had been associated back in the Thirties. I had no sooner come back to Jack and said, 'I've done my stuff, let's have an early bed' than he said, 'Ben, you are the honoured guest in Palmerston North and we're off on a party.'

Lest the reader thinks that Nuffield Scholars live a fast and loose life, nothing could be further from the truth. The truth is that everyone is so hospitable it's hard to make them realise that they, as hosts and hostesses, only have one night but the Nuffield Scholar, in my case, has four months to survive and must not only be gracious to his hosts and hostesses but do his job, which is to learn about farming from his overseas hosts, at the same time projecting a picture of his own style of farming at home. All the host countries were so kind to me that it would be hard to differentiate between them, but I remember my final night in 'Windy Wellington' when the New Zealand Wool Board were determined to give me a proper send-off and gave me one super party. I had to get up early the next morning for a plane to Australia and I was staying in one of those ghastly hotels in Wellington (and in the Sixties they were ghastly).

The scene was something like this: Coutts, not feeling too well, had set his alarm for some horrendous time that wasn't many hours after he kipped down. Alarm goes and Coutts is wandering around in his pyjamas not sure whether it's Christmas or Easter. Enter very stout lady resembling a Gauleiter in the Second World War saying 'Tea', and shoving down the well known British and New Zealand brew beloved by many but hated by Coutts. Minutes later in comes Gauleiter looking more formidable than ever. Meantime Coutts has managed to discard his pyjamas and is standing 'starko bollico'. The Gauleiter, without taking a look at the naked figure, whisks away the empty cup saying, 'Finished!' This, I'm afraid to say, was my last memory of New Zealand. But what super memories I have, and not only from my war experiences, but also those in 1963-64, which leave me with New Zealanders very, but very, high on the list of the people I've met in this short spell we have on earth.

My second spell in Australia was more over in West Australia, and I was sorely tempted to make my home there. At that time land was cheap and generally speaking that part has a fairly useful rainfall. When I got home I did a series of broadcasts on my trip. One family who heard me asked to meet me: after discussion they went out there and have made a great success of their farm. When Sal and I went back to Australia later we went to see this family. The farmer who had heard my broadcast had lost his wife, so he had moved into a tin bungalow and rightly allowed his son and daughter-in-law to live in the farmhouse. Sal and I were to spend the night in the bungalow. I had always thought of Australia as being a country that is too hot for my comfort, but how wrong I was that night. The beds hadn't been slept in for 'yonks' and there was a frost. As the dampness of my sheets turned to steam from the heat of my body I said to Sal, who also wasn't sleeping: 'At least we'll get some porridge and bacon and egg to heat us in the morning.' Imagine my chagrin when at breakfast our host said 'Since I came to Oz I only eat apples for breakfast.' Not my happiest memory of a fabulous country!

At that time the Western Australian farmers were just beginning to realise the potential of breeding sheep for mutton instead of wool, as Perth was beginning to expand. I was asked to judge a carcase competition, something I had never done before, but so bad were most of the carcases that there was one outstanding winner, which I found out later was a Southdown and had no Merino blood in it as had most of them.

In the Sixties there was only one plane a week to South Africa and I nearly missed it, although I was at the aerodrome in plenty of time. I was waiting in the restaurant for the flight to be called, and I found out later that the tannoy system was out of order. Quite by chance I walked out to find everyone else was on board and ,for the first time, and I hope the last, I was rushed across the tarmac as the steps of the aeroplane were being lifted. I shudder to think what the South African Wool Board would have done with their wonderfully organised but very tight month's schedule had I been a week late.

The reason why I had lingered so long in the departure lounge was that I had caught up with Adrian Lamb with whom I had shared digs in Edinburgh in the Thirties. He was going on to pass his medical exams and I to fail my veterinary ones. Adrian specialised in the ophthalmic side of medicine and was the top eye specialist in Perth when I met up with him in 1963. I was able to show him a treasured possession of mine, a receipt from dear Miss Holmes who 'took in' students in Edinburgh. It came to £1.5.6d for five days full board, changed days!

31

South Africa and a Homecoming

Counting my two visits during the war I have been in South Africa on five occasions, but I saw more of the country during my visit in 1964 than on any of the other visits. No one who is a Christian could possibly back apartheid, but many people in this country don't realise how many white South Africans were working like mad to better the situation.

One of my stops was with a lawyer turned farmer who had been legal adviser to the legendary General Smuts, and he was a fund of knowledge. He was one of those octogenarians who always had to be learning something new, and he was taking to farming like a duck to water. He not only had sheep but a more than useful vineyard which required a large cistern for irrigation. In this we used to swim every morning after we had had a short run; the old boy was determined to keep fit and he loved his food and drink. His love of drink included having two large sherries with his breakfast every morning, a habit I found quite catching when I stayed with him. All meals were taken outdoors, and his 'Alto Rouge' red wine was distinctly 'moreish'. He lived in that loveliest of parts, the Stellenbosch area, with its lush vegetation and neat vineyards.

I remember another of my hosts for a completely different reason. It was over near De Witts Berg, where most of the farmers I met were descended from the Dutch Boers whom the British had fought in the Boer war. This farmer, himself of Dutch extraction, had arranged a 'Briflis' (barbecue) in my honour at which I was to speak about Scottish hill farming. After I had finished not one person came forward to speak to me, they just huddled in a corner speaking Afrikaans and left me with a very embarrassed hostess. It may be a coincidence, but it was on a farm in that area that I was to see Africans treated badly—the only time, as most farmers were excellent with their labour. In this incident the farmer in question used a horse-hide whip on an African worker's bare back, so I packed my back and left. I was lucky enough to hitch a lift, and was even more lucky to be let off at a farm where the occupant couldn't stand the farmer that I had left, and gave me a great welcome.

Some of the finest Merino wool in the world comes from a district in

South Africa called the Karoo. It is almost a desert with very sparse vegetation but this goes with fine wool. It was up in this area that I was asked to officiate at a show: it was great fun not knowing a single soul because when one judges at home one is bound to know someone. Their horse classes were of a very high standard. The cattle in that area were all the native Afrikander, which were originally bred as draught oxen but have been improved over the years so that they are very useful beef animals. The sheep were a mixed bunch: some good Merinos and a lot of fat-tailed native sheep, which I'm sure I judged badly. And there were lots of super mohair goats. There were many ostrich farms and I was amazed how fast the ostriches could run. I saw two local boys racing each other on their backs, which was part of the afternoon's entertainment.

But I suppose because I am basically a Highlander, if not by birth then by inclination, I liked the farms up in the Drakensberge mountains, and so attracted to them was I that fifteen years later I was to take my wife Sally back to them for a holiday, one of the best holidays we've had. At Uderdepost I visited one of the most up-to-date animal research stations. This is badly needed in South Africa, as they have a big animal disease problem. On the IWS trip I made my only visit to Port Elizabeth where the main wool warehouses are situated. A namesake of mine was my most generous and interesting host and told me all about the South African wool trade.

At the end of my month in South Africa the IWS had very kindly arranged, as a 'thank you', a few days in the Kruger Game Reserve. Unfortunately it wasn't a good time of year for seeing game but I was glad of the few days' rest. In any case I'd already seen every kind of big game in Uganda, including lion, elephant, cheetah, water buffalo, hippo, giraffe, zebra etc. and every imaginable type of antelope. Altogether that was an unforgettable experience, but had spoilt me for when Sal later got me to go on safari to Kenya.

The farmer with whom I was staying just previously warned me that the Park had no licence, so I went in with my bags well packed with the excellent and cheap South African wines and sherries. It was a quiet time of year, and in the mini-bus there were only three others, two ladies and a gentleman who had been in Cape Town on business and was having a short break before returning to London. This chap hadn't brought any booze, so I shared mine. On the second evening we were listening to the news and it was announced that my good friend George Mackie had won a by-election in Caithness for the Scottish Liberals, which is my party. I was full of cheer and was pouring out drinks for all. Whereupon the gentleman announced, 'My wife can't stand the Scottish Liberals or Scotland and when she comes to power she'll see that they are soundly defeated.' I said (this was 1964), 'It's the Scottish Nationalists that are on the rise just now, not the Liberals. Anyway, who is your wife?' 'Margaret Thatcher,' came the reply. Well, I'd never heard of Mrs Thatcher and when I got back I asked Michael Noble who she was. He told me, and added, 'She and Ted Heath don't see eye to eye.' Prophetic words indeed. I might add that I wrote to Sir Denis after his wife became Prime Minister suggesting that he might reciprocate my generosity in sharing my booze with him by asking me to have a drink with him at No. 10. I'm sad to say I never got a reply, but then, 'Manners maketh the man'.

As I had a full report to write on my four months' trip I had arranged to go home via Cyprus and to stay with my mother's sister, who had, with her husband, retired to Kyrenia. Before leaving home I had met Sally Hutchinson who was staying and working with mutual friends near Gatwick. Sally had worked in Cyprus for a year and it was agreed between us that, as we were attracted to one another, we should meet there and get to know each other better. It was an idyllic week, as I stayed with Aunt May and wrote my report every morning, then Sal would come from her hotel, which Uncle Jimmie had recommended, and all four of us would lunch together. They were uproarious lunch parties with Uncle Jimmie, who had been *The Times* correspondent in Kenya, telling stories of the white settler days in East Africa and, on one occasion, bursting into song much to Aunt May's annoyance. The afternoon was spent swimming, the evening we always walked somewhere and then had dinner in one of the many small restaurants. Forty years ago Cyprus was completely unspoilt and food and wine were very cheap. I haven't been back to Kyrenia since the Turkish invasion, but the Greek part of the island is becoming one huge mass of hideous concrete buildings, and one has to go into the hills to get away from the ugliness which only man can produce. Whether it was Sal that gave me the inspiration, or whether it was the super relaxation of the week I know not, but I got a very nice pat on the back for my report from Bill Vines, an Australian who was Chairman of the International Wool Secretariat, who said that after reading my report he felt that in future the scholars they sent overseas should be older if I was an example. Very conceit-making but, thank goodness, most people of forty-eight are happily married and don't want to leave their wives and family for four months.

While I had factored Ardkinglas, John Noble had been approached by a friend, a Major Philip Fleming, to see if I could also factor his Blackmount Estate at Bridge of Orchy. During the war John Noble had been attached to

MI5 who were based, or some were based, at Barton Abbey in Oxfordshire, Major Fleming's estate. My grandfather on my mother's side was brother to Major Fleming's father, Robert, who had founded the famous Fleming's Bank. Sadly Grandfather decided instead to set up a timber business, become an M.P. and Provost of Aberdeen, none of which made money, unlike the Bank. What money the timber business made was, according to Mother, spent by her eldest brother on high living after he came back from the 1914-18 war. She was given a house in Perthshire, which I must say gave us as a family endless pleasure. The timber business is once more thriving, thanks to the oil finds off Aberdeen, and the banking Flemings have made millions, thanks to being taken over by Chase Manhatten. But I wouldn't have changed my life for that of any of the monied Flemings.

Major Fleming was to become one of the three great influences in my life, the others being Father and Archie McIndoe. I had been managing Blackmount for a couple of years when Major Phil, as he was affectionately known, asked me what I was going to do with myself if I left Ardkinglas. I replied that I didn't know but that I'd always wanted to farm back in Strathearn, which to me, without a doubt, combines everything I hold most dear. 'Well', he said, 'go and buy a farm there on one condition: that is that you continue to factor Blackmount.' I don't know if Major Phil's family are so chuffed with being landed with me for the last twenty-four years, but I was over the moon, and being the biggest Greetin' Geordie of all time I had a wee cry to myself about his generosity.

Unfortunately farms in Strathearn don't come up for sale very often, and I was lucky indeed that Woodburn came on the market. Thanks to the fact that it wasn't then on the mains water supply or the electric grid I got it 'worth the money' as they say. To my knowledge, until 1984 not a single farm was for sale in that area after I had bought Woodburn, so once again I'd been a lucky laddie. The great auctioneer Lovat Fraser said, 'I'm surprised at you, Ben, going in to a bad farm like Woodburn', and my reply was, 'Sir, there are no bad farms, only bad farmers.' Whether I'm right or wrong I leave others to judge, but suffice to say that Lovat's son Roley, now equally famous as a pedigree cattle auctioneer, says the place is transformed.

While I was away on the scholarship my ex-shepherd and friend Robbie McHardy and his wife Ann stayed in the farmhouse of Woodburn and Major Phil and I decided to take up the Capital Grant scheme which allowed us to build a cottage (the one on Woodburn was only a but and ben and too small for most), put in water and electricity, enlarge the steading and generally put the place in working order.

I will never forget my homecoming. Robbie has a marvellous saying which he used at Gaskbeg if I was away for a day broadcasting or for a trip such as I did to America in 1959: 'Weel, you're back again', in that lovely Aberdeenshire twang, so when I came back from Australia, New Zealand and South Africa the welcome was as usual, 'Weel, you're back again.' And back again I was with a vengeance, with a run-out farm to put to rights, my capital spent educating my first family, my first marriage on the rocks and only my salary from Blackmount keeping me from the poorhouse.

32
Blackmount

The Blackmount Estate, all 100,000 acres of it, was bought by Robert Fleming back in 1923 from the Breadalbane family, the second highest Campbell family to the Duke of Argyll himself. The fantastic amount of land owned by the Breadalbane family is celebrated in that lovely poem that begins: 'From Kenmore to Ben More [in Mull] the land is all the Marquis's'—i.e. the Marquis of Breadalbane. The huge Breadalbane estates were starting to be split up in the Twenties and before, and I saw the last of them disposed of in the Forties. It was the old story that we have seen so often in the Highlands: the laird being lured south to the flesh pots just like a moth to a candle. Kilted and with a Highland retinue of handsome clansmen and pipers they must have taken London by storm, but no way could their Highland estates stand the cost of the standard of living in the south any more than these estates can stand it today. Their financial problems were not helped by the fact that one of the Marchionesses was a very heavy gambler; but none of the family in any of the generations learnt anything about the practicalities of running a Highland estate. The result was that the Breadalbanes had to sell off their huge estates piecemeal until today they have nothing left at all. Sadly this has been the story of all too many Highland estates.

Grandfather John was the ambitious one of the brothers, who liked office and became an MP and Lord Provost of Aberdeen, and, of course, with that post went the Lord Lieutenantship of the City. Robert on the other hand was very retiring and shy, but loved his sport as did his wife Kate even more. They took many deer forests annually before eventually buying Blackmount in 1923.

The manager of Glenartney, old John Ferguson, used to enjoy regaling me with stories as to how tough my great-aunt was. His favourite story was that the Ruchil river rose very suddenly in spate just as he and Mrs Fleming were about to cross it behind Auchinner (where the lodge and John's house were). John who, like many stalkers of my acquaintance, hated water, was all for going back up the river some three miles where they could cross by bridge, but, nothing daunted, Kate Fleming said, 'Follow me Ferguson', and raising her skirts up to her oxters and according to old John, 'not being afraid to show her pink bloomers', she launched into the river. She was nearly swept off her feet twice, but she was determined to cross and she did.

Blackmount has been and is a famous deer forest. As in so many other areas the stags are now not so numerous nor so heavy—for a variety of reasons, the main one being the amount of good stag-wintering ground that has been lost to the Forestry Commission. I know that after the 1939-45 war this country was terrified that we would be caught out without enough timber, but so far as I'm concerned the amount of land being allowed to be planted is a national disgrace. Some of the best sheep farms I know have been planted; Highland clearances second only to the famous ones in Sutherland have been perpetrated, because after the Forestry Commission plant trees they take away the labour force, then sell or let the cottages. And villages die. (Having said that, with many of the Commission's forests coming to maturity, in certain districts this pattern is being reversed, as labour is required to fell and market the timber.)

The forests are breeding grounds for vermin, and woe betide any deer that show their noses inside the Forestry fences which in times of blizzards are bound to be flattened. Blackmount now is surrounded with Forestry plantations at Craig, Dalmally, Rannoch and Fasnacloich Appin. Because of the loss of these winterings the stags are not so noteworthy as they were. The sad thing is that Blackmount had first refusal to buy Craig, and they turned it down as they felt they had enough land, even though I told them that a lot of their stags wintered in Glenorchy. It was bought by the Forestry Commission, who fenced it and killed 100 stags in their first year of occupation.

There is a wonderful book, *High Tops of Blackmount*, by one of the Countesses of Breadalbane, which is well worth reading. I love the story told in it of 'The White Hind of Corrie Baa'. It seems that the Marquis of Breadalbane of the time had gone south with his usual retinue of clansmen and pipers and had cut a great dash with the Duke of Richmond and Gordon at Goodwood in Sussex. Goodwood has some lovely park deer, but Breadalbane was saying how he was the only person who owned a white hind in Corrie Baa, Blackmount. The Duke of Richmond and Gordon was determined to get this white hind and it was agreed that he would send up his verderers to capture it. Anyone who knows anything about red deer will know that they were on a hiding to nothing, and although they built a fancy stockade and spent a whole summer on the Blackmount they went back to Sussex without the white hind. Others say it was King James VI who in 1627 wrote to Sir Duncan Campbell (Black Duncan of Cowl) to have the white hind sent down to him. Whichever story is true, the thought of southerners trying to corner a hind on Blackmount on a winter's day tickles me a lot. Hamish

Menzies, the present head stalker, saw a white hind for a year or two quite recently. I have seen a roe deer doe that was white, but not a red deer.

The Fleming family rented the estate for a couple of years before buying it at a reputed price of 5s. per acre, but even if this figure is true few people in the Twenties had that sort of money and there was no Forestry Commission in those days to bump up the price of estates as happens today. Robert Fleming's eldest son was killed in the First World War: Valentine by name, he was father of Peter, to my mind the best writer of travel stories I know. His *News from Tartary* and *Brazilian Adventure* are classics. Peter married that talented actress Celia Johnson and they both came to Blackmount in my time as Factor. As Valentine was killed in the war the estate came to the second brother, Major Philip Fleming, who, as you will have read, was a great benefactor to me. Because 'Uncle Phil' felt he had been lucky in his inheritance he was especially kind to Valentine's family, to Peter perhaps mostly because Peter loved Blackmount.

I happened to be the next gun to Peter when he dropped dead, as I'm sure he would like to have done, on a grouse shooting day on that hill. He always came up a day before the 12th of August, and in the year of his death he looked a very peculiar colour. When he asked me to arrange for a stalker to go out with him I, though a mere employee, asked if he was being wise. Nothing daunted, he went out onto at least one of the high tops of Blackmount and came back completely knackered. As I've said, he would have been delighted to die as he did, having just shot a grouse. (Not a right and a left as Duff Hart-Davis wrote, as I shot one of them!) I was very fond of Peter, who had a real feel for the Highlands, although he was a hopeless farmer.

Then there was Ian who, to my mind, couldn't hold a candle to Peter when it came to writing, but sex and crime are the in-thing nowadays. '007' must have made Ian a fortune, but he was a sybarite, and the hair-shirt atmosphere of Blackmount where one is nearly always cold or wet was not to his taste. (When I knew him Ian loved the soft life, but I understand he had a great war record.) Having said that, there is no house in Britain where one can be more hospitably entertained, but you have to go to the hill wet or dry—and it's usually coming down in stair-rods. Then Valentine's third son was Richard, who joined the family business, and I'm told was more than bright. It may be because of that or it may be because he and my brother Fleming crossed swords, but he was the only one in the family with whom I found it difficult to communicate. Valentine's youngest son Michael was killed in the Second World War, but, as he was a friend of Nigel

Mordaunt, I had met him when I was ponyman on Lochside St Fillans back in the Thirties.

But it was Major Phil Fleming who owned the estate in 1962 when I was appointed the Factor. There had been four in his family: Valentine, Dorothy who married Lord Wyfold, himself, and another sister, Lady Hannay. Although I never knew Lord Wyfold he must have been very astute because he and Uncle Phil drew up a plan to divide the 100,000-acre estate on their respective deaths, or in Lord Wyfold's case on the death of his wife. I took over the factorship when the estate was a complete 100,000 acres and the big lodge at Blackmount, the upkeep of which is phenomenal, was always full of Wyfold relations. Conversely, the Flemings used to stalk a lot of the Wyfold land. All this stopped on the death of Lady Wyfold, as 'My Lord' had cleverly split up Lady Wyfold's share so that there were five possible shooting lodges, the best of the stalking and access to one or other of the salmon rivers.

Families and succession always cause problems, but it has never been as easy to manage the Blackmount 50,000 acres as it was to manage the whole 100,000 acres. This amount of land to someone in the south must sound astronomic, but believe me, who have spent a lifetime managing Highland estates, this one is quite lovely but is miles and miles of damn all. Mainly peat bogs, bad heather, rushes, molinia grass (which is useless for grazing) and boulders. The only possible use is for deer, sheep and forestry (the latter properly planned to integrate with the two foregoing interests).

It was this estate that I was called to manage in 1962, as Major Phil felt that the lawyers, who were then doing the job, weren't in touch with the Jocks. How often estates in the Highlands have been ruined by remote control from London, Edinburgh, Perth, Oban, you name the town, but the resident factor who knew the local problems and the folk is unfortunately a thing of the past.

The staff on the Blackmount end consisted of four stalkers, a housekeeper, a housemaid and a gardener. In the season we took on additional staff as ghillies and also in the lodge. Glenetive also went with Blackmount but was usually let to some of the Fleming relatives, and there the staff was a stalker ghillie and a housekeeper, plus three shepherds.

The Glenkinglass end was much more spread out and the lodge was supplied by boat up Loch Etive. One could walk over the hill to Blackmount but all the supplies had to come in by boat. (Thanks to various grants there is now a road all the way from Taynuilt right up to Glenkinglass Lodge.) The stalker who was resident at Glenkinglass was one McKillop, who was reckoned to be one of the best shots in Scotland with both rifle and shotgun. The story is told that he was having trouble with a gang poaching salmon in the Kinglass river: he positioned himself with his rifle high up above the pool waiting the darkness, and sure enough the poachers arrived. Old Mac shouted that if they didn't clear out he would open fire but they, disbelieving and being four to one, just hurled back abuse. That was enough for McKillop who had a magazine full of wartime coloured tracer bullets which he aimed at the pool and, of course, when the bullets hit the water they ricocheted all over the place. Four ashen-faced men were seen in the Taynuilt pub that night telling the locals that there was a madman living in Glenkinglass, but they were never seen in the glen again.

The McKillops of this world are a dying race. They were brought up the hard way, with no comforts, no wireless or TV, and had to learn a trade. This McKillop did brilliantly, and then at one point he had to go off and fight for his country. As the boat only came up the loch three times a week his food was basic. His housekeeper had a 'kist' (chest) of oatmeal and another of flour. He had a house cow to supply him with milk, and he ate venison day after day. I remember having a meal with him one day and he ate a back roast as I would a corn on the cob. You would think he was playing a mouth organ the way he went from end to end of the roast, but the meat disappeared pretty damned quick!

At the loch side lived the second stalker. Old Mac called him 'the bloody Arab', because he used to bow and scrape to Lady Wyfold. These two men and their ladies lived a lonely life, with the boat only calling three times a week, and when the storms blew they could be cut off for days; but it took quite a storm to deter the intrepid boatman, nicknamed 'The Dooker' because he was always taking a 'dook' in the loch to cut free hawsers that were forever getting tangled round the propeller. But I never knew anyone else who could coax to life, as he could, the ancient engines that his successive boats used to have.

At the Taynuilt end of the estate was the sheep farm of Glenoe, where there were a father and two sons in charge of 2,000 ewes. When I took over in 1962 Glenoe was only accessible by boat, but we got a hill road pushed through and now there is a road right up the lochside to Armaddy. Since those days the shepherd's two sons have gone their own way and done well: one managing an estate and allowed to keep some stock of his own, and the other going on to become first a tenant, then owner, of a farm in Mull where he has prospered.

Clashgour was between the Blackmount and Glenkinglass, but was on

Lady Wyfold's estate. Her stalker there was one Angus Cameron, who was a great clay pigeon shot. He used the name 'The Silver Doctor' when he was at the shooting matches and the name stuck. It is said that all the stalkers and keepers who went to the clay pigeon matches adopted other names so that if they were in the prize list their employers wouldn't know that they had been taking the day off and were probably using the boss's ammunition. Angus had originally been the single stalker at Armaddy, and the story is told of how he had won the Lochaber clay pigeon championship on two occasions and was all set to do so a third time and so win it outright. The wily Lochaber boys, knowing how isolated Angus was, put the date of the match forward a day. But 'there are no secrets on the hill', as the old saying goes, and somehow Angus heard the day before the match day. He set off at some unearthly hour to walk via Glenkinglass, Clashgour and Blackmount to Bridge of Orchy station, took the train to Fort William, duly won the cup, came back by the train and walked all the way back to Armaddy the same night, complete with his beloved cup. Armaddy to Bridge of Orchy is a distance of 22 miles: they bred them tough in those days.

Lady Wyfold was a wonderful character and she and Uncle Phil together at a Blackmount dinner party after a stalking day were worth a guinea a minute. 'Dobs', as Lady Wyfold was called, was as deaf as a post and used to make the most outrageous statements at the top of her voice. Unlike Uncle Phil she was not generous, and expected me to run her estate on a shoe-string. I took her to see a bath in one of the houses: the bath had bits peeling off it which were extremely sore on the backside of those who bathed in it. The old girl took one look at it and said, 'Mine are much worse at Sarsden'— her Oxfordshire estate at which I later stayed, and she was right. I always said to my fellow employees I was sorry for her because she must have been down to her last million (if not two!). As it happens I was hopelessly wrong about the two million as it was much more. What did upset me when I stayed there was to see the number of tin 'potties' set out on the floor to catch the drips from the conservatory roof, and the lovely pictures of race-horses that were getting ruined with the damp. But she was a great character and as hardy as they come: she shot stags well into her eighties.

Another great character, who at the time of writing is still with us, is Joan Fleming, Uncle Phil's widow, who, at the age of eighty-six, is well on her way to having shot 1,000 stags, which when you think of the number shot with old fashioned rifles and over open sights is some going in this chauvinistic world and must be a record. These Flemings are tough and they expect their spouses to be the same! My favourite story about Joan was of an incident after Uncle Phil, who had looked after all her financial dealings, had died. She phoned me to go to Blackmount to see her. I didn't usually go to Blackmount in the season, and so feared something dreadful had happened, like a stalker giving in his notice or something similar. When I got there Joan said, 'Ian [her stalker] reckons as I'm now in my late seventies I ought to have an Agrocat'—one of those wee four-wheeled carts suitable for the hill—'would you be good enough to phone my man of business to see if I can afford one?' When I phoned and said who I was and what it was about I got the most delightful reply: 'Does she want one or a few hundred?'

Then finally there was Glenetive which went, and still does, with Blackmount. It's one of the loveliest glens in the Highlands, but very steep, running down from the main Glencoe road. There used to be a school and a very thriving community, but alas, like so many other isolated communities, the numbers are dwindling and the Forestry, who have planted most of the good downfall land, maintain the servicing of the forest from Ballachulish, so the cottages have been sold off for holiday cottages. It's a great pity but some people look on it as progress.

When I managed the estate first the Kingshouse Hotel was also included, but it was found that unless one was to stay there, with the very short summer season it was not viable, so it was sold off. Major Phil financed the White Corries Ski Lift, but because of the uncertainty of the snowfall and its isolated position it has had its ups and downs. Uncle Phil kindly gave me 100 shares some thirty years ago in the White Corries, but to date they have never given me any return. However as the business has now been taken over by the Glenshee Ski Company, and the White Corries tend to have early snow whereas Glenshee usually has spring snow, and as Glenshee also owns a golf course, there may be a ha' penny to come before I push up the daisies in Trinity Gask churchyard!

When I retired in November 1985 the staff presented me with a beautiful reclining easy chair. They were a great bunch to work with and I was a proud and lucky man to have had that honour. In twenty-four years I only had one man leave and that he did for promotion.

33

Woodburn and the Aberdeen-Angus Society

After that marvellous trip overseas it was extremely hard to settle down to 'auld claes and parritch' at home, and Woodburn had been badly run down since I had known it in the Forties.

It's sad to think that now farms of its size are no longer viable, but forty years ago it kept not only myself but a man as well. Now, in the present century, one would need to work seven days a week, twelve hours a day, to make a living for a family, i.e. a living in the style to which this whole country has become accustomed. In the last few years things have got much worse, and to make a living on Woodburn the present incumbent has had to double the stock, which has cut the moor to ribbons, and has to spend hours working on his computer. As Woodburn has a moor on it I decided to go in for single suckler cows using my old love, the cross-Highlander, as my stock cows and crossing them with an Aberdeen-Angus bull as I had done at Gaskbeg. Breeding these cattle is a long process, as these cows are slow-maturing and don't calve down until they are three or even, in some cases, four years old. Then one has to wait another nine months before one sells the calf crop. The dairy farmer on the other hand gets a monthly milk cheque, and as all businesses depend on cash flow it is obvious why so many small farms are in milk production, but it can be a hard demanding job. Most suckler cows in Scotland today are what I call 'Heinz', i.e. 57 different varieties with all too much continental blood in their veins. This has come about as farmers have, like the rest of the country, gone for a greater financial return. The continental cattle are bigger and therefore weigh more than our native breeds; as one is paid on weight and sadly not on taste (for how can one judge the value of the taste?) the continental breeds win out.

Along with the suckler herd I ran 100 draft Blackfaced ewes, i.e. ewes that had done their five years on a hill farm but could easily do another in a kinder clime and with added feeding. Robbie McHardy was the obvious person to help me with my project, he has always been a first-class stockman and like all good stockmen he didn't rush things, but nothing escaped his beady eye. The old saying goes: 'One never wants a running shepherd or a walking ploughman' and many a time I was grateful for Robbie's slow-thinking ways, as I am a fearful basher and expect things to be done at once (probably because of my army training). One of Robbie's great sayings which I treasure is when he would double check a job: after dividing two lots of stock he would tie the gate with 'tow', as he calls baler twine, and say in his Aberdeenshire twang, 'We'll do it "just for fare" [fear] that anything might go wrong.' Not only was he a first-class shepherd but he was more than a good joiner, which was very useful to me as I can't knock a nail in straight.

Robbie, a shepherd's son, had been brought up the hard way, and like myself married a wife from south of the Border. He left shepherding at the end of the war to take the highest and hardest croft in Strathdon, but just couldn't make it pay, and luckily for me returned to shepherding. He still loves to tell the story of how Anne, his wife, and he were laid up with terrible flu just before one Christmas. Their Christmas presents and the New Year bottle depended on them plucking and selling a dozen geese they had been fattening for the Christmas market. The postman killed the geese and they, lying side by side in a double bed, plucked them. Anyone who has plucked a goose will know what a mess the down can make. It's a wonder the marriage survived!

We bought in lambs from the hill farmers in autumn and fattened them on rape or turnips, and the 'golden hoof' of the lambs greatly helped the fertility of the farm as did vast amounts of hen manure from nearby intensive poultry units. Known locally as 'hen pen', this manure is extremely high in nitrogen and the owners have now, rightly, started to market it, but forty years ago we got it for free.

My aim was to reseed the farm as quickly as possible, i.e. lay it down to grass for the suckler herd, of course using some white clover in the mixture, as white clover when ploughed in also produces nitrogen, from its nodules. Nowadays most nitrogen comes out of a bag, and but little white clover is sown. Looking back on my farming years we were as near organic farmers as makes no difference, since we used so little bought-in fertiliser. Also, I always grew ten acres of oats for feed, and it shows how dramatically things have changed in that forty years ago small farms were still using a binder and we were building stacks with the sheaves. I was lucky that Geordie Wilkie, of Lawhill days, one of the best stackers I ever knew, had retired to nearby Auchterarder, and came over to build my stacks. My benevolent landlord, Major Phil Fleming, agreed to put in an improvement scheme which helped install electricity and mains water, build a cottage for Robbie and modernise the farm buildings. I'm proud to say that in 1985, when the farm was sold, the Major's son got the family money back with interest. I will always be in that family's debt.

Woodburn farmhouse seemed a bit empty without a woman's touch, but in 1966 Sally decided to throw her hand in with me and in March of that year we got married. As a local farmer said, 'The best day's work you ever did, Ben!'

Sally always ribs me that I made it March because Smithfield Show Council have their spring meeting then, and as a councillor I have my fare paid. It happened that in that year they decided to hold the meetings in Sidmouth, Devon, so I was accused of getting a cheap honeymoon thrown in, although we did go on to Cornwall for some halcyon days. I remember only too well that some of my so-called pals filled the matrimonial bed with some extremely prickly rose bushes, and on inspection in the morning we found the attached labels showed that the variety bore an extremely suggestive name.

However, my good friends Forrest Smith and Jimmie Stodhart, well known sheep dealers, were determined to see that Sal got a better honeymoon than a few days in the West Country, and sent us to France. Sadly, Forrest is no longer with us, but I was proud to be asked to give the appreciation at his memorial service.

To be honest, what happened was that they were both determined to break into the French lamb market. Forty years ago virtually nothing was being exported in the way of sheep meat. I expostulated to them that my French wasn't good enough, but they said they were sure I would 'bullshit' my way through. They must have been right, because I made contacts they still have to this day.

These were the days of the old 'Les Halles' mart, and I had the frightening task of having to go out there and make my number. Sally had taken her ancient but trustworthy beetle Volkswagen, and wearing my kilt I set out for the Mart at 4.30 am. I found that the kilt, an interest in rugger and the ability to drink brandy-for-brandy with the French wholesale meat men worked wonders, especially the latter. So far as my French was concerned it improved in leaps and bounds as the morning wore on.

I found myself driving round La Place de la Concorde with complete abandon singing 'Scots wha' hae' at the top of my voice. Luckily there were no gendarmes in sight!

We were then ordered by Forrest down to the South of France, and I remember passing through the Massif Central around Le Puy and thinking that it was crying out for hill sheep stocks such as we have in the Highlands of Scotland. Luckily for us the French are still not self-sufficient in sheep meat, and it will be a bad day for the Scottish, Welsh and English hill farmers when they are. What is it about the French that they do everything in their power to stop having any dealings with us? Is it the memory of Waterloo? Whatever it is, at the hint of B.S.E. in this country they stopped importing British lamb, which especially hurt my particular friends the hill farmers. This was all the more annoying now that it has turned out, as many of us thought, that they too have B.S.E.

Sally came to Woodburn and transformed the place, me included. She brought an Aga stove with her as her dowry, and I thoroughly recommend it to any farmer who is lucky enough to have a generous bride who wishes to bring a dowry with her. Perhaps the ponies that took over the bull pens were not so welcome. But in later years the Highland pony stud became an integral part of the farm, and we have had the honour to sell a mare to Balmoral. More of that anon.

I suppose it was natural that Sal and I should wish to have our own family. Our first daughter decided to arrive in a hurry. The ancient car was being serviced in preparation for the journey to Perth hospital, and the even more ancient Land Rover was hitched to a cart on the night when Sal appeared from a hot bath saying she feared the baby was arriving. I'll never forget that night as long as I live. We had, luckily, just got onto the main Glasgow-Perth road, having travelled some twelve miles on side roads, when bang, one of the tyres blew out. It was then after midnight on a Sunday night. Sal's contractions were getting more and more close together. After what seemed an eternity, and no car approaching going in the Perth direction, I stood in front of the next car coming out of Perth, explained the position and asked if they would be good enough to turn around, which the driver very kindly said he would do. Sal says I never even gave her a helping hand with her night bag but bundled her into the back when the two men got out to let her in.

About an hour later the car came back and when it stopped the driver said he had told the all-night garage of my plight (the wheel studs were rusted on as I'm the world's worst mechanic), but added, 'If your child turns out to be a criminal it's because it went to be born in the company of a well known convict that we're moving from Peterhead to Barlinnie in the middle of the night.' Hence the reason the two men had got out as Sal got in; they were handcuffed together. I understood from the maternity ward sister that it was even funnier at her end because as a matter of routine she had said, 'and who's the father?' only to get a loud reply, 'Neither of us.'

During our time in Woodburn I brought out the odd pedigree animal for sale, and I had a rather showy Highland heifer. That October I had to make the speech at the Annual Highland Cattle Society dinner, so Sal and I were seated at the top table and Robbie and Michael Noble's head shepherd were seated down the dining room, one on each side of Michael. I noticed the whisky bottles, shall we say, diminishing gently, and after the meal when we met in the lounge Robbie, who was standing in front of me, turned his head and said, 'Captain, I'm fu' and slid gently into my arms. Having got him safely to bed I said to Sal, 'that means I'm on duty tomorrow', but I might have known better. When I got along to the Mart at 6.30 a.m. the heifer was watered, fed, bedded and brushed. They don't breed them that way now. Robbie's sort can enjoy themselves with the best but when there is a job to do they're on parade.

One of our great joys at Woodburn were our little pheasant shoots. Pat Wilson, one of the best shots in Scotland, said there were more bottles than pheasants, but everyone seemed to enjoy themselves and we shot on until lunch-time, then packed up and had a jolly time. I've always thought it madness, if one doesn't have a lot of birds, to have to don one's shooting clothes, usually wet, and sally forth again having not done justice to the hostess's lunch. I'm proud to say I always invited some aspiring guns, usually in their teens, to my shoots. So many shoots are now run for syndicates who are willing to pay big money that there are few shoots left that will allow a 'laddie' to make a start. When I was in Speyside and factoring estates I gave the young Max Hastings the thrill of shooting his first grouse.

At one of those shoots Bill Reid, the then President of the Aberdeen-Angus Society, was among the guns and George Mackie (now Lord Mackie of 'Benshie', spelt Ballinshoe) says that I engineered the job of secretary of the Aberdeen-Angus Society at that shoot. True, as I describe in the next chapter, I mentioned to Bill that I was interested, but he and his Council did a lot of heart-searching before they made an appointment. However in 1970 were to start nine of the most challenging years of my life.

34
Aberdeen-Angus Secretary

The Aberdeen-Angus Society is known worldwide in cattle circles: the breed is famous for the quality of its beef. All the great beef-producing countries have used the breed, particularly Canada, USA, Brazil, Argentina, New Zealand and Australia, and it is found in many other countries as well. The breed came from the two Scottish counties after which it is called, and it has gone far. The famous stockbreeder William McCombie of Tillyfour, Aberdeenshire, not only bred good cattle but he was a great publicist (the original Aberdeen-Angus PRO). He not only took cattle to the then top European show in Paris where he swept the boards, but he had no less a personage than Queen Victoria to take tea with him at Tillyfour and paraded his famous cattle in front of her.

The story goes that in order to make it look as if he had more cattle than he really owned he made the cattle go round and round his house, and when they were out of sight behind the farmhouse new leaders took over the same cattle. Her Majesty was not the first or last person to be foxed by the look-alike appearance of Aberdeen-Angus with their black skins and polled (hornless) heads. I've often heard it said in the years that I was secretary, when standing at a show ringside, 'There's no outstanding leader', i.e. they're all much the same. When judging a lot of cattle that are all black and polled one must have one that 'sticks out a mile' above the rest. There was the famous occasion when Bob Adam, one of this generation's great judges and stockmen, had lined up the cattle for ticket presentation and when asked by his steward at which end he should start dishing out the rosettes Bob said jokingly, 'You can start at any end.'

I have always had a tremendous admiration for the Aberdeen-Angus breed, and even in my days at Millhills where I was associated with Beef Shorthorns and Highland cattle I always attended the Aberdeen-Angus Bull Sales which, in the palmy days of the native breed's popularity overseas, used to be in the second week in February, with the Shorthorns in the first week. At Gaskbeg I had set up a small herd of Angus. I also managed the neighbouring estate of Cluny, no longer owned by the Chief of the MacPherson clan, but by the Chairman of Morgan, Crucible, who got me to set up another Aberdeen-Angus herd. This produced the bull 'Elspin of Cluny' that made 2,200 guineas in the fifties—quite a bit of money in those days. Then when the breed society were making a film they asked me, with my broadcasting background, if I would represent the view of the commercial farmer, which I was delighted to do.

This film was shot at Snipe House, the home of the late Bobby Robinson, one of the greatest stockmen and showmen it has been my pleasure to know. When I say showman I don't mean going round the ring with the beast on the end of a halter—it was the way he showed his commercial calves, hundreds of them. All his pens of calves were shown to perfection and drawn as evenly as peas in a pod.

When the lorries came in to Snipe House each lorry driver was given a chit with the numbers of the pens into which his load had to go: that's what I call organisation, and how I admired Bobby. He is one of the characters that are sadly lacking today, but I suppose others will take his place; there is another generation growing up like the 'Terrible Twins', Hogg and Todd, the 'Reiver', John Elliott, and a host more from the same area. I remember all too well after a long and hard working day filming—and believe me filming is one of the hardest jobs I've done, with the constant takes and retakes and the nerves getting the better of one—that we had a marvellous evening, for Bobby and his wife Betty were the most magnanimous hosts. Betty had gone to bed and Alan Grant, Tom Todd and Bobby (all sadly not now with us) plus myself were left and Bobby announced he was hungry and craved for fish; the goldfish were not in their accustomed bowl in the morning and we were not popular with our hostess.

But as usual I digress. When asked to take on the Aberdeen-Angus Society I had, as I've said, already had quite a lot to do with the breed. During the early Sixties they had had tremendous worldwide success and the Perth sales were inundated with stetson hats from the States and Canada and ponchos from Argentina and Brazil. The world record price was paid for Euvulse of Lindertis in 1964 at 60,000 guineas. This bull I didn't see sold, as I was in New Zealand in the February of that year. But though Euvulse made a world record price, which even allowing for inflation has not yet been beaten, he never left a calf. Some cattlemen reckon he was given too much of the stuff out of the 'wee bottle' that promotes the growth of hair, but if given in too large quantities can cause sterility. What is more certain is that the buyer of the bull, Jack Dick, on behalf of Black Watch Farms in the U.S.A., also bought lots of silver from a well-known shop in Perth. Knowing that he had just paid a vast amount for a bull, the people in the shop thought he was creditworthy, only to find later that extracting payment was like getting blood out of a stone. Sadly those high prices of the late Fifties and early

The author clutching the coveted Burke Trophy awarded to the best pair of beef cattle at the Royal Show, Stoneleigh, and won by the Aberdeen-Angus team in 1976

Sixties were the worst thing that ever happened to a breed, as all the high-priced bulls were wee short-legged dumpy animals, 'too wee to bull a cow', as many hard-headed commercial farmers said. We are all human, and everyone in the breed jumped on the bandwagon and tried to breed an 'exporter's' bull. In doing this they forgot their bread and butter which had been, and always will be, the farmers who breed commercial suckled calves for the fattening trade and so for the housewife's beef.

Suddenly in the mid-Sixties the overseas demand dried up, as breeders overseas realised, before Scotland did, that 'when you're stopped weighing you're stopped paying', so they started weight recording and going for big bulls. It was a case of 'Mene Mene Tekel Upharsin' as the old biblical saying goes: 'They were weighed in the balance and found wanting', and we breeders in Scotland were found wanting.

To rectify this the Council of the Aberdeen-Angus Society offered me the job of Secretary in 1970. They had not long ago appointed a 'whizz kid' from a large number of applicants. He had 'borrowed' £8,000 from the Society and had a job paying it back, so after only a year in the post he threw in the towel. The Council were worried about re-advertising the job as it would look bad after such a short time. Bill Reid, who was President that year, was out shooting with me and voiced his concerns. I said to him, 'What about me?' to which he replied 'Are you serious?' and I think the Council were relieved to be got out of a jam. First, I had to go before the Council, with most of whom I was on christian name terms, and was well and truly grilled in my interview. The reactions afterwards were super: 'Never thought you'd call us Mr so-and-so and not by our christian names'; 'Couldn't you have turned up in a better suit, you looked tatty' (something I put right immediately I was appointed); 'You've never stuck a job for very long, can't see you doing us much good', and the classic came from one of our most highly thought-of supporters to a pal of mine, 'He's only a playboy and won't enjoy the hard work involved.'

Only history will relate whether the latter was proved true or not, but after nine years the Society gave me a most handsome cheque and made me an Honorary Life Member of the Society, plus a super engraved silver salver signed by our Patron, that best-loved of all British ladies, HM the Queen Mother. Dad always said nine years is the right stint to do a job. 'The first three years they idolise you, the next three years they criticise you and the last three they scandalise you, get out!' I got out on exactly nine years to the day.

In a very minor degree I took over the Society as Monty took over the Eighth Army, as a demoralised mob. I'm no Monty (I'm not teetotal for a start, as you will know from the foregoing) but in a very minor degree I can get on with the Jocks, as I call them, in this case the small breeders. I had no doubts at all that my first job was to get round every breeder I could in as quick a time as possible, and once having visited them I wished to start writing up my visits in a Breed Newsletter which would let different areas know how others were faring. During their (so-called) halcyon days (with which I disagree), all sorts of monied people had become involved and the story is told that when the Secretary two in front of me was to be sacked, and I still can't think why, Bill Reid, then a Council member, left the Council meeting in Aberdeen early to do some farm business with his lawyer. As he went out he passed the Secretary sitting outside the Council Chamber waiting to be called in. When Bill came back an hour later, he was still sitting there but the President and his cohorts were by this time in the bar. When Bill asked the President if the Secretary had been informed of his fate, he said that the Secretary would be told 'all in good time'. This was the aristocratic outlook I was determined to break, and, with all my many, many faults as Secretary this I firmly did. I was extremely lucky with the staff in the Office, as I am no office-wallah and I depended on them to get on with

The silver tray presented to the author on his retirement as Secretary of the Aberdeen-Angus Society, 1980

things so that I could get out and about and meet the breeders on their own farms. A Breed Society's duty is to maintain the purity of the breed, so to do that each calf must be tattooed in the ear with the owner's tattoo, in my case COT, then a letter denoting its year of birth, and finally a number which showed us which number it was in relation to other calves born in the herd in that particular year. Some breeders started showing what looked like particularly large bulls for their age as the demand increased for bigger bulls, and so we instigated spot checks: some of the worst offenders were my dear friends the Irish. When I say my dear friends, I mean it, as of all the overseas countries I have visited on farming business, and they total the staggering number of fifteen, the Irish were far and away the most welcoming and that is praising them indeed, as I have had some fantastic friendship and hospitality all over the world. But, when it came to registering their calves, some of the Irish thought nothing of 'leaving the calves in the rushes', as we used to say, for a month or two.

Talking of the Irish, no one from Scotland, and especially from the Office, had bothered to go over to see them. I had heard that at their sale in Carrick-on-Shannon there were a lot of good big bulls for sale, so along with an English breeder, the late David Story, a super chap, we set off. After some alarms and excursions, we came back with the first Irish bulls to return to Scotland for many a year. Since then there has been a steady stream, and many have done the breed a lot of good.

Our visit happened to coincide with the first anniversary of a date which the Irish call 'Bloody Sunday', when the big shooting took place in Londonderry. Imagine our surprise, after being feted royally by the Show and Sale Committee as the first Breed Officials to attend their sale, and we were waiting for that sale to commence (they always start at least an hour after the advertised time), when a man came into the ring wearing a black beret and, it was said, with a revolver at his hip. He ordered the Auctioneer to postpone the sale until after the religious services in the two churches, Protestant and Catholic, had been held. So it was back to the hotel, and out of the window I watched the crowds of people entering the two buildings. Much as I would have liked to worship in either, I knew better than to take sides. The hotel owner announced that the hotel and bar would be closed as a sign of respect, but after the service I've never seen so many people crammed into the kitchen, the passages, the lounge, yes, even the loos. All had men in them with bottles, and the drink kept coming from somewhere. It seemed they were having a glorious wake everywhere but in the bar, which, with the front door, remained firmly closed.

How sad that when one goes to a bull sale in Carrick-on-Shannon, the breeders from the North are asked to judge, buy bulls and dram with the men from the South, and all get along together so well, and yet the North/South divide—and hatred in some cases—seems to go on and on, and one wonders if it will ever be resolved.

Some years later I was asked to judge at one of the shows in the West of Ireland. I should have known better, but I drove like Jehu to be there on time, only to find one trailer and a couple of donkeys in the showground, but the pub was going like a fair. That was the day I had three cows by the famous Irish sire, Provider of Drumlone, in front of me and they were stormers, full of character, right on their legs and with bags of size and flesh for ever more. How I would have liked to have owned one of them.

The Spring and Autumn sales in Perth were naturally my most busy times as not only did we have Council meetings at that time, but one got all the moans then as well (and believe me there were plenty). I started up clubs in the different areas and, honour where it is due, it was my predecessor's idea and a good one too as, in England especially, it cemented breed loyalty. I remember having a meeting after the Reading Bull Sale, and our Chairman

*The author with Colin Edwards—the 'luvly' President of the Irish
Aberdeen-Angus Society*

at that time, although brilliant, was going through a problem with the bottle. We had a room in a local hotel with a big sign over it saying 'AA'. The Chairman kept slipping out all the time for more brandy and left me to run the meeting. Eventually the 'Boots' of the hotel pushed the Chairman, then very drunk, through the door saying, 'I think this must be one of yours'— thinking, presumably, that the AA stood for Alcoholics Anonymous.

As I have said, I had a super staff to back me up and I had a fine office in which to work, a Georgian building looking out on the lovely trees and grass of the South Inch, Perth. My predecessor had used the biggest room as his office, but I changed it into a Board Room and bought a lovely table and furniture for it; I was only sad that when our Patron the Queen Mother visited the Perth Sales and lunched in the Board Room I had demitted Office.

Quite the most demanding job for a Breed Society Secretary is the round of the summer shows. These start in the first week of May with Newark and go on right through until August. Some are only one-day shows like the local Scottish ones, but the main ones like the Royal Highland, the Royal and the Great Yorkshire were four-day events, and each breed had to have its presence, which meant the Secretary going off a day earlier to get the photos, breed-promotion literature, hand-outs, accessories etc. all in position. To stand on one's feet for eight hours or more each day can be tiring enough, but to talk endlessly as well is even more so. The dram and hot bath at night were a godsend.

But to me the driving home from the far-away shows like Devon, the Royal Welsh or even the Royal was the worst of it. The year before I retired I had to get one of my friendly cattlemen, Dave Smith, to drive me back from the Royal as I was all-in. It was the constant driving on motorways that got me down—and the constant dramming with all too many friends! I just can't comprehend how some people do it all the year round.

Thanks to Robin Fleming's generosity in allowing me to take on the job at all while still managing his Estate, those nine years were some of the most rewarding in my life, not least the overseas travel the job afforded me.

35

Travel for the Aberdeen-Angus Society

It would be boring to give individual years that I travelled overseas for the Aberdeen-Angus Society. Unfortunately I would have to be the first to admit that few if any sales came from my visits overseas, but Aberdeen-Angus Societies worldwide are a close-knit body and it was essential to keep contact with the other Societies. My Council sent me as we were always hoping for business.

My first trip to the Argentine was before I became the Society Secretary, when one of the most generous people I have ever known, Elizabeth Honeyman of Ballachin in Strathtay, decided she couldn't go on the Society's trip and asked me to take her place, and she would pay my fare. I bless her to this day, as it was during that trip that I got to know Bill Reid, and I'm sure the fact that he often asked me to make the speech on the Society's behalf had a lot to do with my eventually becoming their Secretary.

I can never understand why we as a country got embroiled in the Falklands war, and I'm sure some shrewd talking could have averted it, or it may well be that cattlemen only meet the pro-British Argentinians—but I loved the people and their country. Charlie Duggan, whom I've mentioned before, was extremely generous to the Society's party and, knowing we wouldn't have a lot of spare cash, left whisky and gin at our hotel for us. This was being handed round by Gerry Rankin, Boots Pure Drugs farm factor, who had worked in Argentina and acted as our interpreter. The whisky was the well-known Chivas Regal, quite the most expensive that one could buy out there. Gerry was furious when one of our company pronounced it 'a bit peaty'.

The judging at the Palermo show is a never-to-be-forgotten sight, with day after day judging and hundreds of cattle of all breeds. Our own Bob Adam was judging that year, 1969, which added even more interest for us. I loved the final day when the *Caballeros* showed off their skills on their horses, and I equally loved meeting those chaps. There is a common bond between stockmen in all countries.

When one sees the wonderful land in South America, one realises that if they really farmed it properly as we do in Great Britain (for all the conservationists say about us) we could pack up. I always say that if they planted an umbrella, there would be a clump of umbrellas the next day.

That first visit to Argentina was the last time that Scottish-bred bulls were taken out by exporters to try their luck and test their stock judgement. It was very much the end of an era, as shipping costs and changes in fashion brought about a different approach. The next time I went back to that beautiful country was when they celebrated their Society's centenary, and I have some lovely glasses by which to remember the occasion.

But the two outstanding memories of the centenary visit were that it is the only time I've had to make a public speech with the aid of an interpreter. As a fairly fast speaker I found it very frustrating. The other thing was that their centenary was held well outside of Buenos Aires, and there was a torrential downpour on the way back to the city. I thought having been in Argyll I knew something about rain, but it didn't start to compare with that stuff and luckily we had an excellent driver, but we passed abandoned cars by the dozen and the water was continuously over our floorboards.

I know a lot of my stories in these memoirs have to do with the Demon Drink, but it has given me endless pleasure—and not a little pain! However I recall that some months after the first Argentinian trip I was travelling B-Cal somewhere and the stewardess said, 'Were you not on a trip to Argentina recently?' (I was as usual on A-A business and wearing my kilt.) When I answered in the affirmative she replied, 'That's the only occasion our plane was drunk dry.' 'Nuff said!

But for sheer waste of money, not the Society's I'm glad to say, the Greek visit took the biscuit. A certain Mr Konialides, Onassis' brother-in-law, had decided that as the latter had bred Hereford cattle he, Mr Konialides, would breed Angus. No expense had been spared, not only in buying them but in keeping them on the island of Skiatos, as all their feed had to be ferried out from the mainland. He had both a first-class young manager (now well known in Kent and Sussex NFU circles) and also a resident vet, but he thought it would be nice for a Society representative to pay a visit. Sal and I organised our holiday that year to some of the Greek islands and left some days at the end to visit the cattle. We reported to Athens Airport, where we met Mr Konialides and his many minions and were transported to Skiathos in his private helicopter. After viewing the cattle which were, quite frankly, on bad ground, and had not had time to completely acclimatise, we were bidden to lunch with Mr Konialides at his very posh villa. He had taken the whole staff from his hotel, which he had built in anticipation of the aerodrome which was nearing completion, and they waited on us hand

and foot. During lunch Mr Konialides asked us what we were doing for the remainder of our holiday and when I replied I wasn't sure he said, 'Stay at my hotel on my account.' It was an unforgettable experience, as we were the only residents, and being the boss's guests got first-class treatment. Each evening we walked over to the other side of the island to the most wonderful mile-long silver strand, completely empty, where we bathed 'starko bollico'. I shudder to think how many bodies are each year getting burnt on it now that the aerodrome is complete.

My visit to the States on A-A business was to do with their World Forum, which all A-A Societies ran every fourth year. This was held in Kansas City, and was my insight into the way that the Aberdeen-Angus breed was to go for a period. They held a big show of cattle, where we from Scotland were to see our first sight of what are called 'modern' cattle. I've never liked them and never will. They might be tall-standing but are hard on their tops and shoulders and are split up their backsides, which means they don't have the depth of backside from which one gets the real A-A beef. Whether I liked the cattle or not made no difference to the fact that an old pal, Frank Harding, whom I had known in his great exporting days, got me one of the best steaks I have ever had the pleasure to eat, so perhaps I was wrong about their cattle. And certainly I had one of the best dry Martinis I have ever drunk. Why is it the Yanks can make this lethal drink better than any other nation? I think it's probably because they only wave the cork of the Martini bottle over the gin! Sal and I went back to see Frank Harding in his retirement home in Florida, and he hadn't lost the art of mixing a dry Martini.

The Brazil visit was really one of business. We had decided that as a Society we would buy three bulls at our official sales and take them out to the Porto Allegre Show and Sale in Brazil to promote home-bred cattle. The bulls were put in the safe hands of Jim Donald, Glenalmond, who had made his name with his father's Gaidrew herd, also his own Wester Campsie herd, and has always been a power to reckon with at the Scottish National Fat Stock Show and the Royal Smithfield Show at Earls Court, London. So who better? Michael Noble by that time was Minister of the Board of Trade and warned me that he was to be there, but that our native tipple was some £30 per bottle, so with this tip-off I went to my old friends Matthew Gloag of Famous Grouse fame, and asked if they would sponsor the Society. Which they did and have done ever since. Their Overseas Director said 'Will four dozen do? But don't forget Ben, once they go to Stansted Airport on your head be it.' Jim was going with the cattle from Stansted, so I put the whisky there as cattle food and I was to follow a fortnight later on a normal flight.

I was not entirely surprised to meet a very despondent Jim at the other end saying that the whisky had been impounded in Customs. Nothing daunted, I got hold of our excellent manager-cum-interpreter Gary McRory, of the British Agricultural Export Corporation, put on my grass skirt (my kilt) and sallied forth to see the customs guys at the airport. I'll never forget the electric action that resulted (the only such I saw in fourteen days in Brazil) when I drew myself up to my six-foot-three inches and said, 'There are three bottles for you, two for your second-in-command and one for the driver who takes the bottles to the camp.' The remaining forty-two bottles were back on the show field before we were and, the Lord forgive me, we gave the President of Brazil one of our bottles. But so serious is the feudalism there that the photo that I had arranged for our sponsors was banned, as they didn't want the ordinary folk to see their President accepting whisky from capitalists.

I wished they had seen Woodburn land compared with theirs. As in the Argentine, if they only farmed their land, we as EEC farmers would be in dire trouble. As if we weren't already!

The British Exhibition at Porto Allegre was backed by the BAEC and Michael Noble was there as their president. Also in the party was Sir Henry Plumb, far and away the most popular and flamboyant President the English NFU has ever had. He was there wearing his Ayrshire tie, for he has been a great supporter of that breed all his farming days. He delighted the Jocks by donning a white coat and showing an Ayrshire beast in the show that preceded the Sale. The showground was some miles from Porto Allegre, so we had a bus to transport us back to the hotel, and we always had a Happy Hour before we left; guess why the Aberdeen-Angus stand was the most popular? Jim and the other cattlemen had to leave their stock in the charge of local cattlemen for the night, but they always went back on an early bus in the morning to see to their beasts.

It was a sad morning for me when Jim came bursting into my room to announce that his bulls were not in their pens, and what was I going to do about it? What had happened was they had contracted the deadly foot-and-mouth disease, endemic in South America, and as they were highly insured it turned out it was the best thing that could have happened, as the year before the Brazilians had gone for the big lean types and we had taken out animals with good tops and backsides.

As the song goes 'After the show was over' the A-A contingent were invited to go to the western area where most of the A-A were situated. After a wonderful day or two seeing cattle in really hard country, our schedule home was extremely tight, including a run in one of the owners' super-jeeps driven by a super Jock with practically no English, but we 'ticked'; then a lengthy bus journey with but one stop on the way to Porto Allegre, then Rio, then Lisbon, Heathrow and eventually Edinburgh. Imagine my chagrin when at the one stop of the bus the driver was about to start and we were still missing Jim's second cattleman, who was the son of a very well-known and respected A-A breeder. The bus driver couldn't speak English and I couldn't speak Portuguese, but between us we did make him realise we couldn't go until we found our lost mate. I got off and found him wandering at least three streets away, and when I exploded he said, 'Well, I had to get some cheap cigars before I left Brazil, Ben.' I still wake in the night wondering how he would have got home from the centre of Brazil with the bus and his pals all gone.

But my lasting memory of Brazil is of their gorgeous women. As a stock-breeder all my life I realise how much an outcross is essential, but someone somewhere has put this all together and thank God I was happily married when I went there!

The Council decided that the breed should once more be represented at the prestigious Paris Agricultural Exhibition, where nearly a century before William McCombie had carried all before him. We decided we should not only have a large stock bull on demonstration but also have an Aberdeen-Angus steak bar in the food hall. The Show lasts for a week from Sunday to Sunday, both sabbaths being the favourites with the Parisians. The show area is vast and is staged in four different huge halls. The bull was penned at one end of the exhibition and the steak bar was right at the other. On a Sunday it took me forty minutes to get from one to the other. I have never been so tired in my life as at the end of our first experience there. With the mixture of dust, heat, tiredness and cheap wine I completely lost my voice, and had to depend on Donald Aitchison, the Galloway Cattle Society Secretary (sadly no longer with us) to do all the talking for us on the way home. Donald was called the Japanese Admiral because of his diminutive size and the fact that he was always talking of his war experiences in the Navy when he had commanded the first destroyer to go into St Nazaire. He spoke good French and he succeeded in selling some Galloways into France, but alas, we didn't manage to sell any Aberdeen-Angus. The annoying thing was that the steak bar went like a bomb. I remember well our steak bar being crowded out, whereas the Charolais steak bar which was fairly close by never had as many customers. All our customers were delighted, yet when we told them they ought to ask for A.A. beef we got nothing but blank looks. Is it that in

France the town people, who were the customers in the steak bar, remain still more closely connected to the land than those in this country, and so are more willing to back their farmers? When I was a boy in the twenties a huge proportion of Glaswegians were only a generation or two away from farming folk, and would support them. Now the modern housewife doesn't give a damn where her food comes from, as long as it is cheap. I was responsible for getting the Shipway Brothers to run our steak bar for us. They went back year after year for 16 years, and now run a lamb bar for the Scottish Quality Lamb Association which has done so much to publicise Scottish lamb in France, so perhaps we did some good.

When I got home after that first Paris Exhibition sans voice Sal said, 'You've been up to no good out there, I'm coming with you next year if you go.' She had a slight cold when she left home on this trip, but by the time she had finished her week she had lost her voice too, and didn't come back the following year.

Lest readers think that the author was having holidays abroad at the expense of the A-A Society, I am told by my contacts in the other A-A societies overseas, of which there are many, that my visiting them was one of the reasons why the World Forum of A-A Breeders had so many members, and according to them was the best. Having said that, as the home of the breed, and with all the contacts I and my Council had, we had the ball at our feet and we kicked it, with the help of Famous Grouse Whisky!

36

Aberdeen-Angus Days, Continued

Attending the second Paris Exhibition that we were at was one Bob Hurst, who with his wife had bred A-A cattle in England, but then had emigrated to Spain. He was convinced that there was a future for the breed there and determined that I should go and spy out the land. No less a person than the head of the famous Gonzales Byass firm, of Tio Pepe Sherry fame, had Angus cattle and we were asked to meet him at Jerez after we had attended the Madrid Exhibition. I felt like Scott must have done when he got to the South Pole to find that Amundsen had beaten him: there were some extremely good A-A on a stand sent by the American Aberdeen-Angus Association. However, we still had Jerez to go to and my hopes were high.

We turned up on time but I might have known better, as most of the morning was spent seeing the Bodega and drinking sherry. All the members of the large family gathered each morning and discussed the family business, and some of the assembled company were in their eighties, which says a lot for their sherry. At length the Boss appeared, speaking impeccable English, apologised and said that before we went out to his estancia we must have lunch with him. Sal was with me, as I had arranged with the Society that if they paid my fare I would take Sal and we would make a holiday of it. I'll never forget the ghastly hotel we were in. Our bedroom looked out onto an outdoor cinema that ran on until the small hours, bellowing Spanish at us. The bedroom held the biggest mosquitoes I've ever seen; mosquitoes delight in bombing my McIndoe nose which swells like an elephant's trunk. We finished lunch at 4pm and our host announced, 'I suppose you both ride', whereupon Sal really woke up. Needless to say I was mounted on an ancient old carthorse type and they on cross-thoroughbreds, on which, in true Western movie style, they disappeared into the setting sun leaving me miles behind. But eventually we did see the cattle. Our host promised me faithfully that he would be in contact with me to ship out a Scottish bull, but I'm still awaiting the order. However, he did map out a journey for us through some staggeringly beautiful country. Sadly, although I did my best to get more Scottish A-A into Spain I did not succeed, but at least the sherry I drank didn't cost the Society anything.

Every four years, as I've mentioned, the Aberdeen-Angus Societies of the world hold a World Forum, and Scotland's turn to be host country fell due while I was the incumbent Secretary. I had a wonderful team to help me, but it was a bit of an effort getting everything fitted in. There had to be room for everyone, and there had to be serious discussions on worldwide problems in agriculture and in the breed itself. There had to be herd visits and official banquets. We managed to organise the best class of old bulls ever seen at the Royal Highland Show. We chose Aviemore as our centre because there was enough hotel space plus a good auditorium, also Speyside was one of the original homes of the Aberdeen-Angus breed and at that time still housed the famous Ballindalloch Herd. One day in March when the Forum Committee were up in Aviemore arranging the forthcoming June event, it started to snow heavily and I said to Wyn Colville, our excellent chairman, 'Get this meeting finished early, or we'll get blocked in at Drumochter Pass if we're not careful.'

Having stayed at Gaskbeg for eight years I have a healthy respect for the dreaded Drumochter. Sure enough, just after Dalwhinnie we got stuck, but a little time after that a snowplough appeared heading towards us, the driver alighted and braving the blizzard came over to the car. As I wound down the window he said, 'Oh, it's you Captain, hang on a meenit and we'll take the plough in front of you,' and then he added, 'if you've got a bottle wi' ye.' I have been stuck twice on that infamous stretch of road, once in a lorry and once in a car, and even if the doctors say alcohol isn't the answer to snow it didn't seem to do me any harm. I always carry my 'reserve ration'. So Willie was in luck and so were we as we got through before the darkening.

The Forum was acknowledged as a huge success, but it had so much going for it, although there were the odd hiccups. Brother Frank was Colonel of the King's Own Scottish Borderers who, fortunately for us, were stationed at Fort George. He arranged a super Beating the Retreat on the Sunday evening, but unfortunately, because of transport trouble, the brass band which was to have helped the Sunday Service never turned up. So Tom Nicol, the Queen's Padre at Crathie, and myself had to lead the praise.

Then there was the infamous occasion when the incumbent producer of the Scottish farming programme asked me to represent Scotland in an international debate about A-A cattle; I turned up with two minutes to spare, only to find that he had forgotten to contact the rest and he and I had to do twenty minutes on our own. Not funny.

Looking back one wonders how much business is conducted at these Forums, and the answer would have to be not much, but as in all breeds the world significance is important and the exchange of ideas is also important. For once the Scottish June weather let us down, as, instead of being flaming, it was flaming cold during the period we were in Aviemore, and on the night of the banquet, for which I had bought a new lightweight kilt jacket, I don't think I've ever been so cold. Hoping for good weather we had organised the banquet on the defrosted curling rink of the Coylumbridge Hotel. The roast beef was the best I've ever eaten, and it's a difficult dish to serve to hundreds, but the head waiter, who now has his own excellent restaurant in Aberdeen, organised it with the Committee that his waiters would only have a few yards to go with each helping from specially stationed, portable hot plates; a tip which I will remember. I always get tizzed up before I have to speak publicly, and that night I was so cold I was more tizzed than usual, but luckily we had the Earl of Elgin, one of the top public speakers I know, delivering the main toast of the Society, and what a super job he made of it, finishing off by getting even the most shy Argentinians and Brazilians with one foot on the table to deliver the toast.

This great get-together of the 'clans' was deemed an outstanding success, and apart from the banquet night the weather was as it can be only in June in Scotland, super, as were the speakers. Apart from the Earl of Elgin we had my old friends Bob Urquhart, so long Agricultural Editor of the *Scotsman*, and Sir Henry Plumb who not only kept his promise made to me in Brazil to attend, but so tight was his European schedule that we had to helicopter him out over the dreaded Cairngorms in a thick fog to catch his plane for his next meeting in Sweden.

All the other Societies were longing to do the next Forum, and I regret that instead of sticking to the four-year rotation they decided to have mini-Forums every two years. The snag to my mind was that it used up too many countries too quickly.

However, off I went two years later to represent Scotland in South Africa at their mini-Forum. At least we were in business there: quite a few cattle were shipped there during my years as Secretary. I love that country, and how sad it was that apartheid took over for so many years, but one doesn't interfere with another country's politics and I went there to see their cattle and promote the breed. One of the top breeders there was a George McKenzie, whose wife was a McCombie and owned the famous silver tea pot from which Queen Victoria had 'taken tea'. The McKenzies, terrific hosts, were well known and respected throughout South Africa. The Johannesburg show has a lovely setting and it was fun to meet Anneli Drummond-Hay that was, now established as one of the top show jumpers in South Africa, having married into that country. At the end of a most successful trip, when at last I was able to sell some bulls, Sal and I were given a 'thank you weekend' by two super people, the Barnards, at their coast house. Lest any Aberdeen-Angus breeder reads my memoirs, Sally's fare was paid by me! Unfortunately, the Barnards had forgotten to pay their electricity bill, so we spent the whole weekend without hot water or light, and as we didn't know them well enough, or even have their Bloemfontein phone number, nothing could be done and we've all laughed about it ever since.

Without a doubt the highlight of my years with the Society was the Centenary in 1979, when Her Majesty the Queen Mother, our Patron, graciously consented not only to come to our lunch but also to make a super speech (which I'm damned sure was written by herself because it was delivered from the heart). As Her Majesty was in residence in Birkhall it was obvious that Aberdeen was the place to hold our 'do', and as it was to be Aberdeen what better place than the Elphinstone Hall with all the background of that great name and Her Majesty's upbringing?

It was most unfortunate that our Centenary came just after that awful tragedy of Earl Mountbatten's murder at the hands of the IRA. As a result the security was more than strict, it was rigid. The Aberdeen police were the tops and were more than kind to us, but they had to search not only the cellars but the blooming rafters, as they were certain that the beloved Queen Mum would be next in line.

I unfortunately had to vet each person coming in, and it isn't easy to remember names. It's like the old story: what are four stages of old age in a man? First you forget people's names, secondly you forget people's faces, thirdly you forget to do up your fly buttons and fourthly you forget to undo them. Fortunately I normally wear a kilt, but I still forget people's names and I was most embarrassed when a lady breeder and her daughter came forward and I asked how her husband was, only to be told he had died. Mrs Hedges, I say publicly how sorry I was for that gaffe, as I had the greatest regard for your late husband Bill, he was not only the greatest supporter of Smithfield Show I ever knew, but once held a super night at the Butchers' Hall, no expense spared, with pianist, singers, the lot.

Another memory I have of that Centenary lunch was a hyper-efficient town officer who told me off for not standing in the right place when the Queen Mother arrived (I had been vetting some late-comers). He was extremely curt with me and as Her Majesty arrived and I was one of the welcoming party I had no time to have a few words with him. However, the next night when the Lord Provost of Aberdeen gave the Society a party, I got hold of this chap and asked him where the photos were of the former Lord Provosts. He took me next door, whereupon I pointed at the one of my grandfather, Sir John Fleming, and said, 'That chap presented the gold chain to Aberdeen Town Council that you're now wearing, so less of your lip.' He was more than civil after that.

The Queen Mother's speech was, as one would guess, full of common sense and humour, just like her good self, which I have been lucky enough to find out personally. I had been fortunate to get Mike Mackie, an old pal of mine but since our friendship days highly elevated to be the rightful Lord Lieutenant of the County, to reply to the toast of the guests, apart from Her Majesty, and as always he made a super job of it. There is something very special about the Queen Mother's personality that can bring a gathering of very ordinary people up to an extraordinary high level, and it has been my fortune to experience this in my lifetime more than once. I had the honour of toasting the guests and after doing so had to present Her Majesty with a bronze statue of an Aberdeen-Angus bull and a Caithness Glass goblet suitably inscribed. One only has to look at the resultant photos to see which Her Majesty appreciated.

It is sad indeed that from these halcyon days of the World Forum and the Centenary the breed has been torn apart by internal squabbling. Part of this came about because the Society decided to go into the business of selling Aberdeen-Angus beef, which was never a breed society's job, and partly it is because there are fewer genuine farmer/stocksmen in the breed. As a result of the A.A.'s worldwide reputation, and rightly so, for producing top class beef (because of the marbling, those gossamer strands of fat through the carcase), moneyed people have jumped on the bandwagon, then got onto the breed's Council and made decisions which have done the Society lasting harm. They leave their herds to be looked after by stockmen, who, because of the long hours they have to work and poor pay compared with other jobs, are a dying breed, more's the pity.

Some of the most fervent supporters of the breed from overseas have been the Danes, and but for their veterinary regulations many more cattle would have been exported. Even so there has been a healthy export market there: before I gave up I felt I had to go and see what was happening breed-wise in Denmark. As it was a mainly dairy-producing country, the Aberdeen-Angus breed could only be used on their native breed the red Danes, which is not the worst use for a good beef breed in my view. I flew out Air Icelandic from Edinburgh and went to all three islands that comprise

Denmark. The first real shock I got was a manager who said he sold all the best stock he had and bred from his worst stock; quite contrary to everything I had ever been taught.

After a fabulous week seeing some good and some bad cattle, I was left at Copenhagen Airport by the Secretary of the Danish Aberdeen-Angus Society. What we both didn't realise was that Icelandic Airways were on strike, and I was stranded in Copenhagen until Monday with extremely little money. They tell me Copenhagen is a fun town, but you could fool me. I hadn't two brass farthings, and was only able to pay for a lowly B & B. The snag was I hadn't got any phone numbers of my previous hosts. Even worse, when they shipped me out on the Monday they did it to Amsterdam, saying B-Cal would see me home. When I got there the B-Cal rep said, 'You're joking, we don't fly to-day, but you might get on a Dan Air flight which is about to leave now.' God bless him, he sent his female assistant with my large bag to stop the flight. Who paid for it I will never know, but I'm sad I missed the joys of Copenhagen. Maybe just as well.

But one of the most interesting visits I had overseas had nothing to do with the Aberdeen-Angus Society at all. It was when Michael Noble was Minister of Trade and he was asked by the Government, Heath's, to visit Iran and see what potential there was for trading with them. It was during the reign of the Shah, and Michael decided to take Professor Gordon Dickson to advise on the possibilities of helping the Iranians with their agricultural education, as he had done a great job in that sphere in England both at Cirencester and Durham. Michael asked me to go to see if we could export lamb. The waste of money had to be seen to be believed. An example was a huge slaughterhouse-cum-refrigeration plant that had been erected at vast expense, which had to be pulled down because it was in the flight path to one of the Shah's palaces that he visited once a year.

The first few days were frustrating in the extreme, as we were passed from one ministry official to another and were shown model farms, but I rebelled and at last I was allowed to get out and meet the ordinary farmers. Like all countries that have constant sunshine, water is the secret. Where this had been well used, and they had plenty in the hills, they grew fantastic lucerne. One particular dairy farm managed by an Englishman was a real model. But it was meeting the hill farmers that I enjoyed: there is something about hill farmers all over the world that makes them very special to me. The only difference with the Iranian ones was that their houses were carpeted with the most ornate Persian carpets which in this country would cost a fortune. The land was hopelessly over-grazed, and with some judicious fencing of low ground and the use of irrigation they could have quadrupled their output.

On our last day the three of us had to visit an area up in the hills some four hours' journey north of Teheran. The road was one of the worst I have ever been on, and the driver was certainly the worst (or comparable to some in the Indian Divisions during the war). For the first time in my life I had to ask the driver to stop as I had the you know whats: I've never known fear like it.

When I came home I did a broadcast about my trip and instanced the English farm manager who was doing so well. I suggested there could be a future for more British managers. Luckily no one took me up on it, as shortly afterwards Ayatollah Khomeini overthrew the Shah and the world knows what has happened since. It just shows, if one doesn't have the language, how little one really gets to know about a country, but it was an unforgettable experience.

37

Broadcasting and Public Speaking

If anyone says again, 'It's so easy for you, Ben' after I've made a public speech or done a broadcast, I'll scream. Both Father and Mother were good public speakers; in fact the year that my mother was President of the Church of Scotland Women's Home Board she was written up in the popular daily papers as being the best speaker at that year's Church Assembly when speaking to a full Usher Hall. There is no doubt being born with a good carrying voice is a great advantage, but easy it never is. One has to work at it like every other job in life, but the butterflies in my tummy get bigger every speech or broadcast I make, and it certainly is never easy.

In farming circles and country life public speakers are always in demand, and I suppose it was natural that I should be called on to represent farmers and to speak at NFU dinners and Young Farmers Clubs. I've recently stopped doing the latter, as all too many of them do not have the manners to send an s.a.e. with their invitation or a note of thanks afterwards. It may sound petty of me, but I get a fairly large mail and the physical effort and time spent writing addresses and acceptances or refusals can be consuming.

When a speech comes off it gives one immense pleasure, and one can feel whether one's speech has gone down well or not. In my small way I can see why well-known actors and actresses like performing to a live audience, for if they are appreciative it gives you a tremendous kick. There is a benevolent society connected with the Smithfield Market called The Drovers Club, who help the less fortunate in Smithfield Market. They hold an annual dinner at the Connaught Hotel for 700, and they kindly invited me to be their guest speaker. I was thrilled when I sat down and the Toast Master whispered in my ear, 'Well done sir, just right, amusing and not too long.' The speech to Her Majesty the Queen Mother was another I will always remember, as it was such a super company and all the speeches that day were short, amusing and to the point.

But like everyone else I've made speeches of which I haven't been particularly proud, and I always find it hard to follow someone who is better than myself. This has happened to me on more than one occasion: notably at the World Forum Banquet when the Earl of Elgin spoke brilliantly, and at the Scottish Auctioneers when David Pighills, the Headmaster of Strathallan, was outstanding.

As one gets older one's memory for stories is not so good, and I find a few postcards with headings on them is more than useful for jogging the memory. A stock of stories (clean) is very useful too and I keep different ones for different occasions, such as church stories and agricultural show stories. I've had fun making the speech at one or two of the leading agricultural show dinners. Wedding stories: one of my favourites is of the Church of Scotland minister who wasn't too good at remembering faces or names, and many years after marrying a couple he was reminded by the husband that he, the husband, had been late turning up. The minister, remembering the occasion, said, 'Yes, you got a fright that day all right.' 'I've got her yet', replied the man.

My first broadcast was in 1948 from the October Highland Cattle sales. Alastair Dunnett was the agricultural producer and had been with me at a draft sale of Shorthorns at the famous Calrossie herd in Ross-shire. He mentioned that he couldn't manage to go to Oban so would I send in a report. I was petrified at the thought, but I must have made a half decent job of it as I am still doing regular farming broadcasts all these 50 years on. I am probably the only broadcaster in Scotland who has attained his half century on 'steam radio' and TV. I remember starting that first broadcast by quoting the late Jimmy Bain, a well known cattle dealer, whose saying about Oban was, 'If you can't see Kerrera [the island off Oban] it's raining and if you can it's going to.' I used the same story in October 1984 at the October sales, and luckily my producer, Jan Gavin, hadn't heard it before, God bless her.

In the Fifties, before the advent of TV, we had a lot of farming programmes on steam radio. One was called Farm Forum and the team was always the same: Sandy Main from Windyedge, outside Perth, representing arable farming and chairing the team, who was very quick and an outstanding authority on potatoes; Dougal Fowlie from Aberdeenshire, full of pawky humour and a great feeder of good fat cattle; Robbie Stevenson from Ayrshire, Vice-Chairman of the Scottish Milk Marketing Board, and a breeder of Ayrshire cattle; and myself, at that time resident at Gaskbeg and representing hill farmers. It was a super team: we made each other spark and we were used once a month. When we'd had a frightful harvest and Aberdeenshire had been particularly late, we were asked by Sandy for our district reports, and Dougal, in broad Doric, said, 'Thank God for the Dukes.' Sandy, not understanding the twang asked, 'Did you have some nobility shooting with you or something, Dougal?' 'Na, Na, I just bocht some hundreds o' dukes [ducks] and they ate up the battered hairst.' Sadly I'm now the only living member of that team, but every now and then I meet someone who says 'Ben, I fair miss Farm Forum'. They are always either bald or grey-haired, but certainly not in the first flush of youth!

Then we had broadcasts from different towns and villages chaired by Andrew Biggar who was an excellent chairman. We were once in the tiny hall at Achnacarry and the incomparable Johnnie Bannerman was one of the team. The question from the hall was about the rights and wrongs of poaching, and when Andrew asked Johnnie what his views were on the subject he replied, 'You can't call it poaching when a man takes a salmon', in that lovely lilting west Highland voice. What a great Scot he was and I used to love when he exploded out of his car at Gaskbeg, complete in kilt and cloak (it was he that made me buy my cloak), then din me for ages about Liberal policy and how we must make all the Highland counties Scottish Liberal seats. It was sad he never made the House of Commons, but I understand he took the House of Lords by storm. Those country farming programmes were such fun because whole villages turned out. It was before TV days and to have one's question on the air to be broadcast to the whole of Scotland was quite something.

Then, of course, the producers were all different. My first was Alastair Dunnett who, with his brother Robert, was groomed by their father, like mine a Church of Scotland minister, to go in for broadcasting, and after an education at Fettes they had elocution lessons ad infinitum. They both had beautiful, what I call educated, Scottish voices. They were polished broadcasters and great company, but unfortunately they both had the 'weakness' as we call an addiction to the bottle in the Highlands. (Truth to tell, I have it too but not as badly as they had.) Then, in the heyday of Scottish farm broadcasting before the advent of the 'telly', we had Harry Hoggan who did a super job.

BBC techniques were improving all the time, and I remember the first link-up of farmers from all over the country. I had to be in Aberdeen, which then was a tiny out-station, Robbie Stevenson was in Glasgow, Tony Stodhart (now My Lord Stodhart) was in Edinburgh and I can't remember who were in the English stations. I think Henry Fell and John Cherrington were in London. As it had never been tried before we all had to be in hours earlier for rehearsals and all was completed an hour and a half before link up. I remember Tony signing off and saying, 'I'm going round to the Cafe Royal for a quickie', and Robbie saying, 'Sorry you're not coming to the Curlers, Ben', and there was I stuck in Beechgrove miles from the nearest hostelry with an uninterested engineer and not even a cup of tea on hand, and the thought of going back over the infamous Cockbridge to Tomintoul road after the broadcast. Oh, it was great to be young.

Then we got a new producer who shall remain nameless who, when Tony Stodhart and I were part of the team and demanded our usual pre-programme dram, told us 'You don't drink before you broadcast.' If ever a programme nearly didn't go on the air that was the occasion.

In the Fifties and Sixties Scotland had its own version of 'Any Questions' called 'Matter of Opinion'. At that time the English programme had a farming figure to project the earthy approach, and they used A.G. Street and Ralph Wightman. So I was more than chuffed to appear on 'Matter of Opinion'. I remember in my first broadcast telling a well-known Labour Cabinet Minister, John Strachey, that he was talking a lot of clap-trap. If it had been a farming audience I would have used stronger language. Looking back, I was lucky to meet so many of the Super Scots of their day. Harold Leslie (later Lord Birsay); Lionel Daiches, with that tremendously keen brain; James Shaw Grant, who has done so much for the crofting counties; Tony Stodhart, who went on to the House of Lords and chaired the Committee which produced that excellent report on Local Government; and Jack House, that inimitable Glaswegian. And of course there were always the MPs; some have done well and some not so well. They have a trying and exacting job, and to come off a plane (then with propellers) after a week in the House to appear in a Scottish town can't have been easy.

One of my dearest memories of 'Matter of Opinion' was when it was being held on the island of Islay and one of the team was that super writer Eric Linklater. We had been all too well looked after when the broadcast was finished, as that island is famous for its malt whisky. Eric had left the assembled company to go upstairs to the loo and sometime later a horrific noise could be heard: being the youngest member I was sent off to see what had happened. When I got up to the first landing I heard a tremendous shouting of, 'Let me out, you serfs, let me out.' I just turned the door handle and said, 'It's all right, Eric, your serf's here.' Whether he had claustrophobia or not I will never know, but oh boy! was he glad to see me!

Then there was the memorable occasion during the time when the children had a religious programme (changed days). The regular presenter was off sick, so an old pal of mine (not very religious, I might say) was asked to take over. Coming in after an extremely good lunch, he launched forth by saying, 'I suppose I'd better lower my religious bottom into the famous religious chair.' Knowing the character I'm surprised he was so mild, but thank God he was, he hadn't noticed the green light was on.

The author being interviewed in the Sixties for a TV programme about a Factor's job

Then came the advent of TV, and it was, I suppose, natural that the early producers had to use people who had some broadcasting experience. At Gaskbeg the early English farming units wanted to do something against the 'wicked landlords'. I have never agreed with these sentiments, so I think that the producer in this case finished up with egg on his face, but it was an experience for me with the takes and re-takes one needs. Then I had a TV appearance with MacDonald Hastings in Cliff Michelmore's programme 'Tonight'. Because of this programme, on the problem of marauding deer, MacDonald Hastings, having stayed a couple of nights with us, asked if I would take his son Max to show him what Highland life was all about. This eventually resulted in his Foreword to this book! Thanks also to this I not only had to go to London to put the finishing touches to the feature, but was introduced to Wilfred Pickles, who wanted me to do a piece for his then very popular programme. After this Eddie Straiton, now famous as the TV Vet and the adviser to 'All Creatures Great and Small' (whose author, Alfie Wight, not James Herriott, was at Vet College with me) asked me to go to Birmingham, bring a Highland cow and demonstrate the points of the breed, which was great fun.

After that, TV farming took off, and with my broadcasting experience I was lucky to be used frequently. Although a devotee of the BBC, I must admit, conceitedly, the programme Tyne-Tees did about my life was one of the happiest we did. It was in May in Argyll with snow on the tops, the most lovely weather, when the first takes came off, and I had people I admire like Hamish Menzies and Ian McRae from Blackmount, and Donald and Ernie MacPherson from Cairndow on the programme—these are representative of the people who have made Ben Coutts.

Having been on the Royal Smithfield Show Council for nearly thirty years, I was extremely keen that their history, which stretched back over so many hundreds of years, should be put on film. Arthur Anderson, the current producer of the Scottish farming programme 'Landward' (on which I'm proud to say I launched him), made a first-class job of producing the film, and not only that, he had it shown nationwide and it received much favourable comment, not least from Her Majesty the Queen Mother who appeared in it, and wasn't able to watch it when it was first on because of a previous engagement. Her ADC told me months afterwards that he could have seen me far enough because he had to videotape it. But I have been proud to be the presenter of a record that the Smithfield Club will have for posterity, thanks to video. Since then Eddie Straiton and I have appeared again on 'Landward', talking of 'the days that were'.

There is an age for TV work, and I fear I'm coming to the end of my usefulness to this branch of the media. I was put up to present a new countryside programme, but was turned down because of my age. However, I hope there are some broadcasting years left in me, because I dearly love doing it, even although each time it tears the guts out of me. It makes me concentrate and think: it's a challenge and I've always loved challenges. One should never have regrets in life, but when I sit in a busy Press Room, at, say, the Royal Highland Show—where I presented their bicentenary programme —and the typewriters are chattering all around and I'm knocking out my script in longhand, as I am doing this book, I dearly wish I had learned to type.

38

The Royals

Luckily for agricultural shows, the Royal family are tremendous supporters. A breed society secretary often may have to show off his stand and receive Royalty in his cattle lines, if his breed happens to have Royal patronage, at a county or national show. But as Secretary of the Aberdeen-Angus Society I was luckier than the rest of the society secretaries put together, because every time our Patron went to a show Her Majesty ordered that my President and I were present.

I know it's the in-thing for certain left-wingers to be against the Royal family, although I notice that with monotonous regularity they accept the ermine and go to the House of Lords. But since my boyhood days I have had the greatest admiration for our Royal family, and think many times that we, as a nation, behaving as we do, have better than we deserve. When I think how well our media behaved during the period when King Edward VIII was about to abdicate for the 'woman he loved', and how terribly they have reacted to any foot put out of step by our present Royal family it just makes me fizz. That someone who gave so much for his country as the late Earl Mountbatten should be castigated, as he was recently in one of our leading Sunday papers, makes poor reading to say the least. After all, every one of us, even the greatest in the land, has frailties; is nothing now sacrosanct?

But to the Greatest. HM Queen Elizabeth the Queen Mother had hinted to someone that as Patron of the breed she felt she could help, which God bless her most sincerely she has done. The Aberdeen-Angus Society has had no more fervent nor staunch supporter.

Possibly the first Royal I was to meet was Prince Philip, who was at the Royal Show as its President during my first year as the breed society secretary. No one I have ever met has done his homework better, nor is more forthright. He bluntly told me the Aberdeen-Angus breed were too small (right) and that they were in the wrong hands (right again, at that time) and how was brother Wally? (who had been a good influence in Kenya: doubly right) and one is left rather speechless. Yes, even me.

The next member of the family I was to meet was when the Three Counties Show kindly asked me to judge their Inter-Breed Championship and Princess Anne was to present the prizes. I had been told that Her Royal Highness could be prickly. Whoever got hold of that story wants his head looking at. She was absolutely charming, with a great sense of humour. As an Aberdeen-Angus enthusiast I was expected to put up the breed's Champion as the Overall, but as he was overfat and couldn't walk I made an extremely showy Hereford Bull Overall and a super Welsh Black cow, who unfortunately wasn't too good on her legs, Reserve. I'm glad to say that as these two breeds are strong in the South West my decision was popular with the crowd. But Princess Anne gave me a fair grilling as to why I had made my decisions, and asked me why certain breeds had not been considered. When we came to the Charolais exhibit, which at that time were very much on the up-and-up, Her Royal Highness asked, 'What's wrong with him?' Unfortunately, the animal put in front of me was not a good representative of the breed and I said, 'Do you like soup, your Highness, because this bull has plenty of bone and no flesh to make it?' This remark was followed with peals of laughter and the rest of the programme went like a bomb, mainly thanks to my old pal Mike Simmonds of the Hereford Society who was my Chief Steward. Sadly Mike, who to his dying day bred good old-fashioned Hereford cattle complete with horns, not the modern leggy type, is no longer with us, and his influence on the Hereford breed is sorely missed. Princess Anne I was to meet again, as she was the President of the Royal Highland Show the year I was made a Fellow of the Royal Agricultural Societies (F.R.Ag.S.), and as such she presented me with my certificate.

Then there was that terribly cold, cold Royal Show when Prince Charles was the President. He was passing our stand to go to the Welsh Black Cattle Society stand, of which he is Patron, and I emerged from ours dressed, as usual, in my 'grass skirt', whereupon His Royal Highness stopped and had a super jaw with me, as Donald, my son, had gone to Gordonstoun at the same time as he was at the school—though Donald, now a TV producer and a communist, has never forgiven me for sending him there!

Princess Alice, Duchess of Gloucester, is another fantastic Royal, and I only wish these memoirs of mine were half as good as hers. The East of England Show is naturally her show, as she lives in that area. Her son, the Duke of Gloucester, an ardent farmer, was a most attentive President of the Royal Smithfield Club. Although I have been privileged to meet Princess Alice at the East of England Show on two occasions, without a doubt the happiest one was when brother Frank, as Colonel of the KOSB, and Princess Alice, Colonel in Chief of that illustrious regiment, organised an evening for all those who went to war from Melrose. Jimmy Scott-Aiton, famous (apart from many other things) as the rider of the Foxhunter Chase winner at Cheltenham, the Callant, and I would be two of the few presented who were not KOSB: Jimmy was in the paras at Arnhem and I was, as you know, in the Surrey & Sussex Yeomanry. Who am I to pontificate about the influence of Scottish blood into the country's royalty, but it would be a poor man indeed who didn't admit the great part the Bowes-Lyons and the bold Buccleuchs have done to keep our Royalty in the place which they rightly hold today.

I was fortunate indeed to be asked to judge the Burke Trophy the year after I retired from the Aberdeen-Angus Society Secretaryship. The Burke Trophy is at the Royal Show, and is for a male and female from each beef breed; also from the dairy breeds, but I was obviously doing the beef. The orders to the Judge are that the pair must match. The Judge is allowed to see the pairs in front of him in an outside ring before the big moment when Raymond Brooks Ward does his big commentary in the main ring, by which time the Judge should have made up his mind, ready to slap the lucky winners on their backsides at the time the President arrives—in my year, no less a personage than the Monarch. During my cursory glance in the outside ring (very thorough, actually) I had mentally knocked out all the usual favourites—Aberdeen-Angus: not matched; Herefords: with a wee bad bull; Charolais: unpardonably bad hind legs; Simmentals: useful, but again not right behind. The best pair without a doubt, to my mind, were the Longhorns, now put into the rare breed class. And the South Devons next. I had the courage of my convictions and put up the Longhorns, but I know the Monarch was not amused.

Sally and I went to Balmoral to drive our Highland pony mare at a wonderful driving meet at which one of the obstacle judges, riding a chestnut mare and wearing a headscarf, was none other than our Monarch. When we were presented with special rosettes for attending (and because of security it will never happen again), the Monarch said, to her steward Nigel Thornton-Kemsley after she had presented Sal and me with ours, 'I can never understand why Captain Coutts gave the Burke Trophy to those Longhorn cattle.'

That was a magical weekend, and it coincided with the return of the Prince of Wales and Princess Diana from their honeymoon. Those of us favoured to be up for the driving weekend were allowed to line the avenue to Balmoral to welcome the Royal couple home, a one-off and a never-to-be-forgotten experience. My old friend Martin Leslie, by this time Factor of the Estate, had organised that the employees, as is a tradition in the Highlands, dressed in Balmoral tweed, pulled a brougham, bedecked with heather,

The author with HM The Queen after the author had judged the Longhorns the winners of the coveted Burke trophy at the Royal Show, 1981

from the entrance gates to the Castle. Of course, we were all there to cheer. How sad it is that thanks to the Brighton bombings, Lord Mountbatten's atrocious death etc, the Monarch won't be allowed to hold that sort of weekend again. Sad too that the marriage of Charles and Diana broke up and she came to such a tragic end. However they seem to have bred two super sons, whom I wish well, and hope they get minimal media attention.

Sally and I have been lucky enough to own one or two decent Highland ponies. Her Majesty was needing another good brood mare, and we as it happened had just the right beast. We had two good fillies out of her and we could let her go, and who wouldn't to the Queen? The mare wasn't actually of our own breeding, as when I was given my golden handshake from the Aberdeen-Angus Society there just happened to be a Highland pony sale the next day of Sandy Wright's ponies from Glenalmond, someone for whom I had the greatest regard, and I reckon I bought his best mare. Martin Leslie, having photographed her, eventually closed the deal. Not at the greatest price, but let's be honest, all of us are taxpayers and why should the Royals spend more than the going rate? I said to Martin that Sal and I had been fortunate enough to be asked up to Birkhall for lunch with the Queen Mum and could we bring the mare the same day? The answer was, 'Sure, but I don't think the Monarch will be able to see you.'

It just happened that I was due to be in Grantown-on-Spey the next day doing some recording for the Smithfield Show programme. As a result I said I would take the lorry with the mare and Sal would take the car, which I would need to go over the Lecht to Speyside after our Royal day. As I was early and as I thought Her Majesty was not to meet us, I stopped at the pub just before one comes to Balmoral to wait for Sal, have a dram and see the mare was all right. We were both amazed that, although we had given our lorry and car numbers, we were hardly checked at the Balmoral entrance. We must have looked honest. Now, since our happy driving weekend, security has become frightfully strict at Balmoral.

I had been to Martin's house before, so I knew where to go and parked my lorry in front of his house. When I went in I was given a big dram by his wife Catriona, daughter of my old friend General McDonald, who did such a super job for the Skye NFU. I asked Catriona, who had her hair recently done as she also was lunching at Birkhall, where the mare was to go and she said she would show me. She just got round the corner with me when she saw a Range Rover with pennant up, driven by her husband and carrying the Monarch. Whereupon Catriona fled. Her Majesty, as usual, put me at ease. She said, 'I understand your earlier days were spent with thorough-breds, would you just trot the mare out?'

One of my most lovely memories of this most wonderful person is of this meeting. Highland ponies have long and large tails, and to keep them clean Sal and I always wrap a pair of ladies tights round the tail and cover it with a tail bandage. When I took it off Her Majesty was generous in her praise. I sincerely hope that none of Her Majesty's ladies-in-waiting go short of tights because of that day! I apologised for having on my old dirty dust-coat but Her Majesty, who as always was looking immaculate, replied that she was also in her working clothes, i.e. her kilt.

Then I again had the pleasure of meeting the Monarch when I was doing the TV programme for the bicentenary of the Royal Highland Show. It was indeed a 'Royal' Highland that day as Her Majesty obviously thoroughly enjoyed herself and laughed and joked with lots of us. In fact I was standing behind a row of policemen when Her Majesty spotted me and came over especially to speak to me. Since then Her Majesty has visited my District Council ward and when I was introduced to her said, 'Oh, we know each other of old, he put up those cattle at the Royal Show and even my carriage horses shied at them.'

My father, as a Church of Scotland minister, once preached an excellent sermon about the great lead Her Majesty was giving to her country in her regular church-going. The sermon was shockingly typed, but I thought it so good I 'drew a bow at a venture' and sent it to Her Majesty. Imagine my amazement when I got a letter of thanks from Her Majesty in her own fair hand, which I cherish and keep in a safe place.

But it is Her Majesty Queen Elizabeth the Queen Mother that I have been fortunate enough to meet most. As she was Patron of the Aberdeen-Angus Society and an enthusiastic and knowledgeable breeder of these cattle I was disappointed that no effort had been made by the Society to keep in touch with their Royal Patron, except to ask Her Majesty to open their new offices the year before I became Secretary. Sir Martin Gilliatt, the Queen Mum's Secretary, had worked with brother Wally in Kenya. The first time I went to the Castle of Mey I was petrified as there was a large party, but oh! what a gracious lady that wonderful person is, and she can put you at your ease in seconds. On that first occasion the factor was a local farmer and ex-army officer who knew brother Frank. But then, all those thirty years ago the Queen Mother had big lunch parties, as she was a mere 70! The year after my first visit to the Castle, Martin Leslie took over as factor. Martin I had known in my Gaskbeg days, as when he was filling in his student vacation he 'picked up' grouse with an excellent Labrador on an estate I managed. From that year until 1999 the President and Secretary of the Aberdeen-Angus Society were invited to lunch at the Castle.

On that first occasion I was taken to visit the Royal Gardener, who remembered a broadcast I had done about the different varieties of potatoes I preferred, starting with Sharpe's Express, then Duke of York, followed by Kerr's Pink and finishing with Golden Wonder. But alas, he had the weakness and by the time I went back the next year he was no longer with us.

The Queen Mum's knowledge of gardening is immense and she loves her garden so it's a real experience to be shown by her round the Castle of Mey garden.

For eight years I was invited to the Castle of Mey and naturally the annual visit was taken on by my successor. I thought that would be the end of my invitations, one of which had been to stay the night, when I had the privilege to dance with Her Majesty and to find out how tremendously light she is on her feet. But the year after I retired from the Aberdeen-Angus Society both Sally and I were bidden to Birkhall. My visits to Caithness had been with my Presidents and Sal wasn't invited, so it was super to have her with me. It was the day we delivered the pony to Balmoral and we went with Martin and Catriona, and at the same lunch there were Princess Alexandra and her husband Angus, and Princess Alice, the Duchess of Gloucester. The lunch was in the extremely attractive log cabin that had been presented to the Queen Mother for her eightieth birthday. It was a fun day with the Queen Mother serving up lunch. My bothy days seemed far, far away. She made me feel humble and grateful to have met the most charming and the greatest in the land all in one day.

The Queen Mother's terrific interest in her herd and in the Aberdeen-Angus breed made her an obvious choice to visit the Royal Smithfield Show, and I was deputed to ask Her Majesty if she would do us that honour. Not only did she attend three years in a row, but she has presented a superb new cup for the best pedigreed native animal as she, like many others, felt that the continental cross cattle were winning too often. Not only did the Queen Mum do that for the Club but she invited the whole of Smithfield Council to visit the Castle of Mey and inspect her herd and her North Country Cheviot sheep, after which we took tea and had a 'refresh' with the gracious lady.

Sadly, just before the show in her 100th year, Her Majesty fell and broke her collar-bone, 'just like the jockeys do', as she said. She asked me to present her cup instead, which I was honoured to do. I was also lucky enough to represent the Royal Smithfield Club at the wonderful National Tribute to the Queen Mother on Horse Guards Parade on 19 July 2000, when over 300 organisations with which Her Majesty is associated marched past. It was a wonderful occasion, brilliantly organised as only we, the Brits, can. Her Majesty thanked all who had taken part and all who had attended, and she refused to sit down although there was a chair provided, just as she has refused to use the chair-lift specially installed for her at Sandringham by the Queen. As the old song goes, 'Oh, oh, oh, what a girl!'

What a wonderful effect this truly remarkable lady has had on this old country of ours, and I deem myself a very lucky laddie to have been given so many opportunities to meet her, and to receive her annual Christmas card.

39

Big Ben for Westminster

As already stated I always had a leaning towards Liberal politics. I had had the chance to stand for Inverness-shire back in my Gaskbeg days, but Creina wasn't keen on the idea as she was a socialist. Alastair Duncan Miller, of Remony, near Aberfeldy, had stood twice for West Perth and Kinross and on the second occasion had the hard luck to have that great Scot, then Sir Alec Douglas Home, put up against him by the Tories when they wanted him as Prime Minister. After that Alastair asked me if I would take over his mantle, as he was going to stand as a Regional Councillor, which he not only did but was an excellent Tayside Regional Convener for which he received a well earned CBE: many of us thought it should have been a knighthood.

In the following General Election a young QC, a certain Nicholas Fairbairn, stood for the Tories and beat the Scottish National candidate by under a hundred votes. In later years Nicky made a name for himself in more ways than one. Whether one liked him or not, no one can dispute that he had one of the keenest brains in Scotland, but was also a natural for the press gossip columns with his strange dress taste and his, shall we say, different way of life from that of the ordinary citizen.

By the time the 1983 Election came along Perthshire was one of the constituencies which had been redrawn. West Perth and Kinross no longer comprised only Crieff, Aberfeldy, Callander and Kinross and their surrounding areas, but now Perth, Crieff and Kinross were lumped together with their surrounding rural areas, going as far west as St Fillans and down the Carse of Gowrie to Invergowrie of all stupid places: stupid because it is only four miles from Dundee. So the new constituency of 62,000 voters had 40,000 voters in Perth and I was little known there. However, Liberal Headquarters, knowing my leanings, phoned up and asked me if I would stand, and as the hustings were obviously only two months away I accepted. This came about because Jim Wallace, the original prospective candidate, was lured to Orkney and Shetland. Thanks to Laura Grimond he won this seat, since when he has gone from strength to strength, and is now not only the second minister in the Scottish Assembly, but coped very well when he had to take over on Donald Dewar's death, until Labour appointed a new first minister.

The new constituency party was ill-prepared to fight a campaign. The

Opening the Campaign Office, Crieff, General Election 1983

interests of the old constituencies were entirely different—almost town versus country—as were their ways of raising money (which was almost non-existent). There was neither a club nor headquarters, nor even committee rooms, so we were virtually starting from scratch with an ageing (sixty-seven) prospective Parliamentary Candidate, no agent, virtually no money and no base. Quite a daunting task.

When the Election was actually called there were just four weeks for me to become known to 62,000 voters, an impossible task. I was up against Nicky Fairbairn who, having been MP for West Perth and Kinross, had to be reselected by the new constituency and he had quite a lot of opposition before he actually won through. I also had to contend with Douglas Crawford of the SNP, who had been the MP for Perth in a previous Parliament, was well known and respected in Perth and had been an excellent constituency MP.

So the odds were heavily stacked against me, but I've always thrived on a challenge. Ross Holmes and Alastair Dow, both from Perth Liberal Association, became my Agent and Assistant Agent respectively. Willie Wilson, the only Perth Liberal District Councillor, became my Press Relations Officer, and around them they formed a hard-working committee too numerous to mention. Although too numerous to mention, they were nothing like as numerous as the other two committees of the Tories and the SNP, but ours were all hard-working folk, none of whom could help during the day.

Sally was terrific and backed me all the way, and it was to her that I gave the only promise during that hectic month's campaigning, and that was that I would be her groom at the National Pony Society Show in Alloa two days after the count. (Oh, there was another promise I made, and that was that I wouldn't kiss any babies under sixteen, and those that I did had to be female!) I've become fed up with politicians' promises over the years and decided I'd give none, and judging by the reaction I got on many a doorstep, lots of others are fed up being promised the impossible.

I have had many challenges in my life, but none so satisfying as that month. Broadcasting, TV work, lay preaching, fighting in the war etc, all set the adrenalin flowing, but nothing compared to the experience of wooing votes. As by this time I only had a part-time man helping at Woodburn, I had to be up at 6.30 am to get beasts fed and get ready to move by 9 a.m. I wore my kilt all the time, as a kilt combined with a funny nose made me easily recognisable. Whether that was a good thing I leave to others to judge. So among other chores my black brogues had to be cleaned, one pair for day use and one for evening, as I never let anyone else clean my shoes.

Sometimes with one of my Agents or, if they were unavailable, with a Liberal who had a spare hour or two, I set off to canvass. This I did up until lunchtime when I always returned to Woodburn for two reasons. The first was the mail, which doesn't arrive until 11.30-12 noon (something I would have liked to change had I become the MP) and secondly, since the war years I have, whenever possible, tried to have forty winks at this time, preferably 'on the backs down', but if not, then in a chair.

The mail was huge. Mainly piles of bumph from Liberal HQ which I had no hope of getting through as well as running a campaign. Then there were the nutters—all, I know, with deeply held views, and I respect their beliefs, but how they thought a letter was going to influence a battle-hardened veteran like me, who had formed my own firmly held opinions over sixty-seven years, beats me. I had letters from CND, anti-abortionists (who called my leader and friend, David Steel, a murderer), Age Concern, Community Councils, Institute of Adult Education, Sunday Observance, Women's Campaign for Soviet Jewry to name but a few. But as I didn't become the MP, in the week following the count the sky above Woodburn was red with the size of the bonfire that I lit.

Then in the afternoon I went out (often with Sally) to canvass in one of the areas in which I was to speak that night. I made thirty-two speeches in all, starting off in the rural areas and finishing in Crieff, Kinross and Perth.

I used my farm lorry quite a bit for my canvassing, as it was something different, and I hung my 'Big Ben for Westminster' signs all over it. The slogan was thought out by a delightful member of the SDP Committee called Joe who, like myself, was always a bit drouthy, and I've often said the slogan was worthy of Saatchi and Saatchi.

In this TV-oriented world, evening meetings are no longer a draw, especially as this was in late May and early June when everyone wanted to be in their gardens. But one had to do them, and although I always dreaded the fearfully heavy political questions I did enjoy question time, as it makes the grey-matter tick. I remember getting my knickers properly in a twist when I thought the questioner had asked me my views on what I thought was corporal punishment, and I was extolling its virtues and saying how much good it had done me etc. and wondered why she had such a puzzled look on her face. But she had been asking my views on capital punishment which, as a true blue Tory (having the usual blue-rinsed hair), she would have agreed would have done me a lot of good.

The four weeks were hectic to say the least and I have always all my life enjoyed my Sundays, but never more than during that month.

Towards the end of the campaign Willie Wilson had a brilliant idea when he hired the only available open double-decker bus, with which we toured Perth. We had all sorts of hair-raising experiences in it: one driver tried to decapitate us under the railway bridges, another drove so fast in one section we lost some of our precious 'Big Ben' posters, and it rained so hard one day that the water came down the back stairs like a burn in full spate. We were able literally to look down on our opponents Nicky and Douglas and ask them if they would care for a lift! We were able to stop in the different wards in Perth and canvass and deliver leaflets and then all get in the bus again with the microphones blaring to stop in another ward and do the same thing. Yes, it was not only stimulating, it was the greatest fun, but I slowly realised that it was the same old team that came with me and we were pathetically thin on the ground. No praise can be high enough for the loyal team I had, but compared with the well-oiled Tory efficiency with their fully paid agent, and the Scots Nats who had a committee room and quite a bit of cash, we worked on a shoestring. Dan Scot, our printers in Perth, thanks to Mary Doig lent us their office, which gave us a marvellous H.Q.; but once again one saw the same faithful few manning the office. Looking

Campaign poster, General Election 1983

back I often wonder how, with our slender resources and lack of preparation, we ever amassed three votes short of 11,000, especially as the previous Liberal vote had only been 4,000 in each of the old constituencies. A certain amount of conceit keeps you going. People are invariably kind to you and you think they are going to vote for you, little realising they too have their own views and principles. There's an old saying in Perthshire that they could put up a donkey and hang a blue label around his neck and they'd vote for it. Nicholas Fairbairn was certainly far from a donkey, but I know of any amount of people who said that because of some of his pre-election behaviour they would never vote for him, yet before election day came round they had his posters in their windows. Then there were the floating voters and 'don't knows', of which there were all too many. You've met them in all walks of life: 'They' ought to do this, or 'They' ought to do that, forgetting that the money has to come from the public. At the end of the day the biggest moaners were the ones that didn't know for whom to vote. But after fighting that campaign I realised what a lot of super people there are in this country, and the awful stories that one reads in the paper each day are confined to a small minority.

And if one had decided to stand for Parliament, what better constituency than my own? Often as I motored over the new Tay Bridge going down to the Carse of Gowrie I used to look back up to Perth and its surrounding green countryside and marvel at its beauty; realising only too well why it is known as the Fair City.

But it would be the Fair City that was to beat me. Douglas Crawford was not only well known as an excellent constituency MP but he had a strong force working for him there. Nicky too had the Conservative Club and his full-time agent in this well-known Tory stronghold. As for me, I was only known by the odd shopkeeper, the staff of the local cattle auction mart and the barmen at the different hostelries I had frequented over the years.

As polling day grew near I realised that all the talk I had heard of my possibly winning were false, and our pathetically small, but faithful, band were hopelessly outnumbered by the big battalions. This was especially obvious on polling day, when every single polling station, no matter how small, was manned by a Tory: their ability to muster the troops on the day would do credit to any Field Marshal. People seemed to appear from nowhere, like slater beetles from under stones.

It wasn't quite so bad as the election back in the Fifties when I was a tenant of Sir John Ramsden, and I was told by Sir John that I had to vote for the Tory although he knew I was the local Liberal Chairman. His chauffeur went round in Sir John's car and collected the employees and they too were told for whom they should vote. Luckily, it's changed days now, except that the party that carries my allegiance still seems to be the only one that is dependent on the ordinary voter to supply it with cash.

Anyone who hasn't witnessed a Count after the Polling Day has missed a gripping experience: the fortunes fluctuate backwards and forwards until eventually the winner emerges. Douglas Crawford polled 11,000 odd votes and I about 103 less, and Nicky over 16,000. There is no doubt at all that Douglas and I cut each other's throats, even although we were both ministers' sons and both went to Glasgow Academy.

No way could I be a Scottish Nationalist with their 'here's tae us, wha's like us' mentality. With my worldwide travel I am no isolationist. I am however a fervid Scot and although I served in the Sussex Yeomanry I am fed up with the Home Counties bringing back the gravy while the North gets the bones to pick. I always thought that to my dying day I would vote Liberal albeit, as Sally says, a huntin', shootin' and fishin' one. This I am sad to say has had to change, as the Lib-Dems in the Scottish Assembly have 'got into bed' with the Labour Party. If I wanted to vote Labour I would do so, but no way will I vote Lib-Dem only to find that they are pursuing Labour policies. In my years on the farming scene I have never known a party so anti-countryside, the backbone of which is the farming community, as the present Labour Government is at the beginning of the new millennium.

A year after the General Election I stood for the District Council, when I smelt the sweet scent of success with a majority of 250 votes over the Tory, who had not only been an ex-Provost but also unopposed for too long.

I enjoyed my District Councilling very much. My area, Almondbank, was rural, with rural problems, and if one can sort out even a proportion of the problems one is well rewarded. I was often asked why I, at my age, took on things like PPC for the constituency, or District Councilling, and my answer was quite simple. Life, and Scotland in particular, have been good to me and it's my duty to return that debt no matter how poorly I do it. If one is lucky enough to have gifts one should use them. At the end of both the Parliamentary and District Council campaigns I was so knackered, because I put everything into them, that I think I would have killed myself at Westminster, so it's a good thing, perhaps, that Big Ben didn't go there but left it to the present incumbent (the clock I mean, not the MP).

40

Full Circle

Dad believed that if a person was given a talent he or she must use it. Angus MacDonald, Editor of the *Scottish Farmer*, kindly said of me when I retired from the Aberdeen-Angus Secretaryship: 'He's a great communicator and we'll be hearing more of him.' It was a gift I was given and I use it realising only too well that it was none of my making. It may come as a surprise to readers who don't know me personally to learn that I have a deep faith in God, and am not ashamed of saying so publicly, and I am constantly thanking the Good Lord for the wonderful life he has given me. I can't understand how anyone who works with stock or on the land could not have a faith. The changing seasons never cease to amaze me. I suppose that because of my wound, the resultant years in hospital, plus my time on the raft and my reliance on the goodness of nature for my livelihood, my faith may be stronger than some.

I had the honour to meet Lord Denning when he was Master of the Rolls. Hearing of my interest in the Church he made a remark which I thought was very profound: 'You can't have discipline without morality, and you can't have morality without christianity and you can't have christianity without the church.' Church meetings (yes, and services sometimes too) can be boring affairs, but I have been a great supporter of the Church of Scotland since the war and it grieves me to see it fading all too quickly. As I pen this update to *Bothy to Big Ben*, there is a move afoot to close yet another 500 churches in Scotland. No-one is going to convince me that the ill-discipline in schools, the truancy, the teenage pregnancies and the muggings do not come from the fact that as a nation we are no longer 'kirk-greedy', and thus, as Lord Denning has said, we have lost our morality and discipline. Sunday is no longer the day of rest but the day of pleasure, and churches are used by all too many of us as places where we are baptised, married and where our burial service is held. These foregoing sentences may sound phoney from someone who has obviously enjoyed his dram all his days, but I firmly believe that the Lord came to save sinners like me, not the goodie-goodies.

I am proud to own a certificate showing that I have been an Elder of the Church of Scotland for thirty-five years (thirty-five years of undetected crime, one of my waggish pals said). It was presented to me by Sir John Gilmour when he was the Lord High Commissioner (the Queen's Representative) to the General Assembly of the Church of Scotland. During his year in office he very kindly had Sal and myself to stay at Holyrood Palace. I have never seen anything like the baths: they had wide wooden surrounds and you needed to be a steeplechaser to get in and out of them. Also staying at Holyrood was Jo Grimond for whom I have always had a great admiration. As I write I have been asked to represent the farming community in a procession through St Giles Cathedral, in Her Majesty's presence, depicting all walks of Scottish life, and after this to deliver an address in St Giles. After preaching in St Giles for the Association for the Protection of Rural Scotland I received a letter from the secretary which I cherish:

Dear Ben,

You said you always welcomed a challenge. After hearing you yesterday in St Giles, I understand why. It was a difficult task I set you, and the way you responded was magnificent. The A.P.R.S. is in your debt, because you helped to set the tone for what turned out to be a memorable Jubilee service. I am sorry that I caused you sleepless nights, but from A.P.R.S.'s and the congregation's point of view it was sleep well lost.

All in all, my Church connections have been happy.

With small farms in Britain becoming less and less viable I approached Robin Fleming, my landlord, and asked him what he wanted to do with Woodburn as I was knocking on 'three score years and ten' and wished to quit before farming small farms became a dead loss. Small farms used to be the ideal stepping stones for farm workers to get a start, young lads who would be willing to work twelve hours a day, seven days a week, but the price of land has become artificially high and the taxation system and the land tenure laws have forced landlords to lump small farms together. In many cases they have held on to them themselves.

As Robin didn't want to hold on to Woodburn I approached the two neighbouring landlords who had both shown an interest and we got them both to put in bids. Robin had magnanimously given us a cottage, plus two acres for the ponies, so that we didn't need to move in our retirement. This was in lieu of a pension, as I had factored the Flemings' estates for 25 years. When the farm was bought by his father it was completely run down, so much so you could see rabbits running through my first crop of oats, so thin was the crop in 1965. After I'd built up the fertility, in the year before I

Woodburn Croft, the author's retiral home, seen before he took possession

retired one of the same fields produced, according to the contractor who combined it, one of the heaviest yields in Strathearn. So the farm was more saleable at the end than when it was first bought. We couldn't be more grateful for our cottage and will ever be in his debt, as I have seen all too many farmers retire into a town and then die of boredom. The landlord who eventually bought the farm was none other than Ian Stewart, son of Duncan, my benefactor of forty years ago, so life has gone full circle and I looked forward to be able to wander out of my cottage with my dog and stick through cross-Highland cattle and Blackfaced sheep. Sadly, because of what I call 'brown envelope' farming, i.e. farming to suit the subsidies, this last part of the picture has not become reality, but we have nice neighbours on the farm.

Boredom is not a word in my dictionary, and with my Council work, the Church and helping with the ponies I have plenty on my plate. Talking of the ponies makes me realise that my life really has come full circle, as there are no excuses for me not making their beds as I learnt to do all those years ago at Lavington Stud. Even my horsey daughters admit that Dad makes the horses' beds professionally. I jolly well ought to when I think of the thousands I must have made half a century ago.

Woodburn Croft after the author took over, with his beloved Highland cattle and Blackfaced sheep

I suppose I'll be another of these old dodderers who drive in the middle of the road up to Crieff each day for the papers. And who knows, Auntie Beeb may kindly give me the odd broadcast, something which I particularly enjoy. But of one thing I am certain: I am going to give up judging stock and major public speaking soon, as far too many men have carried on at both these things too long and, in some cases, have made fools of themselves. (I wrote this in the first edition of this book. How wrong I was in this prediction, but of this, more in a further chapter.)

Like my father before me I have educated six of a family, but I had the advantage of having a farm to sell to educate the first four and a herd of cows to sell for the last two, whereas Father had his miserly stipend and, I suspect, some small financial help from a very good friend. I'm proud of all six of mine as I hope Dad was of us. A wee bit of Scottish pride never did anyone any harm.

I became Convenor of the Industry Committee of the Perth & Kinross District Council. I found the Council work time-consuming but rewarding, not financially but in 'something attempted, something done, to earn a night's repose'. Conceitedly, how I would have loved to become the Provost of the 'fair city' of Perth, which was on the cards had I got back onto the Council. However when I was up for re-election there was a rise in the in the fortunes of the S.N.P. and my ward elected an S.N.P. councillor instead of me. This man had to retire from the Council after having a punch-up with a taxi-driver—it takes all sorts to make a world!

A trip to Australia and New Zealand would be nice, with time enough to see things properly without being rushed as I was in 1964. Oh, there are so many things still to be done, and as Louis Armstrong sang: 'There's an awful lot of living to do.' If I'm spared, as they say, I mean to do just that, but so far I literally thank God for a wonderful life.

This was how I ended the original *Bothy to Big Ben* all those 13 years ago, and since then I have done some of that living. Having had time to contemplate the future as far as the countryside is concerned, I'm going to add a couple of chapters to give my thoughts and bring the story up to date.

41
What Happened Next

What a lot has happened since I wrote the original *Bothy to Big Ben* all those twelve years ago! Those who might have read that edition will have noticed that I now have added or updated chapters. In the last paragraph of the first *Bothy to Big Ben* I said that Sal and I would love to have a trip to Australia. Although I had spent two months there on a Nuffield Scholarship in 1964, I had not visited the Northern Territory, where son Shaun was managing a mere twenty thousand cows for the Mount Isa P.L.C., nor had I visited my brother Sir Walter, who retired from Uganda to England as one will have read, but couldn't stand the cold and so went to Perth, Western Australia. As Sal's elder sister lived there also, we decided to see them all and then go to New Zealand, Fiji, the U.S.A. and home. Sadly my brother was to die soon, but it was great to see him. I found Perth a fascinating city: clean, open spaces, parks and of course the pleasure of being beside the Swan River, as I've always had a fondness for being near water, old landlubber that I am. Then there were those lovely 'Veggy Shops', with each day a fantastic supply of fresh vegetables and fruit, the like of which we could never see in our cold Northern climate, Then, next door to that would be a wine shop with the most excellent selection of 'Oz' wines, all right up Coutts' street!

But the journey from Perth up the West Coast to Darwin, where Shaun was to meet us, was a nightmare. One had to stop and get out of the plane at every small town, and each time had to stand under a tin roof with the temperature well over one hundred degrees, so by the time we arrived in Darwin I was knackered.

Shaun's postal address was a P.O. box in Katherine, which was about two hundred miles south of Darwin. When we arrived in Katherine I said, 'Gosh, am I glad we've arrived!' to which Shaun replied, 'Dad, you've two hundred bloody miles to go to get to McArthur' (which was the station he managed). This conversation shows two things, first of all the fantastic distances they have to travel in the Northern Territory, and secondly the way that most people I met up there used swear-words in their everyday speech. Since our visit the N.T., as they call it, has been opened up to tourism: but sadly, for the young, there are few opportunities. I loved watching a calf-cutting competition, a sport at which Shaun had once excelled, but now that he was older he was doing the commentary (I wonder where he got that skill from?) Calf-cutting is a type of rodeo, in which the rider tries to separate a calf out from a mob of cattle.

Having farmed all my life, I was fascinated by the size of Shaun's operation. Water, of course, is the be-all and end-all of everything up in that arid area, and they talk of 'having a good wet' when they get that God-given gift. The Good Lord did rather overdo it when Katherine had floods seven feet deep a couple of years ago. Shaun thought nothing of driving one hundred kilometres to see his stock or a water supply.

He had to do the same when farmers in the N.T. were ordered to test every cattle beast they had for TB, and to shoot those they couldn't gather, just as hill farmers in Scotland often have ewes they can't get in for the normal clippings etc. He reckoned he shot a thousand, but they now have one of the few disease-free cattle stocks in the world. The breed of cattle up there all have to have Brahman blood in them because of the heat. As a Scot used to eating beef from our native breeds, and well hung at that, I found the beef very chewy for my ageing dentures, but with the tremendous rise of tourism to the Far East the N.T. have opened up an expanding market for their beef, with cattle being shipped out of Darwin in their thousands.

He was in charge of what was virtually a village, with a school and a shop, where the employees could get all their supplies apart from the beef which was supplied by the estate. I went out with the hand who had been detailed to get the beast wanted by the cook for the next day. They have a special corral for the steers they consider fit to kill. He shot one, bled it and pulled it onto a canvas sheet he had spread on the sand. He then butchered it on the spot. Not the most hygenic butcher's shop I've seen, but I bet all those who ate it built up antibodies sadly lacking in Britain today. The whole station met for breakfast, and 'stake [steak] and eggs' were on the menu when I was there.

Sadly, as has happened on all too many estates in this country, the accountants moved in. Without looking at the disastrous effects it would have, they ordered Shaun to cut his staff because their wages were the largest item on the expenditure side. This was done to such an extent that it was impossible to carry on running the Station up to the standard to which he was accustomed, and he opted out.

I must say I loved seeing a complete new way of producing beef from that which I had known in Scotland or seen in many other parts of the world. In the N.T. one talked in terms of hundreds of square miles which to my untried eye seemed to have no grazing on it. As for the cattle trains, huge lorries with trailers attached, that took one hundred cattle at a time, they put the fear of death in me. Goodbye, 'Oz', and N.Z., here we come.

From the time I fought beside the New Zealanders in the desert and the friendship I made with Jim Wynyard in Hospital in Alexandria, through to 1964 when I was there on a Nuffield Scholarship for a month, up until the present day, I have gained a tremendous respect for New Zealanders and their country. Is it because they are superb stockmen, or that they are more Scottish than those in other countries I've visited, that they are tremendous rugby players, or that they have the best grazing land in the world? Whatever the reason, I know not, but suffice to say that my daughter, the youngest of my six, has married a New Zealander, is making her home there, and if she has a boy I hope he'll be a rugger player and good enough to play for New Zealand or Scotland—I don't care which country. But having said that, since the game has gone professional some of the physical clashes are terrifying and I fear all too many players will land up like old men at a young age.

Both Sal and I had plenty of friends in New Zealand: in fact Sal had worked there for two years back in the fifties, when that country was looking for immigrants and only charged ten pounds for the trip out. This was on condition that they stayed two years, in the hope that then they would stay for good, but luckily for me Sal didn't. While there she spent a year as a milk tester. I think she liked this job because she had a fast-trotting pony with trap as her means of transport. She still loves her pony driving, and as Max Hasting says is no mean 'whip'. We loved our stay there, but sadly we won't go back as a couple. I am too old now for long flights and we have lost our dearest New Zealand friends, although both families came to visit me in Scotland before they passed on.

Then on to Fiji, where I found being a Scot was an advantage, and being willing to talk about rugger even more so. I little realised back then what an impact Fijians were going to have when the game went professional. What problems that lovely island has gone through recently: but which part of the world, I ask myself, hasn't?

From the time I won my Nuffield Scholarship to the U.S.A. in 1959 1 had always wanted to go back to San Francisco, with 'its little cable cars climbing halfway to the stars', to quote a line of Tony Bennett's world-beating song. Sadly, we hit the town when there was some special holiday, Thanksgiving Day I think, and we couldn't get my favourite meal, breakfast, as our hotel only provided beds! However, much to my amazement and pleasure, I was able to find the super fish restaurant where I had lunched in 1959. One had to pass through a shop in Fisherman's Wharf and pull back a curtain before stepping into the restaurant, which was full of locals who obviously didn't want too many foreigners coming in but served the most excellent fish. A visit to the 'Top of the Mark' was also a must after my previous experiences there, and what glorious views one gets from it of that most fascinating city. Below you is the famous Golden Gate Bridge and, of course, Alcatraz, the prison-island, from which no one ever escaped alive but where the famous prisoner tamed his birds.

Then it was home again after an eventful trip. I'm not the best person in the world when faced with nothing to do—in fact Sal says I'm hopelessly impatient—and sadly, as all my pursuits have been physical ones, I've never been a great reader. So I was thrilled when Pat Chalmers, who had produced the Scottish agricultural T.V. programme but had been promoted to be Controller of BBC Scotland, asked me to be agricultural adviser to a new drama programme they wanted to put on, 'Strathblair'. This was to have an agricultural/Highland theme and to be set in the early fifties. He then introduced me to the producer, Norman McAndlish, and writer, Bill Craig. How sad it was that that team didn't handle the whole series, as during our time together 'Strathblair' had good viewing figures. Sadly, Norman decided to opt out to produce something else, and for some reason unknown to me Bill was dropped. After he left the writers that followed concentrated on crime and sex, and the great appeal of the programme, the Highland way of life and its scenery, was lost.

When we discussed where the programme should be shot, Pat asked me for my opinion. I happened to know the late Duke of Atholl, and my son Hamish was in Glenfender where he had just vacated a croft called Corriebeg. As the rainfall is not as high there as in areas further west, it seemed an ideal location. Blair Atholl is a particularly picturesque village, although the B.B.C. spent a fortune on turning it into something different. From an agricultural point of view I was so lucky, as I had terrific cooperation from the local farmers. John Cameron, on whose farm we did a lot of our film-shooting, was son of a good friend of mine. Then there was Jimmy McFarlane, the local sheepdog trialist who performed wonders with his dogs, which he had to control in such a way that it appeared as if the actor had given the commands.

I will always remember one occasion when Norman couldn't be present and we were dipping the ewes in the spring, just prior to them lambing. One always did this to rid them of any 'beasties' that they might otherwise pass on to their lambs. The producer that day was a lady, and like most of the crew hadn't a clue about the country or the way of life there. Anyway, John Cameron, whose ewes we were dipping, was handling them as they approached the dipper to see if any were close to lambing, in which case he pushed them into a side-pen. The shot of the ewes going through the dipper was about to be taken, the clapper-board announcing the scene-number etc. had been clapped and the producer called 'Quiet!' Thereupon there was a grunt from a ewe about to lamb in the pen behind myself and my fellow shepherds who had gathered the sheep. Once more came the stentorian call: 'Quiet!' A voice was then heard from one of my fellow shepherds, saying: 'You'd be gruntin' too if you were doing what she is!'

The oldies in the cast were terrific. Andrew Keir, sadly no more with us, was wonderful as the grumpy old Grandad. He turned up for a practice session to see how one built a 'cole' of hay, which the young so-called 'star' didn't bother to attend, and as a result couldn't even hold his hay-fork correctly. Alison Peebles got me to show her how to catch and hold Blackfaced ewes without breaking their horns. Francesca, the heroine, was determined to learn to milk, but sadly one can't learn in the short time that we had. As a townee, when she saw the Rhode Island Red cock jump on and off one of his harem that I had to have imported, she remarked, 'No wonder the hens look so unhappy!' Then there was Urbano Barberini, the Italian, who got hopelessly bogged on the grey Fergie tractor, but had the biggest smile I've ever seen on someone in that predicament.

I was seventy-five then, and only wish I'd been in full control of that programme ten years earlier, as it had so much going for it, but the waste of money was frightening. The props team built a wonderful Agricultural Showground, complete with a W.R.I. tent with scones, pancakes etc., a steam engine, pens full of Aberdeen-Angus cattle, Blackfaced sheep, Clydesdale horses etc., etc. However the Director chose to spend most of that scene filming a hill race, girls dancing and a tug-of-war in which the boots shown on the close-up were modern rubber-soled ones that we certainly didn't have in the fifties. Practically none of what I would call real show material was shown. I had been asked by Pat Chalmers to keep the agricultural side as authentic as I could, so I had to go all the way to Northumberland for a dairy shorthorn cow, which was the breed we were all using as 'house-cows' in the fifties. The only shot they took of her was of her tail—I could have got a local cow and saved a lot of money. Also, with the horses, there was a Welsh cob, full of corn, which bucked off David Robb and as a result delayed filming for a day. This beast and its mate had come all the way from Wales, what a waste!

Norman told me that all actors say they can ride, in case they don't get the part they want. The prize example of this was the ageing actor who played the part of the Postman. He had to ride a bicycle, and fell off five times before he actually made the fifty yards he had to cycle, when he got a tremendous cheer from us all. However he got more coverage than many of the rest of the cast, as he was shown on Terry Wogan's 'B.B.C. Bloomers'.

I had to correct all sorts of things with the props team, like changing the English scythe for a Scottish one etc., but that's what I was there for. I had a grand team of real farming folk to help me. My neighbour Bill Heron was invaluable on anything to do with the ways we did things in the fifties. While I was often conferring with the producer or director, he would be with the farm-gang talking about how things were done in 'the days that once were'.

We were so lucky with the weather, as we managed to 'cole' the hay and cut the oats with the binder. The latter, thank the Lord, had a reliable knotter: this so often used to let one down and throw out loose corn instead of sheaves.

The scene I enjoyed most of all was when we threshed the oats. This time we had a young English female director whom we hadn't seen before, but she was a topper and I wish we had had her before. She spent an half hour with me asking sensible questions, then telling me the shots she would like to take. One was of the belts, which had no guards in the old days, goodness knows what the safety boys would have said had they turned up. The main driving belt has a lovely clack-clack sound, but should it happen to come off it is lethal. She wanted to put a cameraman below it but I did manage to dissuade her from that.

It always amazed me how much authority the cameraman had. There was a scene in Corriebeg Cottage when the milk in the old milk dishes, wide so one could skim off the cream, was to be used in a shot. They wanted to do it in front of the fire, because it suited the light. But for once I put my size twelve feet down and said, 'No way, there's a perfectly good wee milk house where it's always done—who wants to try to skim cream from hot milk?'. So of course it took half a day to get the lighting set up in the wee dairy, and Coutts was NOT popular.

The lasting memory for me of a wonderful summer was selling the lambs in the last old fashioned mart in Perthshire. Hays Mart was later bulldozed and is now a housing estate, but I had known it in the late forties when I came back from the war. It was run by the formidable 'Stewarty' Hay who tried to bully farm managers like me into selling everything in his mart. Luckily, fifty years ago, we had two marts in Perth, Hays and MacDonald Fraser. Now we are forced to go bigger and further afield, for what?—huge lorries carrying Foot and Mouth Disease all over the country.

Then, in 1999, the Royal Smithfield Club honoured me twice. Their annual show at Earls Court each December has been my favourite, and at it I have judged, stewarded, commentated and shown cattle and sheep over half a century. Firstly, at the Club's bicentenary dinner at Woburn, where the Club was originally formed by the then Duke of Bedford, I was asked to say the Grace before a very distinguished company. This Grace, with more than a little help from my brother Frank who has a gift for the doggerel (a gift that missed me) was as follows:

'A Grace for Smithfield Bicentenary Dinner'

O Lord, who blessed the loaves and fishes,
Look down upon these Smithfield dishes.
Good meat we're sure, you also blessed,
Thou knowest all—that BEEF IS BEST.

These hundreds of years we've nurtured it,
And always sought a tastier bit
By breeding, culture, elbow grease,
We've shunned grain farmers' life of ease.

God also bless our pigs and lamb,
—Cunningham couldnae give a damn—
You cannot beat a a piece of pork
A-sizzling while you pull the cork.
So let us praise our pigs and sheep,
The prices offered make you weep.

Through wars and drought and BSE,
We've helped to keep our country free—
We've battled with the Min. of Ag.,
And now it's Brussels feet that drag.

God bless our members near and far,
E'en those who lingered at the bar.
You turned the water into wine
These guys will turn it back agine.
And if you've blessings left to spare
Keep Smithfield going for ever mair.
                    Amen.

The author and Laurie Bembridge, the only two Royal Smithfield Club members, and Vice-Presidents, to have been at the pre-war Smithfield Show, unveiling a plaque at the old 'Aggie Hall', Islington, where the Show was held for 77 years

That was in June, then in October, at the instigation of the new owners, the Morris's, of what members of the Smithfield Club called the 'Aggie Hall', a commemorative plaque was to be placed on it. This was to commemorate the fact that it had been used to house the annual Smithfield Show for seventy-seven years! The two remaining members on the Smithfield Council who had been at the last show to be held at the old 'Aggie Hall' in 1938, before the outbreak of World War II, were that well-known, highly respected Lincoln Red breeder, Laurie Bembridge, who had shown cattle there that year, and Yours Truly, who was helping bring out some Sussex cattle as an assistant stockman! But for me it was something rather special, as when Arthur Anderson was producing our Scottish agricultural programme 'Landward', he had asked me to present a programme about Smithfield's two hundred years. We were so lucky in that we were able to take shots of the interior of the old 'Aggie', literally just months before it was gutted and beautifully redesigned as a Business Centre. I love replaying that video. It shows the old floor made up with wooden bricks to allow the cattle wash to get away, the pigeons flying in and out, and probably nesting there, the weeds growing in every corner, and then the transformation into this magnificently designed centre. It beats me why it lay so long unused, from the end of the war until the nineties, but then I never could add two and two, so high finance is (thank goodness) a closed book to me.

Having said that, I ran the Blackmount Estate for the Fleming family who owned Flemings Bank. When they were taken over by the American bankers, Chase Manhattan, the directors of Flemings were given mega golden handshakes. Robin Fleming, who was my boss for most of the time I managed the estate, has most generously put aside some of his money to form a Trust which will enable Sal and me to enjoy the evening of our lives, and if necessary provide enough to pay for (God forbid) an old folks home. I've never had capital for long, as the first I got when I sold Gaskbeg went into educating my first family, and the second lot when I sold off the Woodburn stock educated my last two (and I'm proud of them all). Sal and I live very comfortably day to day, but to buy a new car or do a major repair job on our cottage has presented a problem. Thanks to the Trust there will no longer be any need for me, at the age of eighty-five, to write the odd article, make the odd broadcast, do a commentary at a show or speak at an agricultural discussion group, for all of which I demand a fee. Nor will I have to rack the grey matter I call a brain to produce another book, and receive the princely sum of 99 pence in royalty on a ten pound book!

However I think I will embark on one last chapter as my swan song to a life, the highlights of which I wouldn't have swapped with those of the richest men in the country. I'll describe some of those highlights, and make some suggestions about how I, as an oldie, think farming should go.

42
Some Final Reflections

So here I am at the age of eighty-five, fortunate and thankful to be alive. I am determined not to write any more books, as I find it harder in old age to get the grey cells working, but I feel there are so many things that have given me particular pleasure that I have to say something more about them before I pack up.

As you will have read, Father, on a very modest salary and at great deprivation to himself and Mother, gave all six of us a first-class education. Not only that, but he also passed down to us good voices. Apart from Philip, the youngest, the other five were not fit for opera or anything similar, but Frank and me were endowed with voices that could be heard without the aid of a 'mike' at an after-dinner speech, and certainly on the parade ground when I was a wartime Sergeant-Major.

Looking back over a most marvellous life, my public speaking, broadcasting, lay-preaching and commentating have given me most pleasure, none of which would have been possible without what I call Dad's voice. Little did I realise when I did my first broadcast in 1947 that I would still be broadcasting fifty years on! When it comes to public speaking, e.g. after dinner, Probus, N.F.U., Rotary etc., I started before the era when speakers charged fees for their appearances. I was never too good at Burns' Suppers, but at one supper in Oban I had great delight in 'out-speaking', if there is such a phrase, the late Lord MacKay of Adrbrecknish. He wasn't on form that night, but went on to be a formidable debater in the House of Lords and much missed. Then there was the occasion when I was the main speaker at the Border Agricultural Discussion Society at Peebles in 1989, and the following speakers were David, now Lord, Steel and Paddy Ashdown, quite conceit-making. But much as I enjoyed after-dinner speaking the butterflies in the tummy seemed to be worse then than on any other occasion. Sometimes you know you've done a good job and you can feel the audience are enjoying the speech, yet at other times the speech falls flat, and after all the homework you've put in to make sure your jokes and stories are applicable to the subject, you don't know why.

Two that I did that gave me great pleasure: both had to do with the Aberdeen-Angus Society. The first was at Aviemore where the Scottish Society were hosting the World Forum of A.A. breeders. I had to follow the

Earl of Elgin, who is one of the best after-dinner speakers in the land, which was not easy, but the speech came off. We had the hardest luck that night, as, since it was the second week in June, we had organised the event to be held outside in a marquee. Blow me if there wasn't a 'haar', and even the excellent Aberdeen-Angus beef, beautifully cooked and, thanks to heated trolleys, served really hot to every diner, didn't heat us up, but the Speyside malt whisky did!

The other Aberdeen-Angus occasion was the centenary lunch, when our Patron the Queen Mother graced us with her presence. Not only that, she agreed to reply to my toast to the guests, which was a great honour as she told me she hated public-speaking and seldom agreed to do so. I was able to tell the apocryphal fishing story of the time when she was fishing on a very windy day with her favourite ghillie Sandy. He was wearing his deer-stalker hat, but hadn't tied down his ear flaps and it blew off. When Her Majesty said, 'Why haven't you got your flaps tied down, Sandy?' he replied, 'I've never tied them down since my accident, Ma'am.' 'Accident, what accident, Sandy?' 'The time you asked me to have a dram and I never heard you!'

Then I had to speak at the Canadian, Argentinian and Irish centenary dinners. The latter I will never forget. Sal and I were staying at another hotel to the one where the dinner was being held. The late Colin Edwards (as the Irish would say, 'a luvly man') was their President and had promised to send a taxi for us. Imagine the size of my butterflies when the taxi hadn't arrived at 8 p.m. when the dinner itself was due to start! After frantic phone calls we duly arrived at 8.20 p.m. to find the place going like a fair, and an Irish one at that. We sat down at 9 p.m., and when the Aberdeen-Angus beef was served it was absolutely first-class. How the chef knew we would be an hour late beats me, unless every official dinner in Ireland, and this was a big occasion, runs an hour late. To serve roast beef to a large number of people, properly rare, medium-rare or well-done, is not an easy task, and in too many restaurants and hotels the meat is ruined by being pre-cooked and heated up.

Then, back in 1954 when I was President of the Highland Cattle Society, I had as my first Vice-President Sir Charles MacLean of Duart, who like the Earl of Elgin was a brilliant after-dinner speaker, so I had him to contend with. 'Chips', as he was called, was made the Chief Scout, which meant he had to travel the world and so had to demit office as my Vice-President, and Michael Noble, later my employer but always my friend, was appointed. As 'Chips' went on to become Lord MacLean of Duart, and Michael, Lord

Glenkinglass, I think I will be the only President of a breed society to have had two lords as his Vice-Presidents!

My involvement with the Highland Cattle Society wasn't much at Woodburn, as it wasn't a farming set up where Highland Cattle would be part of the farm policy. Having said that, I did bring out two beasts that won cups at the Oban Sales. But more importantly, I was delighted to be asked to present their breed video, and as Her Majesty has that good fold at Balmoral, and I knew her Factor, that was a must to be featured in it.

Looking back, judging shows is another thing that has given me so much pleasure. It has also given me so many friends—the ones who won!—and others who could take defeat as one should do. Judges differ and some competitors go up, some go down. Whereas when Doctors differ some patients die off, the show people are a race apart: they are tough and come back for more punishment even when beaten in the past. My favourite show story is of the late and great Bertie Marshall, doyen of the Clydesdale horse and Shorthorn cattle breeds and a worldwide judge of both. Re-splendent in a loud checked suit, silk cravat, pork-pie hat and pipe firmly clenched between his teeth, he had just finished judging a large turnout of Shorthorns at one of the large south of England shows when a harassed show secretary came up to him. He said, 'Mr Marshall, the judge of the Jack Russell Terrier section has just suffered a heart attack, would you deputise for him?' To this Bertie replied, 'I'll dae my best'. There was a big turn-out of terriers, and after Bertie had presented the rosette to the Champion, the owner of the Reserve Champion exploded: 'This terrier of mine was Cham-pion at Crufts!' Bertie slowly removed his pipe from his mouth and said to the owner of his Champion: 'Were you at Crufts?' When the answer came back in the negative, Bertie said, 'A pity—you would have been Champion!'

Although I've had the honour of judging the Burke Trophy at the Royal and have judged at the Royal Highland, the Royal Ulster, the super show in Dublin at Ballsbridge, which was Eire's top show, and also at the Royal Welsh, it's the small country shows that have given me most enjoyment. They are so much an essential part of the patchwork that makes up the rural way of life in Britain. Having said that, one of my happiest moments was when I was judging the Aberdeen-Angus in Dublin at that lovely old showground at Ballsbridge. This is surely one of the most lovely showgrounds in the world, and I mean the world, but sadly today it is in the centre of a city where land is at a premium and nowadays is too small for a modern national show. Anyway you could have knocked me down with a feather when I stepped into the ring to find that my steward was my old Colonel when I had been Sergeant-Major in the Surrey and Sussex Yeomanry. He hadn't a clue about the tickets, rosettes, etc. as he had, as an excellent horseman, always been at the show as a competitor in his younger days. But the nicest bit was when we went for lunch and the head waiter, who always recognised my kilt, and I'd been at many Ballsbridge Shows, said, 'You'll have your usual bottle of Burgundy, Sir, and who have you got with you, what would he like to drink?'

But there were lots of small shows where I've really enjoyed judging. Gargunnock in the Carse of Stirling for one, where they had a wonderful turnout of different breeds to celebrate their bicentenary, and also had a tent full of memorabilia of days gone by; and Mull, where everyone on the island converges on one of the small patches of flat ground on the road between Salen and Tobermory. They have a wonderful day out and the hard-working committee put on a great show helped, I might say, by the refreshment tent! Then there is Orkney, which to my mind produces the best-quality beef cattle in Great Britain. The last time I judged there it was, amazingly, a really hot day. After I finished judging my classes, I retired to the Secretary's caravan to have the usual 'wee dram' and was looking forward to some lunch and watching the afternoon's entertainment—only to be told that the entertainment was more judging for special prizes and I was one of the judges! Then there was Hamburg, where Ernst Schonberg had kindly asked me to judge his Highlanders and Galloways. This was prior to a sale he was having in a lovely new mart he had especially erected for the occasion. He had sold rights that he owned for mobile telephones for a large sum, and now was determined to increase the demand for Highland and Galloway beef, as he had the slaughterhouses and butchers shops to process it. Sadly, B.S.E. and now Foot and Mouth have all but brought this excellent idea to a standstill. But what a host he was, paying our fares, our hotel rooms, giving us presents and organising a dinner-dance for us all, of which the Scottish team who produce our agricultural programme 'Landward' were a part. Then, when I was about to board the plane, I was handed an envelope which contained much more than I deserved. Ernst, if you read this, many thanks.

But probably, looking back over the years, I've enjoyed commentating the most. There was the great occasion when the Scottish Winter Fair was being held in the United Auctions Ltd. at Huntingtower, Perth. There was no heating in the mart. I was commentating on the Highland ponies, and knowing how cold all auction marts can be, had worn my old coat, tailored for me at the end of the war by a tailor in East Grinstead, who had lost a son in the Sussex Yeomanry. My family called it Dad's horse blanket. As well as this I had on my woolly boots, scarves, gloves, you name it. because it was perishing cold. The press loved old Coutts all muffled up, and my photo appeared in all the agricultural papers. That year Sal and I went to see son Shaun and family in Bali. When we were there, Sal and I were waiting, as one does, to go to the airport, and lo and behold one of the magazines I was reading to pass the time had that photo in it. The temperature where we were was in the nineties, not sub-zero as it had been in Perth.

Then there is the three-day event in the lovely setting around Blair Castle at Blair Atholl. The late Duke, as I think I've said, is sorely missed. He was a keen supporter of National Hunt racing, and as such knew that supporting eventing would help his sport. Filling in the programme for Thursday was never easy, as unless one is in serious horse competitions dressage is not the ordinary person's idea of a spectator sport, so they introduced a Highland pony day. The Atholl stud was famous at one time, but went through a bad stage, and Iain, the Duke, was determined to get it back to its former glory. So he started off a highly successful trekking centre, and then got the stud of mares going again, but sadly he will not be present to see how they do as it takes years to build up a stud. He also welcomed *Scottish Farmer*'s approach to hold their 'Champion of Champions' of local shows at Blair. This was at the end of the local show season, at the end of August on the Thursday of the three day event. I was asked to do the commentary, and it's one of the happiest I've had to do. At the time of writing I still do it. Sadly, because of Altzheimer's increasingly afflicting the Duke's thoughts and speech, he used to come and sit in my commentating caravan rather than meet the dozens of hangers-on with whoever was the main sponsor. I will never forget that at one show he was sitting with me, and we were discussing the merits of the ponies in front of us, and he was no mean judge of horseflesh. I looked at my watch and said, 'Your Grace, it's one o'clock and you said you were meant to be at the sponsors tent at 12.30.' He replied, 'I suppose I've got to go, but I'd rather stay here'. That was Iain, Duke of Atholl, a great Scot but very shy.

When the show was started I was keen that the spectators learnt something about the different jobs Highland ponies were bred to do in earlier times, as now they have done brilliantly as ridden ponies, having won the Mountain and Moorland Championships two years running at the great Olympia Show. So we started a class for Working Highland Ponies, including ponies with grouse panniers, deer saddles, pulling a log, pulling a plough and, for two shows, we had one yoked to a garron cart full of peat. Sadly the owner has died and the cart has been sold, which is a pity, as it was the last one I know that was made for a Highland pony and it came from Morar. It is now full of flowers outside the building of a well-known company which sells spring water. What a waste, and had I known it was for sale I would have bought it. It added so much to a show, telling the spectators, many from overseas, how ponies were so much part of the Highland scene right up to the last world war.

Then of course there have been the times I have been asked 'to take the pulpit' as a layman. People who know me well think, because of my many faults, I have no right to do this, but I always counter by saying it's because of my faults that I do it.

Judging by the congregations to whom I've preached, they enjoy hearing one of their 'ain folk' not being too theological, as all too many ministers can be, and preaching for no more than ten minutes as all too many ministers do. Dad said, 'If you can't strike gold in ten minutes, stop boring'. How true! And I love the story of the two old ladies sitting at the back of the church. One was terribly deaf, and as the minister was banging on she turned to her pal and said, 'Has he feenished?' Back came the reply, 'Aye, but he hasna stoppit'.

My greatest honour in my preaching days was to be asked by the Association for the Preservation of Rural Scotland to preach the sermon at their Rogation Sunday Service in St Giles. It was a frightening experience, but a wonderful event and congregation, and judging by the following seems to have done what I meant it to do.

From *The Field*, 10th May, 1986:

Sermon of Reconciliation.

A celebration of the Scottish countryside and concern for its future was the theme of the Association for the Preservation of Rural Scotland's Rogation Sunday Service. It was particularly memorable for the torrent of highly evocative words which swept from the immaculately-kilted, craggy figure of one of Scotland's best-kent farmers, Ben Coutts, epitome of all that is best in modern agriculture and rural conservation. Who better to champion both causes than this respected *eminence grise*?

His brilliantly presented plea from the pulpit was a masterpiece of realism tinged with romance. 'What wonderful things can be achieved when God and man get together...' he proclaimed, his vegetable-dyed Farquharson tartan, snowy hair and

commanding stature superbly complementary to the gloomy
vaulting of St Giles Cathedral, Edinburgh.

He conjured up in moments a fleeting vision of his beloved
Highlands, of the wind blowing over the newly-green bracken,
of the cry of lambs on the hillsides, of cattle on the lower
ground—but above all, the awareness of the families living in
and on the countryside, and of families in the cities, all with
their superficially conflicting feelings but similar wants. His
message was one we could all heed.

Now, at the advanced age of eighty-five, and needing to use a stick when I
go to buy my paper, no way am I able to do any of the public speaking, broadcasting etc. that I used to do. However I have conceitedly agreed to preach in
the lovely wee church at Lochbuie on Mull where I have preached before,
was welcomed and had the feeling that I was being listened to, and anyway,
I have a love affair with Mull. And then there are two Highland pony shows
at which I've agreed to commentate and after that it must be 'finito' to all those
fifty years of using Father's voice, before I hear someone in the background
saying 'Not that old bugger again, doesn't he know when to pack up?'

So now to pastures new. Dad always said racing was a 'mugs' game'.
Sadly, I've proved him right, though back in the thirties when I was a
groom I never thought that one day I would be in charge of the Coutts-
MacGregor Clan Syndicate, with a share in the ownership of racing horses.
Having said that, as so far two of our horses have had to be put down and
we've not been able to get a winner, I feel like naming the next horse after
one I backed at Goodwood in 1937 (with at least two shillings) called 'Boozer's
Gloom' and he won! I feel very like his name right now, but that's racing.
There's no way that our syndicate can raise the huge amounts of money that
are now being paid for National Hunt horses. National Hunt used to be the
poor man's sport and the Flat was for the millionaires, but thanks to the
money coming from oil revenues to the sheiks, who love their racing and
will pay anything for the tops, many who owned Flat racehorses have turned
to the jumping game, and this has pushed up the prices.

Our two horses are trained just an hour's drive from here by a lovely
lady, who arranges to have our horses either jumping or galloping up the old
grass field that constitutes their gallops. When I stand halfway up, looking
out at a most lovely view of good horses in the foreground and Loch Leven
(shades of Mary Queen of Scots imprisoned there) in the background, I realise
how lucky I am, compared with people I know who have shares in vast

'Music Blitz', owned by the Coutts-MacGregor Clan Syndicate, of which the author is the Chieftain, being led in at Cheltenham after coming second in his race

syndicates, never see their horses being trained, are paying megabucks compared with 'the Clan', and when they go to a race meeting and into the saddling enclosure, which is half the fun, they don't know many, if any, of the others in their syndicate.

I have a small vegetable patch which grows crops that I know could be bought cheaper in a supermarket (but would the supermarket produce taste as good? No way.) I have my patch because I love the land, and this, with my love of stock, has not only been my mainstay financially, but also (with all due deference to some lovely ladies) the love of my life. This is what has gone wrong with British agriculture: we have too few who love the land and the native breeds of stock in this marvellous country which, second to New Zealand, is the best grass-grazing country in the world. But what has happened? Greed has taken over the farming industry, as it has most of Great Britain, and all too many farmers wait for the brown envelope, which in all too many cases contains a cheque for unwanted grain. Either that, or payment is on the basis of stock numbers of cattle or sheep. If cattle, it is for foreign breeds which are not naturally grass-fed as our breeds are; and if for sheep, the cheques have forced all too many hill farmers to overstock, as the payment is on headage.

So what do I think will happen to British agriculture after this ghastly

Foot and Mouth crisis which, although badly handled at the outset, is, as I write in May 2001, on the wane?

In my broadcasting and writing for agricultural programmes and papers, which I'm proud to say has covered exactly half a century, I have been regularly castigated by the professional agricultural journalists as being an 'oldie' who wants everything in agriculture to revert to the horse era, with yours truly sucking a straw. The latter is the crux of the whole of farming today. Of course I'd like to suck a straw, but it would be in a glass of 'brandy sour', and in Cyprus, not in a harvest field where we'd been turning the sheaves in the stooks because as a result of incessant rain they were starting to sprout. Everyone in this country wants a higher standard of living and farmers are no exception. Where the journalists are wrong is that I know very well one has to move with the times, but I think that in farming some things have moved too fast and we've forgotten to look after the land (about the only thing one can't replace in this country). Of course we can't go back to the horse age or the days of the seven course shift, with four years grass and three arable, but we could sow a mixture of grasses, not just rye grass to which the modern farmer applies two or three doses of nitrogen. I know that those know-alls at the E.U. agricultural headquarters in some form or other no longer allow white clover-sowing, but its nodules when ploughed in were a wonderful source of nitrogen.

Then to potatoes. This strath was famous for producing seed, which not only went to Lincolnshire to produce the ware for the fish and chip trade, but all over the world. I was always told as a laddie that a field with a few stones was good for tatties, as the stones held the heat or the moisture. What happens today? Because modern machinery lifts the crop instead of the school bairns, the stones have to be lifted and disposed of first. How daft can we be? Especially as tatties are now so tasteless that rice and pasta are taking over. But when it comes to taste, the best I ever had were 'Golden Wonders', which had been planted in a disused lazy bed on the side of Loch Etive and of course had had seaweed and cow dung as manure. With a knob of butter in in the centre, no meal produced by those fancy chefs we see on TV could have tasted better.

On the subject of cattle, as I've said and will repeat again and again, why import breeds that need vast amounts of concentrate feeding? The worst case to my mind is the importation of the Belgian Blue, which is not properly made anatomically and was intended in Belgium to live inside and as a result to be fed vast amounts of concentrates. I know they have big bums which give lots of steaks, but I've had one and they are tasteless.

Then there are my beloved hill breeds of sheep, which have not only given me a large part of my livelihood, but also so much pleasure gathering them on those fabulous June mornings when one was on top of a 'Munro' (at three thousand feet) and could see the whole country north and south. And the great camaraderie of the 'neighbourings', when all the surrounding farmers came to help. What is to happen to them? Sadly, few young lads wish to take up shepherding, and some of the larger hill flocks may have to cut back their numbers.

So where do I, as an 'oldie', think we are going to go in agriculture after this ghastly, badly mishandled crisis is past?

I am sure of one thing: the family farm has been the backbone of British agriculture for generations. I have recently met two young lads, whose fathers are farming in these awful times, and they've both said they too are going to farm. These are the sort who will keep the countryside the way the townees think the country should look. I have never had any time for those farmers who enjoyed the good years, bought that Mercedes, curled two nights a week, had holidays abroad twice a year and ran up an overdraft with the bank: these, to me, were never genuine farmers and they'll go. So I see a return to a system of lower input, lower output, even a return to dog and stick in certain areas. As far as cereal growing is concerned, it should always have been confined to the east coast of the country. Why some boffin gave out subsidies to grow grain in straths and even in glens, and so mucked up the excellent agricultural structure there, beats me.

I was more than proud to be made a Fellow of the Royal Agricultural Societies (F.R.Ag.S.), in the farming world equivalent to a top surgeon becoming a Fellow of the Royal College of Surgeons (F.R.C.S.). The Agricultural Fellows have their annual meeting in February, and have two or three top speakers on whatever subject the council feel is most relevant to the year. This year they chose as a subject the effect of globalisation on agriculture, and this was before the Foot and Mouth outbreak which I think might have changed their ideas. The principal speaker was Mike Calvert, who controls the largest acreage of farming in Britain, as he is responsible for all the farmland owned by the Co-op. Not only that, he has been put in charge of sorting out the Royal Show, which has hit some difficulties. After a brilliant speech about how the mega-farms could feed us, and how stressed he and all the major players in the huge farms were, he finished up by telling us something Ben Coutts could have taught him. He said, 'I'm always lecturing about "Big is Beautiful", but I own a cottage in the south of France and am surrounded by small farms, the owners of which smoke Gauloises,

The author making a presentation to the jockey who rode the winner of a race at Perth called 'The Captain Ben Coutts 85th Birthday Race'. Changed days since the author worked as a humble groom!

eat red meat, drink red wine and live to be a hundred'. To which I say, apart from the Gauloises which I gave up years ago, it's a way of life I agree with one hundred per cent.

I sincerely hope we can bring a halt to those huge lorries thundering down our 'B' roads to pick up a few sheep here and some there, and all the stupid things that have crept into agriculture. Of course we could be fed by countries whose standard of living is not as high as ours, but do the townees realise what our countryside will look like if it's devoid of people? I won't be here to see the result of the shake-up there is bound to be after the Foot and Mouth crisis is over, because it will take years to work through.

Meantime, to repeat once again the words of the one and only 'Satchmo', Louis Armstrong, 'there's an awful lot of living to do': and who knows, I might gird my loins, use some of Robin Fleming's kind gift, and travel. After all, one has to die somewhere, so why not, if not in one's native country, then a country one has chosen to visit? After all, I could have died in Tobruk or in the middle of the Atlantic, but I am still here!